Journalists in Film

Journalists in Film
Heroes and Villains

Brian McNair

Edinburgh University Press

© Brian McNair, 2010

Transferred to digital print 2014

Edinburgh University Press Ltd
22 George Square, Edinburgh

www.euppublishing.com

Typeset in Monotype Ehrhardt by
Koinonia, Manchester, and
printed and bound by CPI Group (UK) Ltd
Croydon, CR0 4YY

A CIP record for this book is available
from the British Library

ISBN 978 0 7486 3446 0 (hardback)
ISBN 978 0 7486 3447 7 (paperback)

Contents

List of Figures

Preface and acknowledgements

This book is a film fan's labour of love, and a media scholar's consideration of what journalism – one of our key social and cultural institutions – is in our time, as refracted through the prism of one of our most important cultural forms. The films selected for discussion are those which I have found particularly useful in my academic work as a researcher and teacher of journalism, resonant in what they have to say about how journalism is perceived in liberal democratic societies, and engaging as a film lover. There are omissions, no doubt, and some readers may disagree with my choices and emphases. Suggestions on films which I have neglected to mention are welcome.

My thanks go to the University of Strathclyde for a semester of study leave in which to watch films and write about them, and to those journalists, academics and others who responded to my request for their views on their favourite films about journalism. Thanks to Katherine McNair for help in assembling film stills, tables and formatting of the final typescript, and to Tereza McLaughlin-Vanova for research and office support. Faye Hammill read and provided useful comments on 'Heroines'.

Brian McNair
January 2010

Part I
Introductions and Overviews

CHAPTER I

Introduction

I have been researching, teaching and writing about journalism for more than two decades. I have also written some 200 pieces of journalism of my own – mainly feature articles, travel pieces and commentary columns for the print and online media.[1] Throughout that time I have been fascinated by feature films in which journalism is the subject, or is a central element of the narrative. In my teaching and research work I have found movies a useful, engaging, sometimes inspirational source of knowledge about how, as members of liberal democratic societies in which journalism is highly valued, we view journalists. More often than not they are highly relevant to the analysis and understanding of contemporary debates around news and other forms of journalism.

And debates there always are, heated and high on the public agenda, about journalistic ethics, political bias, the effects of commercialisation and competition on the content and style of journalism, structures of ownership and control of news media, the consequences of new communication technologies, the relationship between news media and politics, the role of the journalist in time of war. The films which have been made about journalism are a fruitful pathway into those debates, with the advantage in terms of grabbing students' attention that they often involve texts which are familiar, even to a non-specialist audience. Mention of Jurgen Habermas' theory of the public sphere will not always prompt excitement in the lecture theatre. Talking about Richard Gere's roguish columnist in *Runaway Bride* (Gary Marshall, 1999)[2] will at least get an audience's attention. This book, necessarily and perhaps fortuitously, makes frequent reference to George Clooney, Angelina Jolie, Kate Winslet, Will Ferrell, and a host of other A-list stars who have made films about journalism and journalists a significant part of their portfolio.

Beyond the opportunity they provide to exploit the celebrity factor (not to be under-estimated in modern media studies pedagogy), we find that films inevitably, and not necessarily by intention, capture something of the prevailing cultural *zeitgeist* in relation to journalism. Film-makers, like the rest of us, live in society. They absorb its changing moods and anxieties and reflect them back to their audiences. Contemporary concerns inevitably inflect their work. Films made decades ago, such as the screwball comedies of the black-and-white era, often speak to and illuminate current debates, contextualising them in relation to a cultural history which, if never quite repeating the same thing twice, seems to recycle social anxieties again and again, teaching us that some things at least don't change; that the unease and, sometimes, outrage we may feel about the performance of some journalists in the twenty-first century, as well as the admiration we have for others, are emotions shared by previous generations. The issues raised more than half a century ago in Billy Wilder's *Ace in the Hole* (1951) are remarkably similar to those which occupy the critics of journalism in our own time.

WHO THIS BOOK IS FOR

Apart from being an academic in the field of media studies, a journalism educator, and an occasional writer of journalism, I am also a film lover who finds few greater satisfactions than that of combining profession and pleasure in a scholarly project. I am therefore delighted to have had the opportunity to write a book about journalism, which uses films about journalism to consider who the journalist is in the twenty-first century, how s/he has got there, and where s/he is going next. It will connect, I hope, with three potential audiences.

First, I intend this book to serve as a resource for the expanding numbers of academics and their students delivering or taking media, journalism and cultural studies courses in colleges and universities across the world, and who wish to better understand the ambivalent relationship we have as publics in liberal democracies with one of our core cultural institutions and the people who work in them. Journalism is hugely important for the effective working of democratic societies, all agree, and so therefore are the journalists. This book explores how that simple truth is reflected in cinema. Introductory chapters trace the evolution of the journalistic role and identity, and the professional practices of journalism in its various guises, before we turn to the cinematic representation of these roles, identities and practices. As we go along, my footnotes provide a scholarly sub-text designed for the use of students and teachers in particular.

My second target reader is the non-academic observer of journalism. The book examines the representation of journalism and journalists in cinema. It asks: how have journalists been imagined by film-makers down the years, and what does this tell us about the changing role of the journalist in society, and of the evolving expectations and tensions in the relationship between journalists and their audiences? These questions are important for students who may have journalistic careers in mind, self-evidently, and for working journalists (who are, like any other professional group, legitimately interested in their public perception), but also for we non-journalists.

Journalism is a job for some, but part of the social and cultural fabric of all (or nearly all) our lives. Everyone who has ever read a newspaper, watched or listened to a broadcast news bulletin, or accessed an online news site, has an interest in how the makers of news and journalism are represented in culture. The cultural commentator Joan Bakewell once referred to journalists, in a book of that name, as *The New Priesthood*[3] signifying that combination of trusted elder and authoritative moral voice which is the liberal journalistic ideal. Priests are not perfect, nor are they infallible, and the movies are a space in our culture where the flaws and weaknesses of the journalistic variety, as well as their strengths, are rehearsed.

I approach the films discussed in the following chapters not only as cultural artefacts worthy of analysis in themselves, but as accessible points of departure for jumping into debates about the state of the news media in the twenty-first century, and the changes and stages they have gone through in getting to this point. I hope that, amongst my non-academic readers, journalists in particular will find this approach interesting and useful, should they wish to reflect on how their profession is perceived by the people who read their articles and watch or listen to their output on radio, TV and online.

A third group of readers, lovers of film in general, may approach this book as a study of one particular cinematic sub-genre which has produced some of the greatest films ever made, as well as some of the worst. For them, and for lovers of lists everywhere, Appendix 1 contains short reviews of all the films about journalism made for the cinema and released in the United Kingdom between 1997 and 2008 – seventy-one titles in all, from Curtis Hanson's *LA Confidential* (1997) to Ron Howard's *Frost/Nixon* (2008).

Richard Ness' filmography, *From Headline Hunter to Superman* (1997), is a comprehensive survey of the history of journalism in cinema from the 1920s up to 1996 and contains some 2,000 such reviews. My appendix does a similar, if much less onerous job for the decade or so after his book ends. While the following chapters explore the changing role of journalism, using movies from as long ago as 1940 to illustrate themes and trends, these reviews, ranging from 100 to 1,000 words in length, address the post-1996 films *as* films. Their focus is on the *aesthetic* dimensions of the movies in question – their qualities (or lack of) as works of cinematic art – as well as the journalism issues they raise. In addition to reviewing the films these short essays contain background information which may be interesting and/or useful to the reader, such as running length and global box office receipts.

By layering the book in this way (thematic chapters, scholarly footnotes, review essays) I hope it will be used by researchers, teachers and students of journalism on the one hand; read and enjoyed by journalists on the other; and read, too, by those who are in neither of the first two categories but merely love the movies and/or care enough about journalism to have an interest in its representation in popular culture; the same non-specialists who attended my lecture on *Journalists in Film* delivered at the Glasgow Film Theatre in 2005, and who stayed on that Sunday afternoon to see George Clooney's *Good Night, and Good Luck* (2005). And by those who have seen *A Mighty Heart* (2007), *Anchorman* (2004), *Zodiac* (2007) or other of the many films about journalism which have been screened in the multiplexes in recent times.

OUTLINE

I begin in Chapter 2 with a discussion of what it is we as publics in democratic societies expect our journalists to be in the twenty-first century, and what we think of how they perform those roles. Chapter 3 presents an overview of the main features of what has been characterised by others such as Richard Ness, Howard Good, Matthew Ehrlich and Joe Saltzman as the 'journalism genre' – the categories and sub-genres of film which have been made about journalism. Chapter 4 focuses on journalism movies released in the period between 1997 and 2008.

The remainder of the book comprises a series of chapters organised thematically around various aspects of the journalist's role which are central to his or her position in democratic societies: the journalist as *watchdog*, and as *witness*, especially in conflict situations; as *artist*, in an era of licensed journalistic subjectivity; as the *king-maker*, or pundit, who has nearly as much celebrity and power as the elites over which he or she is supposed to watch; as the *hack*, or *villain*, the manipulator of the truth and the fabricator of facts.

A chapter is devoted to the representation of female journalists, reflecting the long-standing importance of the discussion of gender in journalism studies. I include, too, in the chapter on king-makers, a section on a category of communication professional who is not a journalist, but whose work is an essential element in the practice of journalism in our time – the public relations practitioner, or 'spin doctor'. That fact justifies, I would argue, some discussion of how PR professionals have been represented in film since the early days when Tony Curtis' delightfully dodgy press agent, Sydney Falco, featured in *Sweet Smell of Success* (Alexander MacKendrick, 1957).

EXCLUSIONS

Cinema is not the first art form to address the subject of journalism. Fiction writers have been doing so for much longer, and many films about journalism are based on literary works. The late Gordon Burns' *Fullalove* (1995) and *Born Yesterday: the news as a novel* (2008), Richard Ford's *The Sportswriter* (1987), Iain McEwan's *Amsterdam* (1998) and Sebastian Faulks' *Engleby* (2007) are some of the best known examples of recent novels about journalism and the people who produce it. Graham Greene, Evelyn Waugh and many other great writers of the past have also tackled the subject, often using experience gained as journalists. I do not attempt to cover the subject of journalism-in-literature in this book, although there are many parallels and commonalities in the approach of writers working in both forms. Cinema and prose fiction are both narrative arts which, aside from their aesthetic attributes, provide observers with a window looking onto a culture's concerns and preoccupations. Space prevents me from including the written word in this volume, however, which could easily fill another book in its own right.

Neither have I included, except here and there in passing, discussion of the representation of journalists in theatre and TV drama. Theatre has been the source of some important movies about journalism, such as Howard Hawks's *His Girl Friday* (made in 1940, and based on Hecht and MacArthur's 1928 play *The Front Page*). The final film of the 1997–2008 period covered for this book was *Frost/Nixon* (Ron Howard, 2008), adapted from Peter Morgan's 2006 stage play of that name. Tim Fountain's *Julie Burchill Is Away*, about the great British controversialist, was produced in London in 2004, its title referencing another successful West End production about a notorious journalist, *Jeffrey Bernard Is Unwell* (Keith Waterhouse, 1989).

There have been some notable TV characterisations of journalists, such as Channel 4's *Drop the Dead Donkey* and *Brass Eye*, BBC's *The Day Today*,[4] and James Nesbitt's character in the 2008 ITV production of *Midnight Man*. In March 2009 Channel 4 broadcast an adaptation of David Peace's *Red Riding* novels, in which investigative journalist William Dunford has a key role. Television programmes tend to be more localised in their references, less familiar to the world beyond the country where they have been produced, than feature films made for the international cinema market. Most of the films about journalism discussed below have had a global audience, and a cultural resonance extending far beyond their country of origin. Although the great majority of them have been made in the English language, and in the United States, reflecting the international dominance of the US film industry, many have become globally iconic as images of journalism, and commercially successful all over the world.[5]

NOTES

1. While this experience does not make me a journalist, it has given me some insight into the professional and editorial practices of the news media, which I hope inform the scholarly argument and evaluations below.
2. Throughout the book the first reference to a film is accompanied by the name of the director and the year of UK cinema release.
3. Bakewell, J., Garnham, N., *The New Priesthood: British television today*, London, Allen Lane, 1970.
4. *Brass Eye* and *The Day Today* were written and performed by a team of British writers including Christopher Morris, Armando Ianucci, Patrick Marber and Steve Coogan. Enormously influential, they parodied the conventions of 1990s TV news and current affairs. Coogan introduced his Alan Partridge character on *The Day Today*, while Marber and Ianucci went on to further success on TV, stage and cinema. Ianucci wrote *In The Thick of It*, a satirical sit com for the BBC about government public relations in the New Labour era, and he directed *In The Loop* about government-media relations in the 2003 Gulf war, which was released to critical and commercial success in 2009.
5. Films about journalism made in languages other than English are included where they have been recognised as particularly important and influential, and where they have crossed over to the international cinema market and been released in the UK (and, by extension, USA) – Fellini's *La Dolce Vita* (1960), for example, or Mereilles' *City of God* (2003), or Danis Tanovic's *No Man's Land*, winner of the Best Foreign Film Oscar in 2002.

CHAPTER 2

A good tradition of love and hate

'People love to hate the journalist', wrote Lynda Ghiglione in 1990,[1] identifying one strand of a long-standing *cultural schizophrenia* in public attitudes to the modern day heirs of Edmund Burke's Fourth Estate.[2] The journalist is a hate figure, on the one hand, held responsible by many for the debasement of public discourse and the coarsening of society in general. The journalist is commonly referred to in these contexts as a hack, a reptile, a sleaze merchant revelling in other's miseries, a purveyor of cultural trash. The outspoken Tory MP and diarist, the late Alan Clark, typified this attitude when he wrote that journalists are 'fellows with, in the main, squalid and unfulfilling private lives, insecure in their careers, and suffering a considerable degree of dependence on alcohol and narcotics'.[3]

Clark was not alone in such thoughts (nor is the journalist alone in harbouring such vices, let us concede at the outset). His comments come from an essay included in a volume entitled *Secrets of the Press: journalists on journalism*. Clark reminds us that much of the loathing expressed for journalists is actually a form of self-loathing. Journalists often hate themselves, it seems, just as much as non-journalists do. In the scabrous words of one of the greatest journalists of the twentieth century, Hunter S. Thompson:

> Journalism is not a profession or a trade. It is a cheap catch-all for fuckoffs and misfits – a false doorway to the backside of life, a filthy piss-ridden little hole nailed off by the building inspector, but just deep enough for a wino to curl up from the sidewalk and masturbate like a chimp in a zoo-cage.[4]

That might be overdoing it, though it is not uncharacteristic of the great gonzo's prose style. Of all the journalists I have met or dealt with, only some of them could be described as 'fuckoffs and misfits'. Thompson's put-down is illustrative, however, of the extreme reactions journalism provokes, even from journalists.

Those in the entertainment industry, sport and other spheres of celebrity who are the objects of unwelcome journalistic attention also tend to be critical of journalists, and who can blame them? In 2004 Mel Gibson co-produced a film called *Paparazzi* (Paul Abascal) in which a Hollywood movie star dishes out summary and lethal punishment to a group of hacks who have been harassing him and his family. The film was not well received critically, but the contempt and hatred for journalists which it displayed are widely shared sentiments amongst the rich and famous who so often feature in the huge sub-sector of the journalism industry that is celebrity news.

Politicians, themselves not the most popular of professional groups, hate journalists because they are often the targets of the news media's disrespect and degeneracy (as they would see it), their thoughts, actions and behaviours exposed to merciless scrutiny before the wide-eyed gaze of a public encouraged (by journalists, who else?) to be evermore voyeuristic and judgemental. From this perspective, journalists are disreputable scandal-mongers, 'pornographers' even, in the words of former British prime minister John Major. 'Are we now in a world', he asked rhetorically, 'in which peephole journalism will print anything, true or false, that is said by anybody, sick or otherwise, on the grounds that the subject is a public figure and therefore the public has a "right to know"?'[5] Himself a victim of relentless press attacks during and after his time in office, Major was referring on this occasion to online coverage of alleged details of the private life of HRH Prince Charles in 2003 which threatened to make it into print (but never did because of the UK's libel and privacy laws).

Tony Blair's director of communications in government, Alistair Campbell, does not bother to disguise his contempt for journalists in his diaries, referring to them repeatedly as 'wankers'. 'Why', he wrote in 1998, after another bruising day with the Westminster lobby journalists, 'should I pretend to respect them when I don't?' (2007: 301). In this case one imagines the feelings were mutual, given the notorious spin doctor's reputation for bullying and abusing journalists with whom he was displeased. But his views are common amongst politicians and their media advisers. Another of Blair's spin doctors in the 1990s, Tim Allan, wrote an impassioned piece denouncing 'punk political journalism' and what he called 'a self-appointed priesthood that believes only relentless attacks will inform our democracy. With their puffed up self-importance, their unelected, unaccountable status and their huge and corrosive influence on political discourse, they have become the trade union barons of our day'.[6]

In January 2005, just as the dust was settling from the Hutton inquiry into the Andrew Gilligan affair,[7] the *Guardian* newspaper ran a special issue headed

'The fourth estate under fire', under which rubric an assortment of distinguished voices lined up to put the boot in to their journalistic fellows. Anthony
Sampson, for example, much-respected author of books on the structure of
power in British society asserted that 'journalists have gained power hugely ...
[and] become much more assertive, aggressive and moralising in confronting
other forms of power'.[8] In his influential book, *What The Media Are Doing To
Our Politics*, journalist John Lloyd concluded of the BBC's performance in the
Gilligan affair that 'we have produced a media culture which in many ways
contradicts the ideals to which we pay homage' (2004: 140). Lloyd's complaint,
echoed by many others, was that his co-professionals had by the early years of
the twenty-first century become locked into a vicious and destructive cycle of
attack journalism, tearing political reputations and careers apart in reckless
pursuit of competitive success. Dressed up as legitimate adversarialism and
the necessary harryings of the Fourth Estate, modern journalism had become
what James Fallows in his 1996 book *Breaking the News* called *hyperadversarial*,
in pursuit of no cause more noble than that of professional vanity and institutional advantage.

As for the publics of those countries where journalism evolved first and
has become a key cultural institution, opinion polls indicate that in the league
of most despised professions journalists feature prominently, listed alongside
lawyers, estate agents and politicians in the 'most hated' charts. An Ipsos-
MORI poll conducted in the United Kingdom in 2006 showed journalists to
be the least trusted to tell the truth among sixteen professional groups,[9] while a
2008 YouGov poll showed steadily declining trust in journalists over a five-year
period.[10]

In the United States research collated by the Pew Center for the People and
the Press on changing attitudes over the period 1985–2007 showed that those
who believe in the morality of journalists had fallen from 54 per cent to 46 per
cent of the population. Nearly one third of those surveyed by Pew believed the
US press to be 'immoral', more than double the figure for 1985.[11] Nearly two
thirds believed US news organisations to be politically biased, while slightly
fewer – 59 per cent – regarded their stories as 'often inaccurate'. Sixty-eight per
cent of those canvassed in this survey did not believe that journalists care about
the people in their stories. And in the wake of such stories as the disappearance
of four-year-old Madeleine McCann while on holiday in the Algarve in 2006,
leading to unsubstantiated newspaper suggestions that the parents had killed
their own daughter, with or without the connivance of their holidaymaking
friends, that belief seems entirely reasonable (Kate and Gerry McCann, and
their friends, were subsequently awarded substantial court damages against
the newspapers who libelled them in this way).

The Project for Excellence in Journalism's 2008 report on *The State of the
Media* found that growing numbers of people in the US regard journalists

as 'immoral' (32 per cent, up from only 13 per cent in 1985), 'inaccurate' (53 per cent), 'politically biased' (55 per cent) and 'unprofessional' (22 per cent). Americans, concluded the PEJ, 'have formed the deep impression that the press is an institution of immense power that should be viewed with suspicion'.[12]

AND NOW ... FOR SOME GOOD NEWS

If journalists are loathed by large numbers of people, or at least disliked and distrusted, they are also admired, respected and, yes, one might even say loved for the work they do, and the crucial role they are recognised to play in liberal democratic societies. The investigative journalist who tirelessly campaigns to get an innocent man out of prison, or a corrupt politician out of office; the foreign correspondent who risks her life to reach a town or village where civilians are under siege from marauding armies; the dedicated seeker-after-truth who fights against the censorial tendencies of advertisers and corporate sponsors – these are esteemed figures in the value system of our culture, before whom we are humbled, sometimes shamed by our own everyday inaction and apathy. The journalist can be our collective conscience, going to places and doing things that we ourselves dare not, and without whose courage we would as societies be very much worse off.

Journalists can be celebrities, idolised for their perceived status and glamour almost as much as rock and movie stars. Wolfe, Thompson, Murrow, Cronkite, Paxman, Frost, Adie, Amanpour – these are the familiar names of journalists past and present who have become 'stars' in the universe of news media because they are perceived to stand for something important, or because their reportage, analyses, insights and judgements are recognised as particularly sharp and revealing. As Alex Gibney's 2008 documentary on *Gonzo* shows, Hunter S. Thompson, at the peak of his journalistic powers in the early 1970s, was more glamorous and exciting a figure than many of the top rank musicians, sporting celebrities and politicians whom he wrote about and with whom he mixed. Larry King's interviews on CNN became the vehicle for the journalist's celebrity as much as, if not more than that of his guests.

Journalists can become too famous, and some notable cinematic representations have satirised the excesses of celebrity journalism. In Oliver Stone's *Natural Born Killers* (1994), about the incestuous relationship between the news media and crime in the United States, Robert Downey Jr plays a TV host whose 'true crime' programme leads to mayhem and death, including his own. Christiane Amanpour, CNN's star foreign correspondent of many years, is loosely parodied in David O. Russell's *Three Kings* (1999), disguised as the female correspondent Adriana Cruz who drops in to the scene of the battle like a celebrity around whom everything else must revolve, utterly convinced of her own importance.

There is, however, more than a grain of truth in this self-perception. At the top of their profession journalists wield huge political influence and command stellar salaries, inspiring those thousands of young people all over the world who enter colleges and universities to study and train to become journalists like their heroes and heroines. In late 2008 Ron Howard's *Frost/Nixon* was released, a study of the famous TV interview given by the disgraced former US president to one of the UK's leading journalistic inquisitors. It was indicative of the degree of name recognition attached to the protagonists in 2008 that the film's title was *Frost/Nixon*, rather than Nixon/Frost.

In the United Kingdom university programmes in journalism are among the most heavily in demand of all higher education degrees in the humanities, a fact for which I and my academic colleagues are duly grateful, and which merely makes more paradoxical the cultural schizophrenia reflected in the opinion polls. In the United States there were 50,000 students taking BAs in journalism-related subjects in 2007, and 3,800 taking Masters courses.[13] For all that public perceptions of journalism, and the expression of these in cinema and other narrative arts are often negative, journalists are at the same time held in admiration, sometimes awe. The journalist is a cultural icon surrounded by both love and loathing, resentment and respect, admiration and anger – a figure perceived as both hero and villain, treated like a rock star at one moment, and a reptile the next. In relation to few professions are cultural stereotypes so extreme and apparently opposed. Nor are there many professions in which the imagined reality is so different from the actual.

JOURNALISTS IN FILM

Film, as Thomas Zynda observed in 1979, and Hollywood film in particular, has been one of the main sources of the representation of journalism in western popular culture. There have been many excellent novels written on the subject, as already noted, and many TV dramas produced, but cinema has a broader popular reach than either of those media, crossing national borders and taste hierarchies as part of cultural globalisation, impacting on the publics of many and diverse countries with a force rarely seen in a particular work of prose fiction or TV drama. Many more people have seen the film of *All the President's Men* (1976) than have read the original book by Woodward and Bernstein (the former took more than $70 million at the US box office on release, and continues to sell to new generations of viewers on DVD. The book was a best-seller too, but not on the scale of the movie). *Citizen Kane* (1941) is an icon of global cinema, familiar (even if only by reputation) to everyone with even a

Figure 1 *Citizen Kane* (Orson Welles, 1941). Source: BFI

passing interest in film history.[14] Global screen stars such as George Clooney and Angelina Jolie play journalists in movies which are often in the box office charts all over the world.

Movies, then, have a reach and a resonance which make it reasonable to consider them a particularly fertile source of how a society perceives and relates to the phenomena which they address. They are not – or rarely are – a 'mirror' held up to society, reflecting us back to ourselves without distortion or error, but they are certainly a prism, through which is refracted a society's conception of itself, or that part of itself which is the subject of the movie, and which is then played back to the audience as a text which may be at one and the same time an entertainment, an ethics lesson and an invitation to reflect on the big domestic and foreign policy issues of the day.

Movies are collective productions, of course, the work of many artists, technicians and producers, all of whom may be presumed to play a larger or smaller part in mediating the final product, but we experience them as single texts comprising a vision, or viewpoint about how things are. They present a statement which can be attributed at least in part to the individual accredited as the director. *Citizen Kane* is perceived as an 'Orson Welles' film, even if it was made with the help of many hundreds of others. Michael Winterbottom's three films discussed in this book (*Welcome To Sarajevo* [1997], *Twenty*

Four Hour Party People [2002], *A Mighty Heart* [2007]) are in large part the products of his particular directorial style.

Narrative film is also a product of its time, weaving prevalent moods and trends into stories which both reflect and reinforce them. In short, the cinema produced by a given society at a given time is one source of data on how that society views itself – in this case, its journalists, and also the publics who consume journalism, in so far as the tastes and demands of audiences determine to some extent which films are made.

Cinema is not bound by the normative principles of journalism, of course, but is structured by aesthetic, commercial, technical and creative factors and constraints. Films in a capitalist cultural economy are first and foremost commodities which must achieve commercial success on the various platforms where they are distributed (including, today, cinemas, DVDs and Blu-ray, and online channels for streaming and downloading). This requires of the film-maker acceptance of those cinematic conventions and tropes expected by an audience. A film is never, therefore, real or true in any simple sense. Like journalism itself, but to a greater extent, it is an *account* of the real. No cinematic text, no matter how 'true' are the events on which it is based, nor how realistically it is directed, can be entirely factually accurate. Incidents in a 'true story' will often be invented, or several incidents collapsed into one, which then comes to stand for the greater whole.

Contemporary film-makers hardly bother to deny this and are more likely to assert merely that their fact-based accounts capture the essence of *a* rather than *the* truth. A writer of prose or poetry may legitimately aspire to capture at least some element of the truth of a phenomenon – love, for example, or sadness, or the beauty of nature – and to find that truth accepted by a reader. The film-maker has the same expectation, to be achieved through the creative manipulation of the elements of the story being represented. This is, and always has been, in the nature of art.

Cinema, like all art, can be viewed as an arena for the mediation of social complexity, a vessel for its reduction down to its key strands and features. Cinematic representations of a particular social type inevitably draw upon the prevailing models of that type which a particular society harbours, and in the process contribute to consolidating and reinforcing their prevalence. In the case of journalism some of these types are clearly based on normative models of the journalist's role – watchdog, witness, sense-maker; others are dysfunctional and toxic, such as the character of Chuck Tatum whom we shall encounter later on. The film-maker is a lightning rod for these competing images of heroism and villainy, licensed to dramatise them, and thus to furnish the material for public debate around the performance of the journalists.

MOVIES AS MYTH

Movies are the central myth-making media of our societies. Films about journalism, by extension, are the main cultural space in which societies (or their artists) articulate their agreed journalistic values, explore and interrogate them, and critique the application of these values both by the journalistic media themselves (as in Billy Ray's *Shattered Glass* [2003]), and by the powerful in their relationship to the news media (*Good Night, and Good Luck* [George Clooney, 2005]). Some films, such as Michael Mann's *The Insider* (1998), critique both journalism and power. I will characterise the movie-maker's cultural roles in this context as:

- *educational* (and *normative*, imparting public knowledge about what journalism is expected to do in a democracy);
- *mythological* and *celebratory* (bringing public attention to, and soliciting praise for, the achievements of journalism at its best);
- *regulatory* (undertaking critical scrutiny of the scrutineers, acting as watchdogs of the watchdogs);
- *defensive*, as against those who would neuter or suppress the critical and dissenting tendencies in liberal journalism.

What, then, do the movies tell us about journalism, and about journalists' relationship to the societies within which they ply their trade? Matthew Ehrlich observes that the movies have 'provided models for real-life journalistic conduct'(2004). Actually, very few movies about journalism can be read as how-to manuals for journalistic professionals. Rather, they are ambivalent, often highly critical explorations of the tensions structured into liberal journalism by the context of its origins in early democratic societies. They form an evolving narrative about what those tensions are, how they have been manifest in particular societies, and how they have changed over time.

Those in power at any given time, as they are monitored by the fourth estate of journalism, monitor in their turn what journalists say about power, and then too what the film-makers and the artists say about both. In democracies the powerful are accountable to the people, who are informed and influenced by the media. What film-makers say about power, and about the relationship between power and journalism, does not go unnoticed by the powerful, because they are aware that these performances, scripts and images comprise an important part of the stock of public knowledge, the knowledge that informs public opinion.

In these respects, movies about journalism are documents of a society's ongoing engagement with this key cultural and political institution. And like all documents, they require to be studied with care. The finished film we see on screen is the work of a collective. Sometimes the influence and signature of a particular director, writer or actor is unmistakeable, and we can speak of a 'Billy Wilder film' with some expectation that others will understand what is meant. On the other hand film-makers are not the only source of the 'messages' on screen. Reading a film is therefore much more than coming to an understanding of who made it, and why. A contemporary auteur is unlikely to wear his politics, or his attitudes to journalism on his sleeve, preferring to leave interpretative space for the audience to read his work in their own way. But film-makers, like it or not, soak up the cultural atmosphere around them, internalise it, reproduce it, and thus cannot help but be viewed as sources for *something*.

My approach to reading film is auteur-based, in so far as I attach significance to the name of the director, writer, actor involved in its production and whose ideas are embodied to some degree in the finished work. But I do not assume a simple translation of those ideas, or of the ideas out there in society into what is up there on screen. The personal visions of the contributors (which are expressed in the cinematography, script, *mise en scène*, and so on), the production constraints on a film (and there are always many), the commercial pressures – all have to be taken into account as factors in interpreting what a film about journalism is trying to say, if indeed it is trying to say anything. But even when a film is *not* trying to say anything very much – take, for example, the lightest of romantic comedies in which journalism features, such as the Angelina Jolie romantic comedy vehicle *Life or Something Like It* (2002) as compared with the message-laden *Good Night, and Good Luck* – we find evidence of what journalism represents at a given moment in US society, of what its producers *assume* journalism to represent in the minds of the broad American public, of what they think journalism represents, or should represent. Such movies – think too of *Bruce Almighty* (Tom Shadyac, 2003) or *Runaway Bride* (Garry Marshall, 1999) – are packed with jokes and asides which make sense only in the context of shared stereotypes and cultural cliches about the nature of journalism and journalists.

THE REGULATORY ROLE OF THE JOURNALISM MOVIE

If journalists are, among other things, the principal cultural watchdogs of our society then movies and movie-makers are part of the apparatus of scrutiny which brings to bear on the journalists. Films, like novels and other forms, draw our attention to the flaws in journalistic practice, often by contrasting it with the normative standards journalism is subject to. Cinema monitors the media, criticises it, and praises it too. Cinema is a place where society's cultural representatives talk back to the media, and thence to power itself.

Within even the most mainstream of cinematic genres the performance of these cultural roles means there is both homage to and substantive, radical critique of the media and its relationship to power.[15] Both can be excessive, in that legitimate praise can tip into panegyric and sycophancy, while criticism may become 'corrosive cynicism' (to use a term often applied to journalists themselves). That being so, it is important for the analyst to maintain a critical evaluative stance towards films about journalism.

It will be my argument in this book that mainstream movies can be and – more often than has tended to be acknowledged – *are* the site of substantive critique, not just of the workings of power in capitalism, but of the media (the journalistic media in this context) and, in some cases, the relationship between media and power. Yes, as we shall see, and as many observers have asserted, the movies perpetuate stereotypes of journalists which are stupid and crass (and why not? Some journalism is certainly possessed of those qualities), but they also contain sophisticated, often radical critiques of how the media work, and of how they relate to political and financial power. The movies represent journalists as heroes *and* villains, and that is appropriate, because journalists are *both*. If the media are a key source of what Niklas Luhman called a society's 'self-recursive myths' (2000) – that is, the narratives through which a society talks about itself to itself – the movies represent a second-tier symbolic system; a set of media representations which function to elucidate, interrogate, and comment on the workings of the first-tier regulatory system of journalism itself.

It is a myth (in the other sense of untruth, unfounded assertion, or false perception) that movies tend to show journalists only or mainly as villains. Some do, and some journalists are, but in many of the films discussed in this book we see sophisticated and, at times, subversive critique of: (1) how journalists and journalism, given the normative functions they are expected to perform within democratic societies, do in fact relate to their publics, their audiences, conceived as non-elite readers, viewers, listeners and (now) internet users; (2) how news media relate to power elites in all those spheres of a society where authority and control are wielded; and (3) the relationship between journalists and power. Narrative feature films – including those financed, distributed and marketed by the biggest and most mainstream of Big Media – are significant locations for the articulation of critical perspectives on the workings of power and media, separately and in their inter-relationship. They are watched by millions upon millions of people, in circumstances which might permit them to have some kind of impact on how those audiences perceive the events and issues being portrayed on screen. They are to this extent a signif-icant mechanism in the self-regulation and management of the public sphere in democracy.

If, for the sake of analytical convenience and using for a moment the language of estates, we think of social and economic power as residing in the first, second and third estates in democratic societies, and journalism as the *fourth estate*, charged with monitoring that power, constraining it and enabling the people to evaluate and debate its acquisition, distribution and performance – a public sphere engaged in the critical scrutiny of power – then movies about journalism sit alongside other cultural forms (novels and TV dramas, satirical comedy, the meta-journalism of journalistic commentary on journalism produced by pundits, essayists and others) as a further level of critical scrutiny, this time including the scrutiny of journalism itself. A fifth estate, as it were.

The film-maker is, at his or her most socially engaged, an important category of public intellectual taking on the work of monitoring the monitors, scrutinising the scrutineers, facilitating public debate about the performance of the news and journalistic media by inserting into the public sphere another kind of knowledge, comprising fact, interpretation and comment. The film-maker's contribution to knowledge is of a more reflective, subjective, aesthetically self-conscious kind than that of the supposedly objective journalist or scientist, embedded within texts which are designed not just to draw attention to the workings of power and prompt public debate, but to entertain.

DEEP IMPACT?

Films reflect the agenda of public debate at any given time, and may help set it if they have sufficient impact. Film-makers, to the degree that their works are well received, construct an arena for debate, often very high profile, and inform the public and the media – or remind them, if they think they know already – of what is expected of journalists, and ask if those expectations are being met. They contribute to an ongoing public conversation within which the role and functions of journalism are never far away from that same public's zone of interest and legitimate concern. That this is true even of the most mainstream films is, when one thinks about it, good news for the state of our political culture, and for the relationship between politics and culture.

As is true for all media, some caution is required in relation to judging a film's impact on its audience, and on the wider public amongst whom it circulates. *All the President's Men* is widely believed to have made a major impact on the practice of journalism in the United States after the Watergate scandal. If ever a film fits Ehrlich's description of a movie which provides a positive model for journalistic work, it is Pakula's study of the Woodward-Bernstein investigation. Others have questioned the extent to which this presumed effect has been mythologised, just as the Watergate investigation itself has become a legend (Schudson 1995). What we can say with certainty is that its production, and its commercial and artistic success both reflected and reinforced US public anxiety about, on the one hand, the state of the presidency, and on the other, the state of the media. If in the Nixon era all US journalists had been like Woodward and Bernstein in their dedication and tenacity perhaps the film would not have been necessary, nor would the Watergate scandal have been allowed to happen. The Watergate investigation can justifiably be seen as a triumph of American liberal journalism. The film of that investigation fed back into a debate which concerned not just the corruption of politics, but the potentially corrupt relationship of journalism to power. Its effectiveness as a work of cinematic art enabled it to provide a model for future journalistic practice, although we cannot know how influential the model was or has been.

In this respect the journalism movie is part of the mythology of American society, part of its ideological foundation (and that of liberal democratic societies more broadly). Ehrlich notes that movies about journalism reflect 'myths coloured by nostalgia' and 'address contradictions at the heart of both journalism and American culture' (2004: 1). Myths can have conservative ideological functions within a society, legitimising the state of things as they are. But myth 'can also critique or change the status quo' (ibid.).

Debates rise and fall on the agenda, cultural and political environments change, and movies about journalism have value in so far as they document this with accuracy. The 1980s TV newsroom featured in *Broadcast News* (James L. Brooks, 1987) is very different from that of *All the President's Men*, both of which are far removed from the monochrome smokiness of the newsroom in Howard Hawks' *His Girl Friday* (1940) or the production offices used by Ed Murrow and his team in *Good Night, and Good Luck*. Future generations of journalists will look back with amazement to those days from their smoke-free, air-conditioned, health-and-safety compliant work stations.

George Clooney's much-admired film addresses what was already, by the 1950s, a prominent debate about the negative impact of commercial pressures on journalistic quality. That debate continues to this day in recognisably similar form, as we shall see, in films such as *Accidental Hero* (Stephen Frears, 1992) and *Mad City* (Costa-Gavras, 1997). If we were to watch either of these movies a half century from now we might conclude that in the late twentieth century when they were made the United States was a society uncomfortable with the tension between the role of journalist as informer and that of entertainer; with the journalist-as-infotainer under pressure to produce news which holds an audience's attention as much as it improves public understanding of current events.

A more recent film such as *Shattered Glass* deals with a phenomenon specific to its time, and the impact of this on journalistic traditions and conventions. Billy Ray's account of the fabrications inflicted on the *New Republic* by Stephen Glass allots a key role to the then-rising online journalism sector. It is an online publication which blows the whistle on Glass, and which leaves the esteemed *New Republic* embarrassed and compromised. Likewise, a film such as *Welcome*

To Sarajevo (Michael Winterbottom, 1997) addresses the role of the foreign correspondent in an era when the ideological certainties of the Cold War had given way to much older, more primitive passions, and the identification of Good and Evil had become much less straightforward than in the days of the Communist menace. By comparing films about foreign correspondence made between, say, the 1940s and the 1990s, we learn much about the changing role of the conflict reporter, and the changing nature of conflict, over this period.

Films about female journalists, such as *Veronica Guerin* (Joel Schumacher, 2003) and David Frankel's *The Devil Wears Prada* (2006) document the outcomes of a century-long process in which women have made great advances in respect of their historically dominant male counterparts. Have the movies accelerated those advances, or allowed them to be embedded more securely in our societies because of the impact they have had on the women who have seen them? This book cannot answer that question, but does view cinema as one way of identifying what has changed in the status of women in society, and within the journalistic profession (see Chapter 7, Heroines).

NOTES

1. 'The American journalist: fiction versus fact', paper delivered in 1990, accessed on the website of *The Image of the Journalist in Popular Culture* (ijpc.org).
2. The first three estates in pre-revolutionary France were the clergy, the aristocracy, and the common citizenry. After the French Revolution, Burke first referred to journalists seated in the Press Gallery of the House of Commons as the Fourth Estate, expressing their political role as watchdogs over the powerful.
3. Clark, Alan, 'Why I hold journalists in low regard', in Glover, Stephen (ed.), *Secrets of the Press*, 1999.
4. Quoted in Wise, Damon, 'Gonzo's back', *Guardian*, 6 December 2008.
5. Major, J., 'We're hurting ourselves as well as Charles', *Sunday Times*, 16 November 2003.
6. Allan, T., 'Puffed up punks', *Guardian*, 4 December 2004.
7. Andrew Gilligan was the BBC correspondent who, on 6 May 2003, asserted that a key document used by the British government to justify its invasion of Iraq had been 'sexed up' in order to exaggerate the threat posed by Saddam Hussein's alleged possession of weapons of mass destruction. The Gilligan report, and the government's furious response to it, led in due course to the death by suicide of a key source for the story, government scientist David Kelly, the forced resignation of the BBC's director general Greg Dyke and its chairman Gavyn Davies, and a wholesale restructuring of the BBC's internal management systems.
8. Sampson, A., 'The fourth estate under fire', *Guardian*, 10 January 2005. Sampson died in 2004, just before this piece was published.
9. Ipsos-MORI, *Opinion of Professions*, April 2008 (http://www.ipsos-mori.com/content/turnout/opinion-of-professions2.ashx).
10. Reported in Barnett, S., 'On the road to self-destruction', *British Journalism Review*, volume 19, number 2, 2008, pp. 5–13.
11. *Views of Press Values and Performance, 1985–2007*, Pew Research Center for the People and the Press, August 2007 (*http://people-press.org/reports/pdf/348.pdf*).

12. *The State of the New Media 2008: an annual report on American journalism* (www.state-ofthenewsmedia.org/2008/narrative_special_attitudes.php?cat=1&media=).

13. From the *Annual Survey of Journalism & Mass Communication Graduates, AEJMC News*, volume 42, number 1, November 2008.

14. In 2008, once again, *Citizen Kane* was named best film ever by the authoritative French periodical *Cahiers De Cinema*, and also by *Sight & Sound*.

15. As Howard Good has observed, 'the narrative patterns of the journalism film genre are mirrors of, and metaphors for, the relationship between the public and the press, its ruined hopes, desperate wishes, and ambiguous promises' (1989: 2).

CHAPTER 3

Heroes and villains – an overview of journalism on film

Richard R. Ness filmography of journalism in the movies lists some 2,166 US-, and around eighty UK-produced films made between the early years of the silent cinema and 1996. In many of these films journalism is present only as a bit player, part of the backdrop to a story which is not really 'about' journalism, but in which journalists are involved to a greater or less extent. In some – the many Superman movies, for example, in which Clark Kent's mild-mannered reporter is the mask behind which a superhero resides – a character's journalistic status is a convenient plot device, a vehicle for a particular kind of narrative (in Superman's case, one in which breaking news is an opportunity for displays of heroism and action-packed battles between Good and Evil). The prevalence of journalism in these contexts reflects the extent to which our contemporary societies are, in so many respects, 'mediated'. News media are the ever-present backdrop to both private and public life, part of the cultural furniture and ambient noise of our society. Cinema reflects this.

In many films, however, the journalist, and his or her profession and its outputs, has been the star of the show, the fulcrum around which the story revolves. These are films in which journalism is unquestionably the *subject* of the work; the source of the dramatic tensions and narrative structures which fuel the plot; the focus of the dilemmas and challenges driving the characters. Within this broad category there are films about virtually nothing except journalism, which I will call *primary representations*, and films – *secondary representations* – in which journalists are certainly centre stage, but which use their journalistic setting as a jumping off point for a movie which is mainly about something else, such as the nature of love, or war.

There is, to repeat, a third category of films in which journalists appear as background characters, with or without lines. In Ridley Scott's *Body of Lies* (2008), for example, TV news footage punctuates the story with 'coverage' of the terrorist atrocities the central characters are trying to prevent.

There are some films, such as *Three Kings* (David O. Russell, 1998), in which journalists play a supporting or minor role, but in which the subject of journalism is still primary rather than incidental. *Three Kings* is superficially a thriller, a heist movie, set in the immediate aftermath of the first Gulf war. A group of US soldiers set out to appropriate Saddam's gold bullion and end up helping refugees from his regime cross the border to safety. Along the way we see the horrific arbitrariness of war, and the chaos and confusion which accompanies it. The narrative is punctuated by appearances from TV news journalist Adriana Cruz, a character reportedly modelled on CNN's Christiane Amanpour, whose presence allows the film to address the role of real-time news in the conflict, and the implications of an environment in which all wars have become 'media wars'. She voices what many people felt about that conflict – what was it for? The impact on war-fighting of the need to provide the news media with stories and images (preferably positive), and for military managers always to be aware of the media dimension of what they do, is a constant theme running through the film. The same is true of Danis Tanovich's *No Man's Land* (2002) about the Bosnian conflict. Again a TV news journalist has a supporting role, but one which allows a focus for much of the film's running time on the exploration of journalism's distorting impact on conflict, and the idea that in observing and reporting such events journalists also affect them, and not always for the better.

Whether primary or secondary in plot terms, journalism's prominence within the cinema of the past 100 years, and in the past decade no less so, leaves us in no doubt that journalism has been and remains a subject with immense appeal to those who make feature films – writers, directors, actors and producers – as well as the audiences who make the movies one of the key popular media forms. Not all of the films discussed in this book are mainstream Hollywood fare. Some have achieved little or no commercial success, remaining within the avant-garde or art-house scene. Such films have often been extremely influential, and here one thinks of Antonioni's *The Passenger* (1975) or Fellini's *La Dolce Vita* (1960). Films about journalism have also been among the biggest earners in cinema.[1]

Films about journalism have also been among the most celebrated as works of art, and regular recipients of Oscars and other awards. The film most often cited in polls as the best film of all time, *Citizen Kane* (Orson Welles, 1941), is a film about journalism as much as it is about power and empire. Kane's acquisition of both is built on journalism, and he spends much of the movie's first act as a working editor and journalist, engaged in the news room with his colleagues to produce the popular progressive newspaper he wishes to own. Although the practice of journalism becomes steadily less important as the story of Kane's rise and fall proceeds, that story is itself presented in the form of a journalistic investigation, in which facts and their meanings are

Figure 2 *His Girl Friday* (Howard Hawks, 1940). Source: BFI

gradually unearthed through interviews with protagonists and the assemblage of secondary sources such as news reel footage, as well as our access to the thoughts of Kane himself. Other acknowledged film classics – *Sweet Smell of Success* (Alexander MacKendrick, 1957), *All the President's Men* (Alan J. Pakula, 1976), *His Girl Friday* (Howard Hawks, 1940) – have journalism at their narrative cores.

The first question to be answered, therefore, is why? What is it about journalism which drives the most talented cinematic artists (and many who are not so talented) to write, produce, direct and perform in movies about it? What is the source of the fourth estate's enduring fascination to film folk and their audiences?

First, as Ness, Ehrlich and others have noted, journalism is highly functional for cinema in that its nature as a professional practice generates the incidents and narratives which make a good movie. Movies tell stories, and therefore require scenarios in which good stories can be credibly and efficiently told. In this the journalist consistently delivers. Journalism, in a manner akin to the policeman or the private detective, is a licensed exposer of the things which some people might wish to remain hidden away from public view. The journalist investigates scandal, cover-ups, corruption, crime. That's his or her

Figure 3 *Sweet Smell of Success* (Alexander MacKendrick, 1957). Source: BFI

job, ordained by four centuries of liberal democratic history and enshrined in the constitutions of many countries,[2] notably the US where most of these films have been made.[3] The journalist, like the private eye, can be a sleazy and distasteful figure, and there have been many such portrayals in film; but where the private eye slinks around on the fringes of respectable society, often a failed law enforcer brought down by personal inadequacy or frailty, the journalist exposes the truth, painful as it may be, with the full support of society, proud and purposeful, and no matter what the opposition. In *The China Syndrome* (James Bridges, 1979) the journalists played by Michael Douglas and Jane Fonda act as the catalyst for the exposure of nuclear hazard.

The business of exposure naturally provokes resistance, and this too is fuel for the story-hungry film-maker. Story-telling often involves a protagonist confronted with an obstacle to reaching a goal, and journalists are all too often obstructed in their profession. Resistance and conflict generate drama, suspense, violence and tragedy. In films based on real life stories, such as *The Insider* (Michael Mann, 1998), conflict and the responses to it by the protagonists – in this case, a tobacco industry whistle-blower and a TV current affairs producer respectively – are the core of the work. *All the President's Men*, too, has little room for characterisation or emotion amidst its narrative of a journalistic struggle for truth against the highest power in the land. The relationship between the journalists and their subject *is* the drama, and there is more than enough of it to sustain a two-hour movie.

Movies about journalists make good stories, then, because the situation of the journalist in society is inherently dramatic. For the majority of actual journalists, of course, the reality of professional life is less exciting than its portrayal in cinema. Movies are not reality, but representations of the real which cut and compress the everyday detail of events – in our case, the often unglamorous details of how news is gathered and distributed – in order to render them engaging for the audiences on whose patronage the industry depends. Movies are mythological – dream factories, indeed – and films about journalism are no less prone to the inclusion of stereotypes, caricatures, and fantasies than any other kind.

The ideal of journalism, and not infrequently the practice of it, neces-sarily takes the journalist, and we as audiences, into the heart of a plausibly real darkness where all manner of twists and turns can be expected. Dennis Hopper's news photographer in *Apocalypse Now* (Francis Ford Coppola, 1978) is in that dark place first imagined by Conrad, captivated by the charismatic magnetism of Brando's Colonel Kurtz as the latter awaits the assassin's bullet. Coppola's film also recreates the work of a TV news crew filming the aftermath of a US attack on a Vietnamese village, and the banal obscenity of a culture which permits such images to be valued as news, and which subordinates the reality of human suffering to the production demands of the network news bulletin.

Films about journalism often take us to the seat of power, as in Pakula's film about Watergate. And for those reasons, too, journalistic stories are often heroic, realisable as simple but stirring tales of Black and White, Good and Evil. Journalists in film often represent a kind of cultural nobility, like the incorruptible cop and the self-sacrificing soldier – an ideal which may be challenged by events, to the benefit of a good story. Journalists can also be – hence the sub-title of this book – screen villains, irredeemably wicked, amoral, worthless. Kirk Douglas' Chuck Tatum in *Ace in the Hole* is such a villain, with his merciless manipulation of a redeemable situation to the point that it destroys lives, including his own. J. J. Hunsecker in *Sweet Smell of Success* is another, played by a sinister Burt Lancaster loosely modelled on the real-life career and persona of Walter Winchell.

The fact that these stories are often true, or based on truth (not, of course, the same thing at all) reminds us of another reason for the appeal of journalists to film-makers: journalism is *important*, in a way that few other professions can be. Film-makers (from now on I will include in this term of convenience all contributors to the film-making process) are people too, fully aware of and engaged in the public debates which occupy the society around them. In recent times Hollywood stars such as George Clooney, Sean Penn and Angelina Jolie have demonstrated their political commitment to such causes as opposing the war in Iraq and world poverty. This has exposed the movie-making elite to a certain degree of mockery from those on the right who see them as a liberal front within the establishment (and from the left, from those who question their motivations and sincerity). They can defend themselves well enough against that caricature, and I will say here only that many cinematic artists are self-evidently intelligent, talented individuals who care about politics, and thus about the media which are so central to the political process in a democracy. Clooney's *Good Night, and Good Luck* exemplifies that concern, in a real-life story from the 1950s made with an eye on the performance of the media in the 'war on terror' which was at its height when the film was released.

Movie-makers, perhaps more than some other categories of professional, are also aware of the impact of the media on public opinion, and thus more inclined to explore issues around the performance of the media. Maybe, too, the experience of at least some of their number in the frenzied arenas of celebrity culture attracts them to stories in which journalists themselves become the scrutinised subject, and often in an unflattering context, in which cinema plays out debates around the ethics of journalism going on in the wider public sphere.

Films about journalism, then, allow film-makers to engage with substantial social issues, and important public debates, and to do so in ways which allow for the telling of compelling stories through characters who resonate in the public imagination. The potential for gripping tales of glamour and grime, of sharply drawn heroes and villains, is a large part of the reason why there has never been any shortage of A-list actors to perform journalistic roles, nor of top directors eager to demonstrate their seriousness and commitment to public affairs through making films about the news media and their often difficult relationship to the societies in which they circulate. Alfred Hitchcock made *Foreign Correspondent* (1940); Orson Welles made *Citizen Kane*; Billy Wilder's *Ace in the Hole* is one of his greatest works. Stephen Frears, Alexander MacKendrick, Oliver Stone, Michael Winterbottom, and many others have hit their creative peaks with films about journalism.

THE JOURNALISM GENRE

Many writers about journalism in the movies refer to them collectively as a 'genre'. I will follow that convention here, although it may be more accurate to say that the 'journalism genre' refers to a wide variety of types of film made about journalism, within a range of genres. There is in film scholarship a long tradition of 'genre studies' which categorises film into various types dependent on subject matter (the western, the war film), the narrative arc (film noir, in which a central male character is brought low or destroyed by a seductive femme fatale), the intended audience (the women's film; the teen film), the production context (independent film, blockbusters, auteur film), or the presence of a particular aesthetic (French New Wave, Dogme 95). According to the Wikipedia definition of the term, 'genres' are recognised as 'vague categories with no fixed boundaries, formed by sets of conventions … many works cross into multiple genres by way of borrowing and recombining these conventions'. To say that a film is a 'genre movie' is to say that it adheres to some or all of the conventions associated with a particular genre, often though not always as a consequence of conscious auteurial choice. The rules of the Danish movement Dogme 95 are clearly articulated by Lars Von Trier and the other directors who wrote them – no artificial lighting, no music on the soundtrack, and so on. Sometimes, genres are recognised as such only retrospectively. How many of those 1950s Hollywood directors of moody, monochrome thrillers recognised that they were making 'film noir'? Though the term was first applied to a particular style of Hollywood movie by French critic Nino Vance in 1946, it was not familiar to the film-makers themselves, and would not achieve common usage until much later.

If films about journalism can be regarded as a genre, then it is one which contains within it, or which crosses over into, many other recognised genres. *Ace in the Hole* may be viewed as 'film noir', for example, given the relationship between the main male and female protagonists, and the classic 'noir' trajectory of the former's story. *Citizen Kane* is sometimes described as 'noir-ish', as is *Sweet Smell of Success*, because of their cinematography and also the role played by female characters as 'femme fatales' in their stories. The 2007 film version of the life of Jesse James,[4] and Clint Eastwood's *Unforgiven* (1992) are westerns in which journalists feature prominently, if not centrally, as part of the myth-making apparatus of the old west. These are westerns made against the backdrop of awareness of the media's power to construct legends, and to manufacture celebrity.

Many of the screwball comedies of the 1930s and 1940s, including *His Girl Friday*, *The Philadelphia Story* (George Cukor, 1940), and *It Happened One Night* (Frank Capra, 1934), are also part of the genre of journalism films, the journalists' roles often being played by the leading Hollywood men (and women) of the day such as Clark Gable, Cary Grant and James Stewart. More recent romantic comedies starring today's leading men and women, in which journalists often feature as protagonists – *Runaway Bride*, for example – are thus often described as 'screwball'.

When I refer to the 'genre' of journalism movies, therefore, I have in mind all those films of which it can be said that one or more of the main characters is a journalist. This is a smaller category than the set of films in which journalists appear as characters, and can be further sub-divided into two categories.

First, and the main focus of this book, are those films which are, in an unambiguous way, *primary* (or instrumental) representations, *about* journalists and journalism. Whether marketed as period dramas, or romantic comedies, or bio-pics, or thrillers, journalists and journalism are their subject. *Capote* would be such a film, or *A Mighty Heart*. In *Shattered Glass* the lead characters are all journalists, the main location is an editorial office, and the subject of the work is unmistakeably the state of US journalism at a particular moment in its history. George Clooney's *Good Night, and Good Luck* is similarly focused on questions to do with the role of journalism as a democratic support.

Second, which I will call *secondary* representations, is that category of films which feature journalists, often as central characters, but in which journalism is an incidental element of the story. One thinks here of *The Shipping News* (Lasse Halstrom, 2004), where the subject of journalism – the job into which the central character is propelled by events – is less important to the playing out of the story than the movie's main themes of personal redemption and rediscovery. The same point can be made of *Dan in Real Life* (Peter Hedges, 2007), which stars Steve Carell as a recently bereaved newspaper 'agony uncle'. Secondary representations may be concerned with the life issues which a person who just happens to be a journalist might encounter in or out of the working environment. Journalism may in this context function as an important

Figure 4 *Shattered Glass* (Billy Ray, 2003). Source: BFI

plot device, as in *Dan in Real Life*, where the lead character's journalistic status is principally a vehicle for establishing him as a certain kind of personality – intellectual, sensitive – with a certain kind of romantic potential, here developed in his relationship with Juliette Binoche's character. The nature of his journalism, or the processes which lead to its production are not discussed or explored in any depth in the film – it is simply there in the background. Steve Carell's Dan could have been a poet or a novelist, if the aim were simply to construct a character who is a writer. Creating him as a columnist allows the script to play on the ironies of a man who gives public advice on relationships to his readers, but is somewhat dysfunctional in his own private life. Beyond this, his journalism is marginal to the story.

Vantage Point (Pete Travis, 2008) is also a secondary representation, in so far as the film features a TV news team led by producer Sigourney Weaver, who provide one of five points of view on the action (the apparent assassination of a US president). The journalists are positioned as witnesses to an event, alongside the tourist, the policeman, the presidential bodyguard and so on. The film is not in any sense 'about' journalism, although the successive presentations of the five perspectives on the event do serve to highlight the relativity of truth, the limits of objectivity, and the fact that what one believes to be true is at least partly determined by one's view, or vantage point. Like Antonioni's *Blow Up* (1966), although it is unlikely ever to be praised as that film was, *Vantage Point* plays with the idea that one cannot always believe what one sees with one's own eyes. Films in this category often have insightful, humorous and thought-provoking observations to make about journalism, but they are incidental rather than core to the plot.

JOURNALISM IN THE MOVIES: A GENERIC MATRIX

If films about journalism are a category defined by their subject matter (journalism and journalists), we can identify the many genres and sub-genres into which these films can be fitted. Movies about journalism are not *a* genre, but encompass a variety of generic conventions.

DRAMA

Defined by Wikipedia as a genre that 'depends on in-depth development of realistic characters dealing with emotional themes',[5] dramas about journalism include early classics such as *Citizen Kane*, with its examination of the destructive (and self-destructive) impact of media power on relationships and lives. *Good Night, and Good Luck* is a drama based on actual events about the struggle for media freedom at a time of heightened political anxieties. *Broadcast*

News (James L. Brooks, 1987) is described on the sleeve of its 2004 DVD release as a 'quirky romantic comedy' but could just as easily be classified as drama, exploring as it does not only the personal relationships between a group of journalists working for a local TV news organisation, but complex issues around the perceived commercialisation of news in the 1980s. William Hurt's newsreader represents not just the love interest for Holly Hunter's producer, but the mounting superficiality of TV news in an era when (the film suggests) good looks and smooth delivery (including, in one key scene, Hurt's fake tears as he interviews a rape victim) count for more than journalistic integrity. Dramas can contain humour, of course, but in a subsidiary relationship to the main themes, which will rarely be funny in themselves. *The Devil Wears Prada* has many funny scenes which gently mock the fashion industry and those who see it as only marginally less important than life itself, but beneath its glossy exterior lies a serious exploration of what modern journalism is about, particularly for the increasing numbers of women entering the profession. It is also, in its most dramatic moments, an impassioned defence of the seriousness with which successful women in the style journalism sector – represented in this film by Meryl Streep's Miranda – approach their work.

COMEDY

Speaking of romantic comedies, this genre is among the most common in films about journalism. Themselves a sub-genre of comedy, romantic comedies typically present a battle of wills between a male and female lead, resolving in a more or less happy ending. The screwball comedies of the black and white era famously featured sparkling, witty verbal exchanges between their stars, and remain much loved to this day. More recent examples of the journalistic romantic comedy include *Runaway Bride*, in which Richard Gere plays a roguish, unethical columnist working on an exposé of a woman (Julia Roberts) who repeatedly absconds from her wedding arrangements. As in the classic screwball comedies, the humour arising from the Gere-Roberts duel is set against a more serious engagement with the nature of journalism itself. Gere's character is sacked for getting his facts wrong in a story about Roberts' character. 'Journalism lesson number one', his editor explains, 'if you fabricate your facts, you get fired', and the film is genuinely interested in the ethics of the intrusive, human interest journalism which features in much of the news media today. In the balance of the piece, however, these reflections are of far lesser importance than the comic interplay of the stars. The film, and the genre, are comedy first, drama second.

The broader category of comedy is represented by films such as *Bruce Almighty* (Tom Shadyac, 2003) and *Anchorman* (Adam Mackay, 2004). In the

Figure 5 *Runaway Bride* (Gary Marshall, 1999). Source: BFI

first, Jim Carrey's jaded local TV news reporter acquires the powers of divine intervention, which he uses to enhance his chances of getting the girl, and to extract revenge on his rivals, such as Steve Carell's anally-retentive news presenter. The film is typical Carrey-esque comedy, and often very funny, but it also contains a message about the importance of local journalism. Carrey's character begins the film with a view of local journalism as inferior and boring, reflecting its low status in the journalistic hierarchy (where people learn their trade in local papers and broadcast news organisations, before graduating to the big time and the big city). By the film's end Carrey has rediscovered his enthusiasm for local homespun stories such as the 'world's biggest cookie'. The local journalist has gone from loser to community lynchpin.[6]

Anchorman fits into a recent sub-genre of film comedy which takes us back to the recent past, and has fun with the startlingly (from this distance) non-PC attitudes of the 1970s in which it is set. The film-makers have been associated with a variety of retro-comic projects of this kind, such as *Starsky and Hutch* (Todd Phillips, 2004), and the film delights in its defiantly sexist humour (from the safety of a post-feminist perspective, within which it is permitted to laugh at how reactionary and backward we used to be without being accused of actually endorsing those views). The hypermasculinity of the 1970s TV news room, the treatment of the pretty blonde female journalist who joins the team, and turns out to be a more dangerous adversary to Will Ferrell's anchorman than he could have imagined – all are played for laughs which come mainly at the expense of men and 1970s notions of masculinity. As with the other comedies mentioned above, though, as we laugh at the downfall of Ron Burgundy, there is a serious kernel for the student of journalism who wishes to know what life was like in the news media before feminism and its critique of patriarchal news culture became accepted. Athough its status as satire is challenged by at least one reviewer, 'its one explicit message has to do with the sexism of 1970s television'.[7]

SATIRE

Somewhere between comedy and drama sits *satire*, of which there have been many excellent examples in the journalism genre. Satire uses techniques of exaggeration and ironic humour to comment on those individuals, institutions and social trends which it targets. Humour, to the extent that it is used in satire, tends to be bitter-sweet, cerebral, dark-edged, and happy endings are by no means guaranteed. Satire is political comedy which aims to show up the absurdities and hypocrisies of the social world. Sydney Lumet's *Network* explores the encroaching commercialisation of TV news in the United States in the 1970s – the rise of infotainment, as we would characterise the trend today – through the eyes of its central character, a jaded journalist of the old guard who submits to the corporate agenda and turns his programme into a freak show. The plot is absurd, but just close enough to actual trends in the actual news media of the time to be believable – could a news presenter ever be shot live on air, by a member of the studio audience, professional journalistic integrity literally sacrificed in the name of the ratings war? An extreme idea, but one which in the era of Jerry Springer and Jeremy Kyle seems at least within the realm of the possible.

The best satires are those which achieve believability, or the suspension of disbelief within imagined worlds which are just real and consistent enough to be true. Barry Levinson's *Wag the Dog* (1997) tells the story of a US president who manipulates the media by staging a fictional war to detract from a looming sex scandal. Inspired by the mediated nature of the first Gulf War in 1991, the critical success of the film was heightened by the convergences between its plot and the news management practices of the Clinton administration which, if it never actually faked a war for publicity purposes, was accused in 1998 of launching cruise missiles at a chemical factory in Sudan as a diversionary tactic to deal with the Monica Lewinsky sex scandal.[8]

Gus Van Sant's *To Die For* (1995) satirises the vacuity of the American media with the story of how a pathological career-climber (Nicole Kidman) is prepared to do anything, from sleeping with the producer to arranging her husband's death, for the sake of advancement as a TV presenter. The film's exaggerated vision of the industry might be read as an indictment of the self-centred amorality of the media profession. It also plays into stereotypes of the competitive young woman who achieves success not through talent but through the calculated use of her own body.

Oliver Stone's *Natural Born Killers* (1994), hugely controversial on release because of its violent content, is also one of the most biting satires about media ever made. *Natural Born Killers* makes the media complicit in the construction of celebrity criminals Mickey and Mallory (Woody Harrelson and Juliette Lewis) as they go on a mammoth killing spree across America. Robert Downey Jr's Wayne Gale, who conducts a live, televised interview with Mickey in a high security prison, sparking off a riot which will lead to many more deaths, and ultimately his own, is an extreme caricature of that type of TV presenter/journalist who actively cultivates trauma and dysfunction in the pursuit of ratings. He is wholly amoral, and painted so unsympathetically that when he is summarily executed by the killers at the end of the film we are inclined to approve. The closing credits include scenes from the real-life case of the Menendez brothers, who became celebrity criminals after killing their parents. Stone's point is clear – there is something far wrong with a system in which the media make spectacle out of crime, and celebrities out of criminals.

THE THRILLER

Another staple type of the journalism genre is the thriller. As noted above, the role of the journalist can be the vehicle for exciting tales of investigation, discovery, cover-up, confrontation. The journalist is a kind of detective, whose progress towards the resolution of a mystery or injustice often follows the classic thriller structure. Denzel Washington's character in *The Pelican Brief* (Alan J. Pakula, 1993) is one example, as is Cate Blanchett in Joel Schumacher's *Veronica Guerin* (2003). The latter's plot, based on actual events involving the assassination of investigative reporter Veronica Guerin in Ireland, follows the journalist as she seeks to resolve corruption and incompetence in the name of justice. As is typical of the thriller form, the protagonist is in jeopardy throughout the story, and indeed is eventually killed. A similar fate awaits the central character of Michael Winterbottom's *A Mighty Heart* – Daniel Pearl. This 'true' story has a pre-ordained conclusion, thanks to the worldwide publicity which followed Pearl's decapitation by his Pakistani kidnappers, but getting to that point, and the harrowing experience of his wife (played by Angelina Jolie), is as thrilling as any thriller could be, and more tragic than most, because we know that the events depicted on screen did actually happen.

The film noir works of the 1940s and 1950s are often placed within the thriller genre. Some, such as *Ace in the Hole*, have journalists at their heart.

In noir, however, the question posed by the narrative, and answered by the journalist, is not 'who did it?' but what will befall the protagonist because of his transgression? In film noir the central male character is someone who crosses the line between right and wrong, good and evil, often under the influence of an alluring femme fatale. This transgression brings about his own downfall. When Kirk Douglas' character, Chuck Tatum, puts a man's life needlessly in jeopardy for the sake of a good story and his own personal gain, he is on a path to his own death.

David Fincher's *Zodiac* (2007) adopts a thriller structure in its account of a serial killing spree which took place in San Francisco in the late 1960s. We might regard *All the President's Men* as a thriller too, rather than a drama, as its mounting tension leads towards the climax we all know. Of course, no one died in Woodward and Bernstein's investigation, and the narrative ends before the villain gets caught (the final scenes are found news reel footage of Nixon's final months). But the meticulous progress of the case is as compelling and nerve-wracking as any serial killer thriller.

THE BIO-PIC

Many films about journalism have been true stories, or stories based on actual events, and actual persons. Recent times have seen bio-pics about Truman Capote as well as Veronica Guerin and Daniel Pearl. In *Up Close and Personal* (Jon Avnet, 1996) Michelle Pfeiffer plays a character based on Jessica Savitch, who became the first female network TV news anchor in the United States. Warren Beatty told the story of John Reed (author of the classic *Ten Days That Shook the World*) in *Reds* (1981).

Bio-pics and other 'true' stories about journalism are true, of course, only in the sense that in all narratives, fictional or factual, the gap between what actually happened and what is represented is wide, filled by the writer's creative licence, the producers' demands for a well known actor who can carry the movie to commercial success (Clooney, Gere, Redford, Jolie, Winslet), and the inevitable narrative compressions required by a predominantly visual medium working within the constraints of mainstream popular taste.

THE ACTION HERO MOVIE

Richard Ness titles his filmography *From Headline Hunter to Superman*, a reference to the fact that many of the best known films about journalism have been within the superhero action genre. There have been many versions of Superman, on TV and in the movies; and Spider-Man too. Both of these comic book superheroes are journalists in their day jobs. This is convenient in plot terms, because it gives them access to breaking news, and thus allows them to be on the scene quickly. Both Clark Kent and Peter Parker are somewhat nondescript employees, doing their jobs of reporter and photojournalist with quiet competence. But as they prowl around the newsrooms and editorial offices they are in prime position to hear about and respond to the latest outrage by the bad guys. The status of these characters as media workers also places them in an ambivalent relationship to the truth, which intensifies the central mystery around which the superhero genre often revolves – will his true identity be revealed? In a scenario where the hero's work colleagues and best buddies are journalists, the urgency of this question is highlighted, because it is precisely the work of the journalist to discover the truth. Spider-Man's career is particularly bedevilled by the brutal tabloid practices of the editor of Parker's paper, *The Daily Bugle*, J. Jonah Jameson. Jameson's mistaken view of Spider-Man as a criminal provides an important element of the plot's tension, and plays into a popular perception of the tabloid press as bigoted and irresponsible.

SOME OTHER GENRES

Journalists have also featured in many war movies, particularly in the context of the post-Soviet conflicts in the former Yugoslavia and the genocide in Rwanda. Musicals about journalism are less common, although *Chicago* harbours amongst its song and dance numbers a quite sophisticated critique of the role of tabloid journalism in the construction of celebrity, and the damage this can do to individuals. The Chicago-set *His Girl Friday* remakes *The Front Page* for late 1930s America, and focuses on the journalists. *Chicago* shows the effects of the popular journalism of that era on those who become its subjects, or victims. There have been a few horror films made with journalists in their stories, such as John Erick Dowdle's *Quarantine* (2008). Westerns are not a genre usually associated with journalism, but, as noted above, two recent examples feature journalists in contexts which highlight the birth of celebrity culture and the role of the media in the construction of myth. We should also note the inclusion of films about journalism within the upsurge of documentaries in the mainstream movie market which has been evident since the late 1990s, such as *Control Room* (Jehane Noujaim, 2004) and *Gonzo* (Alex Gibney, 2008).

NOTES

1. The *Variety* list of the top 390 box office earners of US films (http://www.variety.com/index.asp?layout=chart_pass&charttype=chart_top_domestic&dept=Film) includes three in our category of movies about journalism: *All the President's Men* (number 359, with $70,600,000 earned), *Superman* (number 112 – $134,218,018) and *Runaway Bride* (number 80 – $152,257,409). This list calculates only US box office receipts, and only goes up to 2001.
2. See Martin Conboy's *Journalism: a critical history* (2004), and Joad Raymond's *The Invention of the Newspaper* (1996).
3. For a history of the American media and the formation of journalism in what would become the United States, see Paul Starr's *The Creation of the Media* (2004). John Hartley's *Understanding Popular Culture* (1996) is a thought-provoking account of the role of journalism in the French Revolution.
4. *The Assassination of Jesse James by the Coward Robert Ford* (Andrew Dominick, 2007)
5. http://en.wikipedia.org/wiki/Drama_film.
6. *Bruce Almighty* shares some features with *Groundhog Day* (Harold Ramis, 1993), in which Bill Murray's local TV weatherman becomes trapped in a parallel universe of infinitely repeating days. Armed with the knowledge that every day, which begins with a report on the annual ritual of groundhog day in a Pennsylvanian town, will be the same, but that in knowing the future he has the power to shape it, he embarks on a campaign to win the affection of his producer, played by Andie McDowell. Again, the contempt for local journalism with which Murray's character begins the film is transformed by the end into a celebration of its centrality to communities.
7. From review by Lawrenson, E., *Sight & Sound*, volume 14, number 10, 2004.
8. Levinson's later *Man of the Year* (2007), starring Robin Williams as a Jon Stewart-type broadcaster who runs for the presidency, was less successful as a satire of the mediated excesses of contemporary US politics.

CHAPTER 4

Journalism in Film: 1997–2008

In the period from 1997 to 2008 seventy-one films were made about journalism for cinema release in the UK[1] (see Table 1). As noted in the previous chapter, by films 'about' journalism I refer to films in which one or more of the main characters is a journalist. Within this category there will be *primary* and *secondary* representations, depending on whether the role of the journalist is instrumental or incidental.

If that distinction is clear enough, let me note that, given the blurred nature of the contemporary media environment, deciding who is and who is not a journalist is less straightforward than was once the case. One of the features of our age is the blurring of many social and cultural categories, including those which mark out professions and distinguish them from each other, and from other occupational categories.

Is a radio talk show host, or the folksy presenter who talks about him or herself on radio and TV, a journalist? I will say yes, for the same reason that the lifestyle columnist in print (as played by Steve Carell in *Dan in Real Life*) is reasonably categorised as a journalist, even though he undertakes no reportage, and rarely discusses anything to do with politics, economics or the state of foreign relations. Steve's Dan, like the kind of character who appears in Oliver Stone's *Talk Show* (1988), and again in *The Brave One* (Neil Jordan, 2007), reflects the emergence in the twentieth century of a journalistic culture infused with licensed introspection and personalised reflection on the issues of the day. It is the journalism of the 'I', the me, the subject, which increasingly engages with its audience as participants in the form of callers to phone-in shows, letter writers, emailers and text messagers.

Journalism originated as reportage – a medium of monitoring and surveillance required for sound management and administration of social systems. However, it long ago branched into opinion, commentary, analysis. It became polemical, partisan, propagandistic. With the rise of mass culture it also

Table 1 Journalism in film, 1997–2008

Title	Year	Director	Genre	Male/Female	Primary/Secondary	Hero/Villain	Subject
Frost/Nixon	2008	Ron Howard	Drama	Male	Primary	Hero	Political journalism
Gonzo: The Life and Works of Hunter S Thompson	2008	Alex Gibney	Documentary	Male	Primary	Hero	Literary journalism
Quarantine	2008	John Eric Dowdle	Horror	Female	Primary	Hero	TV documentary
How To Lose Friends and Alienate People	2008	Robert B Weide	Comedy (satire)	M/F	Primary	Hero	Style journalism
Sex and the City	2008	Michael Patrick King	Comedy (romantic)	Female	Secondary	Hero	Lifestyle journalism
Vantage Point	2008	Pete Travis	Thriller	Female	Secondary	Hero	TV news
Definitely Maybe	2008	Adam Brook	Comedy	Female	Secondary	Hero	Features
Control	2008	Anton Corbijn	Drama	Male	Secondary	Hero	Current affairs
Leatherheads	2007	George Clooney	Comedy	Female	Primary	Hero	Sport/celebrity culture
REC	2007	Jaume Balaguero, Paco Plaza	Horror	Female	Primary	Hero	TV documentary
Dan in Real Life	2007	Peter Hodges	Comedy: romantic	Male	Secondary	Hero	Style column
Lions for Lambs	2007	Robert Redford	Drama	Female	Primary	Hero	Political journalism
Perfect Stanger	2007	James Foley	thriller	Female	Primary	Villain	Investigative journalism
Zodiac	2007	David Fincher	Thriller	Male	Primary	Hero	Investigative journalism
Spider Man 3	2007	Sam Raimi	Action	Male	Secondary	Hero	Print journalism
The Bourne Ultimatum	2007	Paul Greengrass	Action	Male	Secondary	Hero	Investigative journalism
A Mighty Heart	2007	Michael Winterbottom	Thriller	Female	Primary	Hero	Foreign correspondence
The Brave One	2007	Neil Jordan	Drama	Female	Secondary	Hero	Talk radio
The Weather	2007	Gore Vestvey	Drama	Male	Secondary	Hero	Weather news
The Hunting Party	2007	Richard Shepherd	Thriller	Male	Primary	Hero	Foreign correspondence
Thank You For Smoking	2006	Jason Reitman	Drama	Female	Secondary	Hero	Investigative report
Blood Diamond	2006	Edward Zwick	Drama	Female	Secondary	Hero	Foreign correspondence
Interview	2006	Steve Buscemi	Drama	Male	Primary	Villain	Celebrity journalism
Infamous	2006	Douglas McGrath	Drama	Male	Primary	Hero	Literary journalism
The Good German	2006	Steven Soderberg	Thriller	Male	Secondary	Hero	Foreign correspondence
Borat	2006	Larry Charles	Comedy (satire)	Male	Primary	Hero	TV documentary
Superman Returns	2006	Bryan Singer	Action	Female	Secondary	Hero	Print journalism
Scoop	2006	Woody Allen	Comedy	Female	Primary	Hero	Investigative journalism
The Devil Wears Prada	2006	David Frankel	Drama	Female	Primary	Hero	Style journalism
Capote	2005	Bennett Miller	Drama	Male	Primary	Hero	Literary journalism
Good Night, and Good Luck	2005	George Clooney	Drama	Male	Primary	Hero	Investigative journalism
	2005	Mary McGuckian	Comedy (satire)	M/Fe	Primary	Villain	Tabloid journalism

Year	Film	Director	Genre	Gender	Role	Hero/Villain	Journalism type
2004	2046	Wong Kar Wai	Drama	Male	Secondary	Hero	Columnist
2004	Paparazzi	Paul Abascal	Thriller	Male	Primary	Villain	Celebrity photojournalism
2004	Anchorman	Adam Mckay	Comedy	M/F	Primary	Villain	TV news
2004	The Life Aquatic	Wes Anderson	Comedy	Female	Secondary	Hero	Feature journalism
2004	Spiderman 2	Sam Raimi	Action	Male	Secondary	Hero	Print journalism
2004	13 Going on 30	Gary Winick	Comedy	Female	Secondary	Hero	Style journalism
2003	City of God	Fernando Meirelles	Drama	Male	Secondary	Hero	Photojournalism
2003	How to Lose a Guy in Ten Days	Donald Petrie	Comedy	Female	Secondary	Hero	Style journalism
2003	Shattered Glass	Billy Ray	Drama	M/F	Primary	Hero	Print journalism
2003	Bruce Almighty	Tom Shadyac	Comedy	Male	Primary	Hero	Local journalism
2002	Veronica Guerin	Joel Schumacher	Thriller	Female	Primary	Hero	Investigative journalism
2002	The Quiet American	Philip Noyce	Drama	Male	Primary	Hero	Foreign correspondence
2002	Chicago	Rob Marshall	Musical	Male	Secondary	Villain	Tabloid journalism
2002	Spiderman	Sam Raimi	Action	Male	Secondary	Villain	Print journalism
2002	The Life of David Gale	Alan Parker	Thriller	Female	Primary	Hero	Investigative journalism
2002	Life or Something Like It	Stephen Herek	Comedy (romantic)	Female	Primary	Hero	TV news
2002	Black and White	Craig Lahiff	Drama	Male	Secondary	Hero	Print journalism
2002	No Man's Land	Danis Tanovich	Drama	Female	Secondary	Villain	Foreign correspondence
2002	24 Hour Party People	Michael Winterbottom	Drama	Male	Primary	Hero	Current affairs
2001	Cat's Meow	Peter Bogdanovich	Drama	M/F	Secondary	Villain	Media power
2001	15 Minutes	John Herzfeld	Thriller	Male	Secondary	Villain	Tabloid TV
2001	Kissing Jessica Stein	Charles Herman-Wurmfeld	Comedy	Female	Secondary	Hero	Features journalism
2000	Almost Famous	Cameron Crowe	Drama	Female	Secondary	hero	Music journalism
2000	In the Mood for Love	Wong Kar Wai	Drama	Male	Primary	Hero	Print journalism
1999	Three Kings	David O. Russell	War	Male	Secondary	Hero	Foreign correspondence
1999	The Insider	Michael Mann	Drama	Female	Secondary	Hero	Investigative journalism
1999	Complicity	Gavin Millar	Thriller	Male	Primary	Villain	Print journalism
1999	Runaway Bride	Gary Marshall	Comedy (romantic)	M/F	Primary	Hero	Print journalism
1999	In the Garden of Good and Evil	Clint Eastwood	drama	Male	Primary	Hero	Features journalism
1999	True Crime	Clint Eastwood	Thriller	Male	Secondary	Hero	investigative journalism
1998	Celebrity	Woody Allen	Comedy (satire)	Male	Primary	Villain	Celebrity journalism
1997	Fear and Loathing in Las Vegas	Terry Gilliam	Comedy (satire)	Male	Primary	Hero	Literary journalism
1997	Deep Impact	Mimi Leder	Disaster	Female	Primary	Hero	Investigative journalism
1997	Velvet Goldmine	Todd Haynes	Drama	Male	Secondary	Hero	Investigative journalism
1997	Mad City	Costa-Gavras	Drama	Male	Secondary	Hero	TV news
1997	Welcome to Sarayevo	Michael Winterbottom	Drama	M/F	Primary	Hero	Foreign correspondence
1997	LA Confidential	Cameron Crowe	Thriller	Male	Primary	Villain	Celebrity journalism
1997	Tomorrow Never Dies	Roger Spottiswood	Action	Male	Secondary	Villain	Media power

became entertainment. As leisure and affluence increased, journalism became the vehicle for monitoring and talking about culture, high and low, and about the relationship of the individual to the collective, social world. Within the news package, space was made for non-reportorial journalistic forms, linked to straight news by the fact that they addressed the real, the actual, the factual. This kind of journalism often sits next to more conventional journalistic forms, but is distanced from its rules and standards. Talk show hosts, radio presenters, lifestyle columnists are not generally expected to be objective or detached. On the contrary, their subjectivity and projection of personality are key to their success as media performers. The output of the radio presenter played by Jodie Foster in *The Brave One* belongs to that more personalised journalism of the self which, if it is far removed from the conventions of objective reportage, is nonetheless part of the expanded, privatised, often feminised public sphere in which women address women's issues, to audiences comprising both women and men.

And what of the weather man, or woman, as played by Nicole Kidman in *To Die For*, Bill Murray in *Groundhog Day* and, in our 1997–2008 sample period, Nicolas Cage in *The Weather Man* (Gore Verbinski, 2007)? Reporting the weather is not the kind of journalism likely to win a Pulitzer prize, clearly, but it has been a staple of the news package since the nineteenth century. Like the musings of the lifestyle columnist, weather reports are among the most frequently used services of any news outlet, and I have no hesitation in treating the weatherman as a category of journalist in this book. In this I am following the precedent set by previous writers on journalism in the movies, many of whom refer to Nicole Kidman's performance in *To Die For* as a classic representation. Bill Murray's character in *Groundhog Day*, stuck in Poughkeepsie with his camera crew and apparently condemned to repeat the same twenty-four-hour cycle forever, is a weatherman whose comic predicament does not prevent the subversion of commonly held assumptions about the triviality of weather news, and of local journalism in general.

THE CULT OF REALITY

Weather news has been around for centuries. More recent are those forms of reality culture in which journalism is hybridised and combined with forms which deal in the representation of factuality rather than the creation of imagined or made-up worlds, but are not widely recognised as 'journalism'. The best example of this is the reality TV format common in popular factual TV all over the world. Reality TV began as an outgrowth of the fly-on-the-wall documentary, itself a relatively recent cultural form, but one which is generally recognised as journalism.[2] Is reality TV thereby a hybrid form of journalism, or a form of popular entertainment which has more in common with the game show? Might one thus include *The Truman Show* (Peter Weir, 1998), or *My Little Eye* (Marc Evans, 2002), or *Quarantine* (John Erick Dowdle, 2008) in a book such as this?

The latter *is* included, because its central character is a journalist who becomes trapped in a house of horrors (and is thus, being a journalist, in a narratively convenient but existentially precarious position to film the action and leave a record of what happened, *Cloverfield*-style). The first two films are, on the other hand, part of a sub-genre of movies made in the past decade which engage with the fascinating cultural and existential issues raised by the reality TV phenomenon, but still seem to me distant from the journalism genre. Truman's God-like producer in the sky is precisely that, a producer who sees his show more as a soap opera than a fly-on-the-wall documentary. The audiences who follow it live on TV are addicted to the unfolding narrative, as they would be to that of the UK's *EastEnders* at its melodramatic peak. They are knowing spectators of a long-running drama which, though it involves one 'real' person, Truman, has no reality beyond the confines of Sea Haven, his made-for-TV home. It is an invented, controlled, scripted reality.

A further exclusion concerns films about the communication practice which since the start of the twentieth century has developed in parallel with journalism and as an organised response to it: public relations, and associated activities such as political campaigning. In Chapter 10, 'King-makers', I discuss these films in some detail. They are not films 'about' journalism, however, so much as films about the consequences of journalism on other spheres such as politics and business. Rod Tiffen in his perceptive study of *News and Power* (1989) argued that the effects of news media were to be seen not least on institutions and organisations, and the responses of these organisations to the emergence of a mediatised political culture requiring intensive management and, if possible, manipulation. Films such as *Wag the Dog*, *The Contender* (Rod Lurie, 2000), *Primary Colors* (Mike Nichols, 1998) and *Man of the Year* (Barry Levinson, 2007) are built around this idea, and address the effects of our contemporary media environment on the management of politics. Journalists are not the subject of these movies, however, which are more interested in exploring, usually through satire, the ways in which political actors seek to influence and manage the news media. They are about the consequences of modern journalism for non-news organisations. I exclude them from the 'about journalism' list, therefore.

In *Thank You for Smoking* (Jason Reitman, 2006), also a film about public relations, a key supporting character is a journalist, and her investigative work is central to the story of the downfall of an arrogant and cynical tobacco lobbyist. It can therefore be categorised here as a film about journalism.

JOURNALISM ON SCREEN, 1997–2008:
A CONTENT ANALYSIS

Table 1 shows all the films about journalism made for cinema and released in the UK between the years 1997 and 2008 inclusive (for reviews and synopses, see Appendix 1). The list does not include films such as *Edison* (David Burke, 2005), released straight to DVD. Gavin Millar's *Complicity* (2000) is included, although poor critical reception ensured that it was released not in the UK as a whole but only in Scotland where Iain Banks' source novel is set (and it then had limited theatrical release in the US).

With above exclusions, we find that seventy-one films were made about journalism and released in cinemas in the 1997–2008 period. The peak years for production were 2006–8, when thirty-one films about journalism were released. Film-makers' interest in the subject dipped in 1998 with just two films released, and only two came out in 2000. I attach no particular significance to these variations, given the small number of productions concerned. It is at least noteworthy, however, that in the final four years of the period under review more than thirty films were made with journalism at their heart, suggesting a sustained and growing interest in the subject as the 2000s advanced.

The director whose name appears most regularly in my list of films about journalism (excluding Sam Raimi, who directed the three *Spider-Man* movies) is Michael Winterbottom, with three films (*Welcome To Sarajevo* (1997); *Twenty Four Hour Party People* (2004), about TV journalist and founder of Factory Records Tony Wilson; and *A Mighty Heart* (2007). George Clooney is also prominent, both as director (*Good Night, and Good Luck*; *Leatherheads*) and actor (*The Good German*, *Three Kings*). Meryl Streep and Angelina Jolie portrayed journalists in two films apiece, as did Richard Gere and comic actor Steve Carell.

Breaking the films down by generic category, twenty-six films were classified as drama. These included Ron Howard's *Frost/Nixon* (2008), Costa-Gavras' *Mad City* (1997) and the pair of films made about Truman Capote and released in 2005–06. Another common genre was the thriller (thirteen titles) – dramas laced with suspense and which build to often violent resolutions, including Clint Eastwood's *True Crime* (1999), *Veronica Guerin* (Joel Schumacher, 2003) and David Fincher's *Zodiac* (2007).

As the above examples indicate, many of these films – eighteen in all – tell stories which were presented to the audience as 'based on true events'. Four titles (*How To Lose Friends and Alienate People* (Robert L. Weide, 2008), *The Devil Wears Prada*, *Welcome To Sarajevo*, *The Hunting Party*) were widely advertised as loosely based on the real-life experiences of journalists, albeit disguised with fictionalised names and other details. As noted earlier, 'true stories' are never quite that, with even the most realistic of screenplays incorporating numerous compressions and narrative short cuts, dramatic exaggerations and aesthetic flourishes intended to maximise a story's impact as cinema. Thus *The Hunting Party*, based on an Esquire feature article by foreign correspondent Scott Anderson about his adventures in post-war Serbia, changes not only his name but major elements of the original, rendering it more Indiana Jones than Woodward and Bernstein.

The frequency of true stories in cinema highlights that aspect of journalism which has made it such a popular subject for film-makers: its inherently dramatic, often dangerous qualities, be it the tension and suspense of Daniel Pearl's kidnapping and subsequent execution, Lowell Bergman's struggle to have Jeffrey Wigand's whistle-blowing reported on NBC, or the battle of wits between David Frost and Richard Nixon depicted in *Frost/Nixon*. Journalism's true stories are frequently more dramatic and compelling than the lurid fictions about journalism presented in films such as *Paparazzi* (Paul Abascal, 2004) or *A Perfect Stranger* (James Foley, 2007).

Six of the films made about journalism between 1997 and 2008 depicted action or superheroes: *Spider-Man* (three releases), *Superman Returns*, James Bond and Jason Bourne (I include the Bond-vehicle *Tomorrow Never Dies* (Roger Spottiswoode, 1998) because of its portrayal of a megalomaniac media baron and his use of media power to attempt to take over the world – see Chapter 11). Several of the US scholars referenced in the previous chapter have noted the link between superheroes and journalism in the movies. Richard Ness' filmography is titled *From Headline Hunter to Superman*, and with Bryan Singer's *Superman Returns* (2006), alongside the phenomenally successful *Spider-Man* franchise (nearly $3 billion at the global box office), that connection clearly continues. Superheroes, as they go about saving people from villains, tend to attract the attention of the media, and thus provide rich material for the exploration of celebrity culture, the ethics of crime journalism and other matters of public concern (the violation of privacy by tabloids, for example – *Daily Bugle* editor J. Jonah Jameson devotes his professional life to unmasking the Spider-Man, whom he wrongly believes to be a force for evil in the city. This tension, with the journalist presented as the source of injustice, has been central to the franchise ever since its first incarnation). *Superman Returns*, meanwhile, provides in the figure of Lois Lane an evolving portrayal of women in journalism which at the same time as balancing the hero's hyper-masculinity reflects prevailing gender stereotypes.

Next to dramas, the most frequently used genre for films about journalism in the 1997–2008 period was comedy, including romantic comedy, teen comedy, satire and what we might call 'retro' – that recent sub-genre of comedy which has postmodern fun with the conventions and quaintly incorrect prejudices of

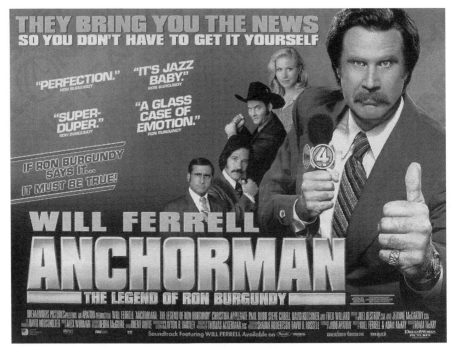

Figure 6 *Anchorman* (Adam McKay, 2004). Source: BFI

the pre-feminist, pre-gay liberation, pre-civil rights past. *Anchorman*, with its parody of a 1970s TV newsroom, belongs to this genre in being a comedy fully aware of the feminist critique of sexism in journalism, and it both celebrates and rejects that sexism in its affection for Ron Burgundy. It then delights in his downfall at the hands of blonde beauty Veronica Corningstone (herself a stereotype of hard-bodied blondeness, but refracted through the post-Madonna lens, where the female body is wielded as a weapon in the sex wars by knowing, powerful women).

A total of nineteen comedies of various types were made with journalism at their core, often with serious underlying messages. In *Borat*, for example (subtitled *Cultural learnings of America for make benefit glorious nation of Kazakhstan*) Sacha Baron Cohen's character moves from mocking his own assumed country of Kazakhstan (in a manner condemned by many as racist) to a merciless exposure of the racism, anti-semitism and general boorishness of so much that is American. Using the mock-documentary, reality-style format which had become familiar to audiences in the mid-2000s *Borat* is both hilarious and disturbing in the picture it paints of a pre-Obama United States where, in some places at least, attitudes appear to have progressed little since the days of the Civil War.

A popular sub-genre in journalism movies remains that of the romantic comedy. The screwball comedies of the 1930s and 1940s established the dramatic compatibility of journalism and humour, often by fusing the farcical, do-or-die atmosphere of the tabloid newsroom with quite sophisticated treatment of the nature of the news business. Ever since, the film industry's leading men and women have appeared together in rom coms involving journalistic plots. In our sample period Richard Gere is the roguish columnist to Julia Roberts *Runaway Bride* (Gary Marshall, 1999). In *Life or Something Like It* (Stephen Herek, 2002) Angelina Jolie is the superficial TV news reporter who receives advance warning of her impending death, playing opposite Edward Burns as the sensitive cameraman who teaches her the real priorities of life. In *Sex and the City* (Michael Patrick King, 2008) Sarah Jessica Parker is lifestyle columnist Carrie Bradshaw, wooed, then dumped, then wooed again by her handsome but anonymous co-star.

The remainder of the 1997–2008 sample comprises two documentaries about journalism: Alex Gibney's *Gonzo*, about Hunter S. Thompson, and Jehane Noujaim's *Control Room*, a record of Al Jazeera's performance during the 2003 invasion of Iraq. There were two horror movies (*Quarantine* (John Erick Dowdle, 2008), and the Spanish language film of which it was a remake, REC (Jaume Balaguero, Paco Plaza, 2007), one disaster film (*Deep Impact*, Mimi Leder, 1998), one war film (*Three Kings*), and one musical. *Chicago* (Rob Marshall, 2002) is based on a stage show about the popular media's tendency towards the construction of criminal celebrity. Amidst the great song and dance routines (and another interesting performance from Richard Gere as a combination of lawyer and public relations man who uses the media to win sympathy for his client, Roxie) is a 1930s-set tale of tabloid excess which speaks to the news values and ethical lapses of the present-day popular media.

Categorised by subject matter, the seventy-one films in the sample were dominated by the familiar themes of foreign correspondence, which featured in eight titles, and investigative journalism, in twelve. As noted earlier, filmmakers' interest in these categories of journalism reflects the inherently dramatic and cinematic qualities of investigation and war news respectively. Investigative journalists are a kind of quasi-legal detective, often up against corruption, power and vested interests as they strive towards their end point of exclusive exposure. Their stories are suspenseful, sometimes violent and often, as in the case of *Veronica Guerin*, depressingly true. Foreign correspondence on the other hand takes the film-maker to exotic locations, and allows him to witness and publicise human suffering in ways which s/he may hope will impact on public opinion and policy. Again there is danger and suspense, a thrilling quality to these stories, the opportunity for redemptive and uplifting tales of journalistic heroism in the face of violence and threat.

HEROES OR VILLAINS?

In so far as journalists on screen can be divided into heroes and villains (and this is not always easy since, as film-makers know, the most interesting characters tend to combine elements of both – Richard Gere's columnist in *Runaway Bride* begins the film as a villain, but ends it as a hero; Simon Pegg's shallow and selfish style journalist in *How To Lose Friends and Alienate People*, modelled on the real-life *Vanity Fair* writer Toby Young, is hardly heroic, but nor is he entirely a villain). It is the characters who are either investigative reporters or foreign correspondents who are most likely to be portrayed heroically: Daniel Pearl, his wife Marianne Pearl (*A Mighty Heart*); Michael Henderson in *Welcome To Sarajevo*; Kate Winslet's Bitsy Bloom in *The Life of David Gale* (Alan Parker, 2004). Journalistic heroes tend to be those journalists engaged in fulfilling the normatively approved functions of journalism in a democracy: witnessing injustice, holding power to account, defending freedom. In portraying these heroes, cinema performs its mythical function of dramatising those normative ideals, and translating them into a popular cultural idiom.

Let us note here the perhaps surprising finding that journalists are portrayed heroically in the large majority of the seventy-one films under discussion. In fifty-eight of the titles listed in Table 1 (82 per cent) we are presented with journalists who are, despite their flaws (which in the case of the lovable rogues such as Richard Gere's Ike are frequently attractive in any case), good, courageous people devoted to their profession and to upholding its best traditions and ideals.

Some observers have detected in recent films about journalism a tendency to negative representations of the profession. James Caryn, writing in the *New York Times* in 2005, argued that since the highpoint of *All the President's Men* and that film's portrayal of the quiet heroism of Woodward and Bernstein it has been all downhill for journalists on screen. As evidence he cites the Spanish language film *Cronicos* (Sebastian Cordero, 2004, not included in this study, since it was not released in cinemas in the UK), starring John Leguziamo as a tabloid reporter who will stop at nothing to get his story. His character, asserts Caryn, 'embodies the reporter as seen in current films: he's a sleaze'.[3] In 2008, Stephen Armstrong in the *Guardian* argued in similar fashion that 'with the odd exception, the 1,000 or so screen appearances by journalists mostly portray them as hardworking forces for good. Recently, however, the screen seems to have fallen out with the trade'.[4]

Neither of these readings accurately captures the positivity and lack of cynicism seen in recent screen representations of journalism, which signify nothing so much as the film-makers' evident desire to praise and pay respect to the principles, if not always the practice of liberal journalism. There is in many of the 1997–2008 films a sincere, almost naïve adherence to the nobility of the fourth estate, often set against the background of a post-9/11 world where terror, torture and governmental mendacity loom large.

If it is true to say that the majority of past representations have been 'positive' in the sense described by Armstrong we should take note that the past portrayals of journalism which are today most highly valued by critics and commentators, including journalists themselves, feature some memorable villains. Villains dominate three of the undisputed classics of the genre – *Citizen Kane*, *Ace in the Hole*, and *Sweet Smell of Success*. Charles Foster Kane begins his screen life as a victim, then becomes a youthful idealist, then a cynic and a monster. Chuck Tatum in *Ace in the Hole* is the kind of journalist for whom the term 'reptile' seems entirely appropriate, while J. J. Hunsecker in *Sweet Smell of Success* is entirely beyond redemption. All are compelling characters, but rotten to the core. Then there is Sally Field's Regan in *Absence of Malice* (Sydney Pollack, 1981), who betrays her source and causes a suicide; Nicole Kidman's Suzanna Stone, who has her husband murdered to advance her career prospects; and Robert Downey Jr's true crime TV journalist in *Natural Born Killers*, who is happy to see people die at the hands of Mickey and Mallory because it makes good television. Some of the best films about journalism, in short, have portrayed the most villainous of journalists.

By contrast, in most of the films made between 1997 and 2008, such as *A Mighty Heart*, *Good Night, and Good Luck*, and *Welcome To Sarajevo*, journalists are portrayed as heroic, to the point of reckless disregard for their own safety

Figure 7 *Natural Born Killers* (Oliver Stone, 1994). Source: BFI

Figure 8 *A Mighty Heart* (Michael Winterbottom, 2007). Source: BFI

(and for the well-being of their families and loved ones). Veronica Guerin is portrayed by Cate Blanchett as a heroine, undisputably, in Joel Schumacher's account of her ill-fated investigation into organised crime in Ireland. This heroism is contextualised by repeated references to the husband and children who wait for her at home, fearful and uncertain of what will happen to her next. In the end, her determination to uncover the truth costs her her life, and her family a wife and mother. Her behaviour is portrayed as reckless, even selfish, but heroic nonetheless. Though not as forcefully presented, Michael Winterbottom's portrayal of Daniel Pearl likewise leads the viewer to question the personal cost, not only to himself but to his pregnant wife and unborn child, of pursuing the story. That he is a courageous figure is never questioned. Indeed, we might say that over the decade under discussion journalists have become, in reality and in their representation in cinema, more heroic and more troublesome to dysfunctional authority and abusive power than ever before.

The villains of the journalism genre in the years 1997–2008 tend to be found, as they always have been, in movies about popular journalism, or what used to be known as the tabloid sector. In our sample, there were only fourteen films in which journalists were portrayed in negative terms, and in even fewer as out-and-out villains, devoid of redeeming features. In the latter category is *Paparazzi*, Paul Abascal's crude revenge thriller about a movie star whose life is ruined by a group of remorseless tabloid photographers. In *15 Minutes* (John Herzfeld) Kelsey Grammar plays an unscrupulous 'true crime' presenter of *Top Story*, 'the nation's newsreel', driven by the need for 'bad news'. 'We're a tabloid show', he proclaims, while working with an alcoholic cop played by Robert De Niro to be there on the scene when the heat is going down. Grammar's character can be compared to Robert Downey Jr's in *Natural Born Killers*, another tabloid villain.

Mary McGuckian's *Rag Tale* presents a similarly unforgiving portrait of the UK's notorious 'red top' journalism, while *Celebrity* (Woody Allen, 1999) and *Perfect Stranger* (James Foley, 2007) present what one might read as their directors' deep hatred of the celebrity journalism which surrounds them and makes their lives miserable (as they may believe). Steve Buscemi's *Interview* (2006) has an embittered political journalist who lies and cheats his way into his TV star interviewee's confidence, and then her pants, only to be betrayed by her in turn.

The balance of good and evil in journalism movies can be summarised, therefore, as:

- foreign correspondents and investigative reporters, good;
- tabloid hacks, celebrity interviewers, paparazzi and other agents of the gutter press, bad.

Figure 9   *The Devil Wears Prada* (David Frankel, 2006). Source: BFI

This dichotomy reflects the long-standing and deep-rooted public status of these different sectors of the journalism industry, seen in *His Girl Friday* as much as *Chicago* and *LA Confidential*.

There is a trend which complicates this polarity, however, and which reflects the rise of feminism and enhanced female socio-economic power since the 1970s. Eight of the 1997–2008 movies had as their subject 'style' or lifestyle journalism – the kind of journalism which fills the pages of *Cosmopolitan* and *Vanity Fair* and addresses fashion, health and lifestyle, sexuality and celebrity. *How To Lose Friends and Alienate People*, *Sex and the City*, *The Devil Wears Prada* and *13 Going On 30*, though very different in tone, each in its way reflects the extent to which journalism in the early twenty-first century was undergoing a process of feminisation, both in terms of its content (more coverage of fashion, lifestyle, and so on), and in terms of the respect accorded these categories of content by a hitherto suspicious cultural elite.

MALE AND FEMALE

This brings us to what some might regard as the most surprising finding of all. In thirty-two of the films made about journalism in 1997–2008 (45 per cent) at least one of the main journalistic characters was a female. Women indeed outnumbered their male counterparts in films about foreign correspondence and investigative journalism, traditionally (and on celluloid no less so) male preserves of the profession.

Chapter 7 discusses the representation of female journalists, past and present, in detail, noting the paradoxical fact that cinema has since the 1930s and the Torchy Blane series been a cultural space in which there have been strong positive female characters (in the sense in which feminism would use those terms). It is nonetheless striking that in the cinema of the 1997–2008 period so many of the lead journalistic roles were occupied by women, and that these women were neither the 'sob sisters' nor the 'superbitches' of past celluloid convention. Angelina Jolie in *A Mighty Heart*; Cate Blanchett in *Veronica Guerin*; Meryl Streep and Anne Hathaway in *The Devil Wears Prada*; Tea Leoni in *Deep Impact* – the list goes on, reflecting a period in which, if women had not yet achieved professional parity within journalism, they had made huge progress in the news room and, perhaps as important, had become much more valuable as consumers and taste arbiters of journalism than in the pre-feminist era. If journalism remained a male-dominated profession in the 2000s it was also true that the news industry by then faced an audience populated by women who were more educated, more affluent, more demanding in all things than any previous generation, and who were entirely comfortable with the thought of women reporters on the front line, or being beaten up by Irish gangsters, or out-brutalising the brutes in the tabloid editorial board (as occurs in Mary McGuckian's *Rag Tale*).

They also, many of them, wanted to see women journalists in nice frocks and shoes to die for, with little to worry about except the fashion sense and personal income of their next suitor. By the 2000s films about journalism were broad enough in their scope to permit both models of women's identity – one celebrating the femin*ine*, the other the femin*ist*.

The finding of substantial female representation in movies about journalism should be qualified with the equally revealing fact that of seventy-one films made about journalism in the 1997–2008 period only three were directed by women – just over 4 per cent. The continuing scarcity of women behind the cameras, as opposed to the evolving nature of their representation on screen, is a feature noted in Martha M. Lauzen's 2005 report on *The Celluloid Ceiling*.[5] Lauzen observes that only 7 per cent of directors of the 250 top grossing films in the US that year were women, a decline on previous years (the highest number being 11 per cent in 2000). Women are even less involved as directors in the making of films about journalism, taking the decade as a whole.

NOTES

1. Based on listings in *Sight & Sound*, which contains synopses and reviews of every film released in the UK. There is a pleasing circularity in the fact that the period covered by this chapter is topped and tailed with films about Hunter S. Thompson – Terry Gilliam's 1997 adaptation of Thompson's autobiographical text, *Fear and Loathing in Las Vegas*, released in the autumn of 1998, and Alex Gibney's documentary about Thompson, *Gonzo*, released in the UK in December 2008. It is also fortuituous, if entirely accidental, that the very end of the period saw the release of Ron Howard's *Frost/Nixon*, about the television interviews of the disgraced ex-president conducted in 1976. Howard made *The Paper* in 1994, a news room farce/satire modelled on *The Front Page*. *Frost/Nixon* came along just in time to reinforce what is one of this book's key arguments – that the journalist is a cultural figure of immense and growing importance in democratic societies, his or her role constantly under scrutiny by the very best of our film-making talent (and sometimes by the worst).
2. For a scholarly history of the rise of reality TV, and its roots in other journalistic forms, see Annette Hill's two volumes, *Reality TV* (2005) and *Restyling Factual TV* (2007).
3. Caryn, J., 'The decline and fall of journalists on film', *New York Times*, 19 July 2005.
4. Armstrong, S., 'From hero to zero', *Guardian*, 12 May 2008.
5. Lauzen, Martha M., *The Celluloid Ceiling: behind-the-scenes employment of women in the top 250 films of 2005* (://moviesbywomen.com/stats_celluloid_ceiling_2005.php).

Part II
Heroes

CHAPTER 5

Watchdogs

In the real world, as in the cinema, the idea of the journalist-as-hero finds its purest, most noble expression in the figure of the watchdog. Since a recognisably modern form of journalism first developed in the seventeenth century[1] fuelled by the English civil war and other anti-feudal movements in Europe and north America (culminating in the American War of Independence of 1776 and the French Revolution of 1789), the journalist in liberal democratic societies has been expected to occupy the social and cultural space between governing elite and governed non-elite; to act as a buffer, or bridge, between those who wield power and those on whose behalf, in a democratic polity, it is supposed to be wielded. In this respect the journalist is a deeply political figure, called upon to be the champion of the people, their advocate and representative. In this representative capacity the journalist is also the *watchdog*, standing guard over the democratic constitution, the system of law and order which underpins it, and the adherence of the powerful to those rules which, in the defence of the public as a whole, a society has decreed should govern its economy, politics and culture.

The watchdog function of journalism arises logically from news' fundamental function of environmental surveillance. When, as occurred in early modern Europe and north America between the early seventeenth and late eighteenth centuries, the political environment becomes one characterised by democratic structures and acceptance of the belief that the popular will is sovereign, monitoring it, informing the people about it, must include those zones and spheres of society where power resides and is exercised. The struggle for democratic freedom was first and foremost a struggle against the arbitrariness of absolute power, a rejection of the right of despots to govern in their own interests without regard to the needs or desires of the people. The propensity of power to corrupt was built into the various forms of democratic constitution which emerged out of these struggles, informing such principles as the separation of legislative and judicial power in the US, and the independence of the judiciary in the United Kingdom. Democratic societies from the outset put heavy stress on the preservation of mechanisms for ensuring 'checks and balances' in the accumulation and management of power, including a 'free' media – i.e., a media which is institutionally independent of the state on the one hand, and corporate and other power elites on the other. The importance of a free media underpins the reverence with which the first amendment to the US constitution is held, and the ferocity with which it is protected when perceived to be under threat.

So journalists in a democracy must, if they are doing their jobs properly, inform the people about what power is doing in their name, or to them, or to others on their behalf. Journalists must watch over power, then, and sound the alarm when fault is found. Journalistic scrutiny becomes at an early stage in liberal capitalism's development a central element in the self-regulation of democracy; the main means by which dysfunction in the workings of the system, or structural flaws in the system itself, can be identified, publicly debated, and rectified. The news media in this regard form a self-reflective, 'autopoetic' system, to use Luhmann's phrase in *The Reality of the Mass Media* (2000), permitting abuses and corruptions of power to be exposed and debated, correcting for errors.

Journalists are the communicative heart of what Habermas called the public sphere (1989), notionally independent from party and furnishing citizens with the information required to make sound decisions about who shall govern them and how, and also providing the space for that information to be properly considered, debated, contradicted, tested. The role of the journalist in a functioning public sphere is to exercise critical scrutiny over the actions of the powerful, the members of those elites whose activities impact on the life of a society and its citizens. Authoritarian societies past and present have no comparable conception of the journalist as watchdog, or scrutineer of power. In such societies, and regardless of whether the authority to exercise power is derived from some notion of divine right, or the nominally secular appeal to class, the critical journalist is perceived as a threat to power and treated accordingly.

For the five centuries and more which have elapsed since Gutenberg's invention of movable type, journalists have been imprisoned, exiled, executed and assassinated by those who feel their power to be at risk from what they write. Journalists remain at risk in those countries in which the need for a public sphere, and for the critical, scrutinising journalism required to make it a meaningful democratic mechanism, are not accepted by ruling elites. In Russia, for example, recent years have seen the deaths of a number of journalists, including the death by radiation poisoning of Alexander Litvinenko and the execution of Anna Politovskaya.

WATCHDOGS IN THE MOVIES

Given the central importance of the watchdog role to the mythology of liberal journalism, it is perhaps unsurprising that films with this theme at their heart tend to be taken with great seriousness by the critical community. They can also be viewed as core teaching texts of liberal democratic ideology, promoting, warning their audiences, in popular cultural idiom, why this kind of journalism is and should be important to them, how and why it is threatened, and why it must be defended. They contain, if in a manner shaped by the subjective, creative and imaginative powers of their producers, a society's reflections on its democratic health and fitness, and the role which journalistic media have played. If cinema is a medium where dreams are manufactured and legends forged, and in which film-makers articulate and enact their society's central myths for popular consumption, films about journalistic watchdogs have been among the highest profile productions.

Watchdog movies often come with their status as 'events' clearly signalled. They tend to involve big budgets, A-list stars with reputations for seriousness and commitment to causes, and are accompanied by extensive debate in the public sphere, inspired by their arrival. The three films discussed in this chapter – *All the President's Men*, *The Insider* and *Good Night, and Good Luck* – each travelled with this baggage, marketed and reviewed as statements about something bigger than Hollywood celebrity, and more important than mere entertainment. They were mainstream films, all three, and played in multiplexes as star vehicles, but they also had the status of what are sometimes called 'issue movies', where it is acknowledged in critical discourse round the film that it is 'about' something of relevance to political life and public debate.

Movies about watchdogs are always concerned with the encounter between journalism – the fourth estate – and power, an encounter usually staged on the terrain of investigative journalism, that sphere of journalistic work focused on the discovery and exposure of information which some would rather remained secret. Watchdog movies are premised on the notion that information is itself a form of power, and a weapon to be wielded in its pursuit and preservation. Watchdog movies are about the struggle which takes place around information, and the crucial role of the journalist in that struggle.

They are often 'true' stories, based on actual events. In *All the President's Men* the power under investigation, being watched over, is of the very highest order – the executive, the President in the White House, the most powerful person in the most powerful country on earth. There could be no purer demonstration of the watchdog role in action than this true tale of how two *Washington Post* staff reporters pursued an investigation which would lead, in the end, to the downfall of a two-term landslide president in time of war (the Vietnam war was still going on when the Watergate break-in and subsequent investigation by Woodward and Bernstein occurred). The power being watched over in Michael Mann's *The Insider* is, by contrast, corporate – the power of big business, Big Tobacco in particular – in the wealthiest country on earth. *The Insider* is about watching over the financial power of capitalism. *Good Night, and Good Luck*, thirdly, is about watching over the media itself, and those working in it who would lend their status and influence to the communication of fear, anxiety and panic. Clooney's film, set at the height of the Cold War of the 1950s, is really about the war on terror of the 2000s and the role of at least some journalists in colluding with or contributing to the climate of paranoia which characterised those years.

ALL THE PRESIDENT'S MEN

What Bonnie Brennen calls an *ur-text* of journalism movies, and probably the best known example of a film in which the journalist is represented as a positive figure watching over American democracy, is *All the President's Men* (Alan J. Pakula, 1976).[2] This film adaptation of the book by the reporters who pursued the story of the Watergate break-in and contributed substantially to Richard Nixon's resignation in 1974 has become *the* leading example not just of cinema's portrayal of journalists-as-heroes, but of what the watchdog role of journalism is all about.

Bob Woodward and Carl Bernstein were relative novices at the *Post* and pursued their investigation against the resistance of sources, the scepticism of editors, the dismissals of professional peers, and the opposition of the politicians who stood to lose from this story of corruption and abuse of office. They persevered, as is well known to every student of journalism, and their story has come to exemplify the positive ideal of American journalism, and of liberal journalism in general – the fourth estate's finest hour.

The film adopts a spare, semi-documentary approach to telling a story which had, even by 1976, become mythical. The opening scene eavesdrops on the Watergate burglars as they attempt to bug the offices of the National Democratic Committee in 1971, only to get caught in the act. Then it moves to the newsroom of the *Washington Post*, a working environment of stark white light, noisily clacking typewriters, desks covered in papers and documents. The authenticity of this location is one of the film's most admired features, and still used in many journalism classes today as a guide to what news rooms looked like in the days before computers, mobile phones and the internet. Big, chunky phones ring noisily and incessantly, staff wander around in the background, convening meetings and conversations, while Bernstein smokes everywhere, even in the elevator (although Dustin Hoffman's portrayal of a smoker is perhaps the least convincing aspect of the film – he looks like a teenager trying to smoke so that he can be one of the big boys, and finding the experience rather more unpleasant than he bargained for).

From this point on the film gives an account of how an apparently minor crime story – a hotel break-in – builds into the biggest political scandal the United States had ever seen. Hoffman and Robert Redford (Bob Woodward) spend most of their time on screen laboriously putting together the pieces of a jigsaw – 'a puzzle', Woodward says in desperation to a source at one point – from snippets of information and small irregularities which gradually accumulate to hint at a cover-up of political corruption. 'They're hungry', says their editor in justification of their doggedness to pursue this story despite opposition. And determined. The film is a straightforwardly linear narrative of how an investigative story is conducted, a master class in journalistic technique.

Each scene moves the viewer on to another piece of the jigsaw, like a police procedural. The journalists are like detectives, taking evidence, checking and double-checking their sources, comparing notes, building up their case. And as every maverick detective has his sceptical boss who presents a well-meaning but misguided obstacle to the progress of an investigation, so Woodward and Bernstein have to fight against the doubts of their editor-in-chief Ben Bradlee (Jason Robards), their more senior colleagues on the political desk (who resent that these young upstarts have a head start on this most political of news stories), and other news media. In the end, of course, they triumph, though we do not get to see the moment of their victory. As the film ends in 1972, before the re-election of Nixon for a second term, Woodward and Bernstein have been given the backing of Bradlee to pursue the investigation to its conclusion, and we see them working at their desks in the news room, battering away on their typewriters as a TV screen shows actual news footage of Nixon's campaign victory. The closing scene shows only a news wire churning out the headlines of subsequent months and years – the beginning of the Watergate hearings; the first convictions; Nixon's denials; Nixon's resignation. Credits rolling on a black screen.

The casting of Redford and Hoffman lends the film Hollywood glamour (both were huge stars in the 1970s), but a minimalist tone is maintained throughout. There is no musical soundtrack to add atmosphere, and no back story for the two journalists. We know only that Woodward has been on the paper for just nine months, while Bernstein has sixteen months 'in the business'. We see nothing of their private lives, except one interior of Woodward's apartment. As in *Good Night, and Good Luck* the story of journalists doing their job, determinedly and professionally, is judged to be enough to carry the movie. The Watergate investigation was so important, Pakula seems to be saying, that character development and emotional depth would be distracting. Let's just see how it happened, interview by interview, telephone call by telephone call. It is even less embroidered than Clooney's film, which despite its superficial simplicity works hard with monochrome cinematography and artfully lit cigarette smoke to evoke its 1950s ambience. *All the President's Men* is as close to documentary in feel and structure as it is possible to imagine in a mainstream production starring two of Hollywood's most eligible leading men.

The story, of course, *is* important enough to carry this narrative strategy, and the two lead actors convincingly portray two very different personalities who come together to make a good team. More than three decades later the film retains its relevance and aesthetic power, and is recognised as a showcase for what is considered exemplary in liberal journalism – a re-enactment, or master class in the practice of investigation which is still used on journalism programmes to illustrate how it should be done. For *Financial Times* editor Lionel Barber, who worked on the *Washington Post* in the 1980s, the film documents and also celebrates an era of print journalism which is now disappearing due to financial and technological pressures, but should be remembered as a time when 'reporters were given days, often weeks, to research stories. The editing process was exhausting: copy passed through at least four pairs of hands'.[3]

All the President's Men depicts the progression of a story from initial hunch to publication in all its drudgery, the tedium and repetition of its narrative progression justified only by the audience's knowledge that, in the end, it was precisely this slow, methodical, unglamorous rigour which allowed the story to survive the political and corporate pressures to drop or bury it. The film's message is profoundly opposed to the view of journalism as a glamorous, exciting business, showing instead that the path to uncovering an important truth is long and difficult, and that short cuts are inadmissible. Bob Woodward looks like Robert Redford, and that is a Hollywoodisation of the facts, yes, but even Robert Redford, if he wants to write a story accusing a newly elected White House administration of corruption, has, in the time before googling became the preferred method of doing journalistic research, to spend hundreds of hours checking library records, invoices, and other documents. In the days before mobile phones and faxes, Carl Bernstein (played by Dustin Hoffman) has to get on a plane and fly five hours south to check some obscure invoices which will later turn out to have a key role in piecing together the story. From such drudgery, we see, the epochal exposé of a White House cover-up emerges.

All the President's Men, then, has come to be regarded as a 'how-to' movie by journalists and educators alike – a two-hour long tutorial in the principles and practice of investigative journalism, where the quiet tenacity of the central characters serves only to highlight how shocking and dramatic is the corruption they have exposed at the heart of American government. The journalists, we see, are not in the least political in the performance of their professional duties, and would pursue their story in exactly the same way were it a Democrat in the Oval Office. The investigation is conducted by the book with scrupulous

Figure 10 *All the President's Men* (Alan J. Pakula, 1976). Source BFI

observance of such rules as 'double sourcing' (nothing can be printed that has not been confirmed by at least one reliable source). There is no 'whodunnit' quality to the story, since there can be no doubt as to who the culprits were – just a relentless pursuit of the facts of the case, upon which others will in due course act. The film ends with snippets from congressional and other hearings which took place after the main action of the movie is concluded, as if to say, the watchdogs have done their work, now the forces of law and order will make their judgment.

THE LEGACY OF *ALL THE PRESIDENT'S MEN*

For many observers the lasting legacy of the film's simple message and understated seriousness is the importance of investigative journalism in democratic societies, at a time when competitive pressures and financial constraints are reducing the amount of editorial resource devoted to the specialism. Journalism scholars and practitioners alike have been critical of what they argue to be the weakening of investigative journalism in media organisations. This most expensive of journalistic endeavours (because of the time and person power required to pursue it effectively, as depicted in Pakula's film) is in serious decline, goes the argument. The continuing value of *All the President's Men* lies, for many commentators, in the importance it allots to properly resourced, editorially supported investigation, especially when the trail leads right to the top.[4] In October 2008 a *Financial Times* article (penned by editor Lionel Barber) about the state of contemporary journalism in the US and the UK was illustrated with a still from *All the President's Men*, showing Robert Redford addressing Dustin Hoffman in the *Washington Post* newsroom as they go about their investigation.[5] For Barber, as for many others, the film continues to symbolise journalistic excellence with its portrayal of how the fourth estate can change things for the better.

Not all observers are so gushing in their praise, however. Michael Schudson challenges the myth of Watergate, as he characterises it:

> That two young *Washington Post* reporters brought down the President of the United States. This is a myth of David and Goliath, of powerless individuals overturning an institution of overwhelming might. It is high noon in Washington, with two white-hatted young reporters at one end of the street and the black-hatted President at the other, protected by his minions. And the good guys win. The press, truth its only weapon, saves the day. (1995: 143)

Schudson is not the only one to have questioned the myth of Watergate as presented in *All the President's Men*. Nor is he wrong to point out the simplifications, exaggerations and distortions made inevitable by the translation of the facts into cinematic form. Richard Nixon was brought down by legislative oversight of his administration's actions, assisted and encouraged but not entirely caused by journalistic revelations (although who can say what would have happened in the absence of the kind of critical scrutiny of Nixon's 'dirty tricks' operation initiated by Woodward and Bernstein, and supported, as the film shows, by editor Bradlee?).

Schudson also argues that the myth of the Watergate investigation is at least partly responsible for the steadily more intrusive political journalism of the post-Nixon era, a journalism which achieved its greatest 'success' with the humiliation of Bill Clinton in 1998–9 (and which occurred after the above article was written). Lionel Barber, meanwhile, attributes to *All the President's Men* (the book and the film) the unwelcome rise of 'celebrity' journalism.

FROM WATERGATE TO MONICA-GATE, AND THE CRISIS OF INVESTIGATIVE JOURNALISM

In considering these qualifications to what is a revered film we should concede, first, that no film about anything, based on true events or not, ever did anything other than exaggerate, distort, misrepresent and manipulate the 'facts' of the case to suit the storytelling demands of the cinematic medium. This observation is not intended as a criticism, but a recognition that 'realism' in cinema can only ever be a relative term, an aspiration, and that to expect any film account of actual events to be 'true' to real life in any absolute or objective sense is naïve. The subjectivity of the choices made by writers, directors, editors, actors, cinematographers and the rest of the many people involved in making a film renders it an impression, an interpretation, an account, which at best will capture some essential element of the reality being represented, but never the full richness and complexity of a story, or anything like it. Despite its considerable length and attention to detail, its quasi-documentary style and its patient, low-key progress to a deliberately anti-climactic conclusion, *All the President's Men* is no less a construction than the book by Woodward and Bernstein on which it is based, or the many other movies which have been made about fictional scandals and cover-ups. It is shaped by personal subjectivity, compromises made in the production process, the storytelling techniques required to make a narrative feature film acceptable to the audience on whom its commercial success depends.

I make these points, to repeat, not to criticise what is by near universal consent an excellent piece of film-making as deserving of its 'classic' status as any of the films discussed in this book, but to downgrade expectations of what such a text can achieve. *All the President's Men* is an adaptation of one, inevitably slanted account of a sequence of events which could be narrated from many other perspectives, and not necessarily in such glamorous terms. The film is far from being a crowd pleaser in its style, but the involvement of two of America's leading male stars – Robert Redford and Dustin Hoffman – as the reporters places it firmly in the realm of Hollywood fantasy. For Lionel Barber this A-list casting has had unfortunate ramifications.

> In retrospect, the Watergate scandal was a curse as well as a blessing for US journalism. *All the President's Men* made celebrity a goal to which many journalists now aspire.[6]

Redford and Hoffman were sex symbols. One could argue that this was an asset for the film, in so far as it gave a complex and difficult story a recognisably human face to the millions of people who were encouraged by their involvement to go and see it in cinemas. It may not have had the same impact as a cultural event without these actors. Moreover, the sincerity of the two lead actors, and their interest in the exploration of journalism in their work, cannot be in question given their later and frequent involvement in films about journalism (Redford directed and starred in *Lions For Lambs* (2007), for example; Hoffmann was a TV journalist in Costa-Gavras' *Mad City* (1997), and a victim of tabloid frenzy in *Accidental Hero* (Stephen Frears, 1992).

Barber's more serious point is that *All the President's Men* launched a trend towards what he calls 'celebrity journalism' – the notion of the journalist-as-star, more famous and self-important (perhaps) than the subjects of his or her coverage. This is unfair, it seems to me. Was there ever a time in the history of journalism when its practitioners did not seek celebrity? Were Walter Winchell and Louella Parsons in the 1930s and 1940s not famous and admired (or loathed)? Ed Murrow and Walter Cronkite in the 1950s and 1960s? The portrayal of the character of J. J. Hunsecker in *Sweet Smell of Success*, modelled on Winchell, shows that the celebrity of some journalists and the abuses to which it might be put was an issue even in the 1950s, long before Redford and Hoffman became the glamorous personification of Woodward and Bernstein.

We might revise Barber's point to say that Pakula's film, and the sexiness of the lead performances at its heart, made journalists in the US and elsewhere aspire to be famous for being good journalists, and for bringing corrupt power to heel as Woodward and Bernstein so dramatically did. And if that is true, then good. The film undoubtedly created a myth, from the movie-star casting of its reporters to the suggestion made in the script that investigative journalism was the principal, if not only cause of the scandal and its outcome. But it is a functional myth, with a progressive, pro-democratic meaning, which if it has inspired real journalists to attempt to follow in Woodward's and Bernstein's footsteps need not be regretted. Young journalists, like other categories of professional, *need* role models, and this is what *All the President's Men* provided like no other work of popular cinema before or since.

FROM WATERGATE TO MONICA-GATE

What of Schudson's suggestion that there is a line of development from the normatively approved scrutiny depicted in *All the President's Men* to the less welcome, because personally intrusive style of watchdog journalism seen in the Clinton–Lewinsky scandal, for example? Schudson's essay on 'Watergate and the Press' appears in a 1995 publication, before the Lewinsky scandal but after Bill Clinton's ascendancy to the presidency. As such, he may be considered prescient in noting that a particularly intrusive style of political reporting had become more prevalent in western journalism, and was soon to become much more so. We had, after all, never seen anything like the voyeuristic frenzy of 1998–9.[7] It is simplistic, however, to link this trend to the success of the Watergate investigation, or to its representation in film. The significance of Watergate was not in creating a vogue for political scandal, which is in itself nothing new, but in proving that the watchdog role of the journalist could have a truly cleansing impact on the highest levels of the executive government of the most powerful country on earth. That this role was then extended to the private lives of politicians cannot be attributed to Woodward and Bernstein, nor should it be dismissed, as it so often is by scholars, as a degeneration of the function.

The rise of intrusive political journalism can be viewed as part of the broader decline in social deference which has characterised western societies since, roughly speaking, the 1950s. In the 1960s in the US this trend had not progressed so far as to threaten exposure of President Kennedy's serial womanising in and around the White House (Hersh 1997). In Britain, as late as the 1990s, politicians were largely sheltered from intrusive coverage of their private lives, unless they were implicated in criminal acts. In France this remained true until the ascendacy of Nicola Sarkozy and his much reported romance of and marriage to Carla Bruni.[8] Politicians in all democratic countries had alcohol and substance abuse problems, affairs, debts and much else, without it ever becoming public knowledge through media coverage. Journalists, like their audiences, largely accepted that these aspects of political life were, unless directly impacting on public duties, out of bounds. That changed in the 1990s, as politics and celebrity became more entwined on the one hand, and on the other, the lines between public and private affairs dissolved in celebrity journalism (see the scandals afflicting Silvio Berlusconi in 2009).[9]

Where some view this as an unfortunate trend, because of its coarsening of the public sphere (and there has been that at times, for sure), I and others have greeted it as a positive expression of what journalistic scrunity can mean in a mass democracy.[10] Take, for example, the case of Charles and Diana, whose marriage and (as it turned out) highly dysfunctional lives were exposed to public scrutiny in the 1990s, fuelled by interviews given by Diana to writer Andrew Morton and celebrity TV interviewer Bashir Mann. In a country where a substantial proportion of the public still believed in the 1950s in the divine right of kings, the knowledge that aristocrats were fallible human beings with marriage problems, eating disorders and personality flaws like the rest of us was liberating. Henceforth, the monarch's claims to exercise power and authority in the UK were subject to a degree of questioning which must be considered healthy by all democrats.

The excesses of celebrity journalism, and the extent to which political journalism blurs the public/private line and crosses into the zone of prurient voyeurism, can certainly be criticised on ethical grounds. The politician who does not make 'family values' or 'personal morality' the foundation of his or her identity should not be attacked in the media for behaviour which some may question or even find offensive. He or she who does – New York state governor Elliot Spitzer, for example – may reasonably expect to be vilified if found in breach of those values. Where extremes do occur, they are less the consequence of what Woodward and Bernstein achieved more than three decades ago and much more to do with a media marketplace which has become steadily more competitive over the years, and which is stoked into frenzied speculation by the activities of public relations professionals, or spin doctors working in the political sphere. Rod Lurie's rarely seen and under-rated 2000 film based on precisely this premise, *The Contender*, has a conservative congressman played by Gary Oldman manufacture a sex scandal in order to prevent a woman (Joan Allen) being nominated as vice-president.

In addition to the factors of media competitiveness and political manipulativeness, the availability of live, networked, always-on, globalised media means that any scandal quickly becomes news, from where it can go on to become a full blown crisis. The evolution of journalism's watchdog role, its intrusion into the private lives of elites, may on occasion mean an excess of voyeuristic spectacle. That, however, is the price of an unprecedentedly combative and adversarial journalism, and one which we would as citizens come to regret losing were it closed down.

GOOD NIGHT, AND GOOD LUCK

Three decades and six presidents on from the events depicted in *All the President's Men*, *Good Night, and Good Luck* was released. Like its illustrious predecessor, George Clooney's second film as director was favourably received by both critics and audiences as a well crafted study of the best of US journalism (the film took $31.5 million at the US box office, and was nominated for six Oscars in 2006, athough it won none). Released in the United States in 2005, the display of best practice on screen was this time read not as a self-congratulatory master class in how to perform the watchdog function, but as a critical comment on the current performance of the US news media in relation to the 'war on terror' and the 2003 invasion of Iraq. Where Pakula's film is the unadorned re-enactment of an honourable episode in the history of American journalism, *Good Night, and Good Luck* is a psychological drama about the journalistic confrontation with right wing populism, and how that confrontation is negotiated in the face of corporate pressure to kowtow.

Reviewing *Good Night, and Good Luck* on its release, Philip Kemp described it as a film which 'celebrates a hero – a principled journalist who took a stand against a malignant demagogue and helped bring him down'.[11] For Geoffrey McNab, the film is also 'a celebration of professionalism' which 'evokes a lost era of journalism, long before the excesses of Jayson Blair, Stephen Glass and Fox News besmirched the reputation of the US media'.[12] The inclusion of Fox News in this triad of journalistic villains refers to the fact that it is the overtly partisan, frequently jingoistic style of News Corp's US TV news channel which most observers read as the target of Clooney's film.

Where Murrow and his colleagues are seen to stand up for what they believe to be truth and objectivity in their treatment of the Radulovich story, at considerable risk to themselves (and one of their team is dead by the end of the film, having killed himself because of negative press coverage), Fox News has been widely criticised inside and out of the US for its blatantly biased treatment of the war on terror and its related conflicts. And indeed, to any observer of Fox more used to the studied impartiality of TV news as practised by the BBC and the US terrestrial networks, the style of the channel's coverage seems more akin to the tabloid and red-top newspapers owned by News Corp in the US and the UK. Fox News presenters such as Bill O'Reilly make little effort to hide their ideological and political preferences, and during the invasion and occupation of Iraq seemed to view themselves as war-time propagandists rather than objective reporters, far less watchdogs over executive power in the White House. This writer recalls watching Fox News on a 2004 visit to the USA, at the time when the Abu Ghraib scandal was dominating the news agenda there and elsewhere, and being startled to hear the atrocious human rights abuses inflicted by US soldiers on their Iraqi charges as 'wrong doing by our boys' and other, equally anodyne phrases. Likewise, those who dared to criticise aspects of US policy in the Middle East, or in relation to the detention camp at Guantanamo were regularly pilloried by Fox News as unpatriotic traitors to the cause of freedom and democracy. In marked contrast to the style of Sky News in the UK, which has always sought to compete with the BBC and ITN

Figure 11   *Good Night, and Good Luck* (George Clooney, 2005). Source: BFL

(the two providers of British public service broadcast journalism) on quality and ethical grounds, Fox routinely banged the drum for the Bush administration, right or wrong, and railed against its critics, justified or not.

The power over which journalists watch in *Good Night …* is not that of the president, nor of corporate interests as in *The Insider*, but the power of fear when it is used as a weapon, manipulated and exploited to justify the erosion of civil liberties. In so far as big US business is seen here to exert pressure on the CBS journalists (pressure which is in the end successfully resisted), we are clear that the real enemy of freedom and democracy is Senator Joe McCarthy, the figure head of the anti-communist witch-hunts of the 1950s. The film depicts an era in the United States when even big firms such as Alcoa were afraid of taking on McCarthy and his supporters, and risking their anger. The drama of the Radulovich case may have been sufficient to propel the film on its own, but against the background of director and star Clooney's known views on the war on terror it was widely read as a reference to, and commentary on the US media's collusion with the climate of fear stoked up by the Bush administration post-9/11. If there is a specific target of the script (which Clooney co-wrote), it is the Fox News presenters O'Reilly and Hannity.

As with *All the President's Men*, there were some dissenters from the generally positive reception enjoyed by Clooney's film. Jeff Jarvis refers to Murrow in a column written at the time as 'a god of American journalism'. *Good Night, and Good Luck* 'conjures up Murrow's ghost just as America's scandal-scarred and budget-bruised journalistic institutions are taking on the mood of haunted houses'. Jarvis, however, questions the reverence extended to Murrow and his generation, representing as they do, in his view, 'a half-century of journalistic haughtiness, self-importance and separation from the public'.[13] That seems ungenerous, if only because Murrow's *was* the preferred mode of journalistic performance and delivery in those days. Irrespective of its elitist and patrician style as seen from the era of Jon Stewart or Michael Moore, his authority and 'haughtiness' was crucial to puncturing the McCarthy bubble and ending an unfortunate period in American political history.

THE INSIDER

One of the most serious health issues for a democracy is the corporate pressure which exists on journalistic watchdogs to turn their gaze away from corruption and wrongdoing. *Good Night, and Good Luck* treats this problem with reference to the influence of advertiser Alcoa on CBS current affairs show *See It Now*, where producer Fred Friendly must confront his executives on the importance of not giving in (Alcoa did not wish to be seen to support CBS coverage of the Radulovich story through its advertising because it was a major military contractor, and risked losing business). Corporate pressure on journalistic watchdogs is the theme of another much praised film based on actual events, Michael Mann's *The Insider* (1999).

Adapted from a *Vanity Fair* article by Marie Brenner,[14] the film attracted seven Oscar nominations, and just over $29 million at the US box office. Starring Russell Crowe as tobacco company whistle-blower Jeffrey Wigand, it tells the story of the efforts of CBS current affairs producer Lowell Bergman (Al Pacino) to get Wigand's explosive revelations into the public domain. Pacino plays what reviewer Nick James described as 'a tenacious figure who lives and breathes that near-mythical force for good: journalistic integrity'.[15] This integrity is established in an opening segment where Bergman travels to the Middle East to interview a muslim cleric with affiliations to a terrorist organisation. The sheikh's representatives demand prior approval of the questions which CBS will put to him. Producer Lowell Bergman, hooded and blindfolded, refuses: 'You've seen *60 Minutes*. You've seen Mike Wallace (the programme presenter), so you know our reputation for objectivity and integrity.' And he gets his way. The interview is set up, senior presenter Mike Wallace gets to ask his questions the way he wants to, as gun-toting, leather-jacketed Arab fighters stand by. Viewed in a post-9/11 environment, this is a poignant reminder of how things were in an earlier, more rule-governed age. As the fate of Daniel Pearl would show (see Chapter 6) the days when a US media crew could travel to the Middle East and make demands of islamic fundamentalist fighters on the basis of appeals to journalistic 'objectivity' and 'integrity' would soon be over.

Bergman stumbles onto Wigand's desire to blow the whistle on Big Tobacco by accident, setting off a chain of events in which the producer first has to persuade the whistle-blower to go on the record with his allegations, then persuade his bosses and CBS executives to permit the resulting programme to be transmitted. He succeeds in the first objective, but fails in the second, as CBS corporate interests begin to conflict with those of the journalists.

Mann's film differs from those of Pakula and Clooney in that it addresses not only the ethical violations of a powerful sector of the American elite but the ethics of a journalist who, like the lawyers seeking Wigand's public deposition in the pursuit of their claims against Big Tobacco, put their own definition of the public interest above the private needs of their whistle blower. Both Bergman and the lawyers insist that it is Wigand's choice, and responsibility, whether or not he testifies, but they make it very difficult for him to resist their appeals and at the same time preserve any sense of personal honour.

Bergman's ethical dilemma arises when his source is left abandoned by corporate interests. As he puts it to Mike Wallace when explaining his decision to resign as *60 Minutes* producer, no source will ever believe his promises again. His integrity as an investigative journalist is fatally and permanently

Figure 12 *The Insider* (Michael Mann, 1999)

destroyed. And while the script is critical of the cowardice and self-interest of CBS in the face of Big Tobacco, the film also asks the important question – is any story worth the potential destruction of a news organisation like CBS (the same dilemma arises in *Good Night, and Good Luck*)?

Unlike *All the President's Men, The Insider* is a psychological drama bearing all the stylistic flourishes of a Michael Mann movie. Ethical dilemmas are personalised and we see the human cost of applying liberal journalistic principles in situations where powerful interests are under attack. These are men with families and private lives, unlike Woodward and Bernstein in Pakula's film (or Murrow and Friendly in *Good Night, and Good Luck* for that matter). Despite a number of speeches about the ethics of investigative journalism and references to 'the legacy of Edward R. Murrow', this is not a procedural quasi-documentary but a thriller. No one gets killed in *The Insider*, and as with *All the President's Men* we know the ending before the film starts, but the tension builds as courage leads to betrayal, and betrayal leads back to the courage of Bergman in effectively giving away his 'scoop' to the competition. By doing so, he fulfils his obligation to Wigand, and forces the broadcast of the damaging allegations, but destroys his own career at CBS. At the conclusion of *The Insider*, then, the whistle-blower can claim a victory of sorts, and claims amounting to billions of dollars in compensation were subsequently lodged against the tobacco companies. The personal cost to Wigand was enormous, however, as it was to Bergman.

In *Good Night, and Good Luck* Ed Murrow and his team emerge triumphant from their tussle with corporate interests, and get to report their story more or less as they would wish. The script sheds light on some of their own professional deficiencies, but in the end it is Senator McCarthy who goes down. *The Insider*, on the other hand, is the story of how US corporate interests – the big tobacco companies in particular – successfully smothered an attempt by journalist Lowell Bergman to expose the research evidence that the risks of cancer caused by smoking had been known about by the companies for many years. In terms of cinema's myth-making function, *The Insider* is an articulation of the normative values of investigative journalism, and a critique of the performance of these, both by the media (CBS's concern with profit) and big business power (their attempt to stifle Wigand). *The Insider* thus emerges as a film principally about the tensions between news and business, or between the role of journalism as watchdog over power (corporate power, in this case), and the function of journalism as commodity in the infotainment sector of the media. The last act is peppered with exchanges between Bergman and Wallace, Bergman and the CBS corporate lawyer, Begman and the CBS senior executive officer, about which takes precedence – CBS Corporate, or CBS News. As the company lawyers intervene to have the Wigand interview removed from the story that will go out, Bergman asks in exasperation: 'Since when has the paragon of investigative journalism allowed lawyers to determine the content of *60 Minutes?*' Reviewer Mark Kermode observed that:

> One is tempted to compare it to *All the President's Men*, but that hardly does service to *The Insider*'s brash effrontery. After all, everyone knew that Nixon was corrupt and had resigned by the time Alan Pakula's movie hit the screens. He was, therefore, a sitting duck, while Mann's target (the tobacco corporations) is still powerful and on the move.[16]

CONCLUSION

The three films discussed in this chapter are widely regarded as among the best ever made about journalism. All were critically and commercially successful, engaging some of the most high-powered writers, directors and actors working in mainstream cinema. The seriousness with which they were made, and the resources poured into them, allow us to say with some confidence that the heroic status of the journalist as watchdog is genuinely valued, and that threats to that status continue to be viewed with dismay and suspicion. In these films, as in few others, the scrutinising, watchdog function of journalism is placed at the very heart of democratic societies, its performance itself scrutinised and evaluated. If, as we have seen, it might be argued that *All the President's Men* is a somewhat idealised account of the Woodward-Bernstein investigation, or that *Good Night, and Good Luck* overstates the supience of the US media towards the Bush administration – it was released, after all, in the year after Michael Moore's *Fahrenheit 9/11* beat *Spider-Man II* at the US box office – that such films have been made at all, and have been received with such appreciation by audiences all over the world, is a cause for modest celebration of the civic potential of popular cinema. Each of these films was made on the premise of a shared social consensus – the belief that independent, courageous, critical and well-resourced journalism matters in modern democracies. Today's student journalists could do worse than watch these movies for sound instruction on how to perform their watchdog role.

NOTES

1. The early history of journalism in England is explored in Raymond Joad's *The Invention of the Newspaper* (1996). Martin Conboy's *Journalism: a critical history* (2004) is also recommended for further reading. Paul Starr's *The Creation of the Media* (2004) tells the story of the origins of US journalistic traditions in the struggle for independence.
2. She defines the 'ur-text' as 'a seminal text that illustrates a specific structure of feeling regarding the construction of contemporary journalistic practices' (Brennen 1998: 115).
3. Barber, L., 'Why journalism wins my vote', *Financial Times*, 11/12 October 2008 (http://www.ft.com/cms/s/0/35dadeac-9662-11dd-9dce-000077b07658.html).
4. For a recent collection of scholarly and practitioner essays on the history and contemporary practice of inestigative journalism see De Burgh (ed.) (2008).
5. Barber, L., 'Why journalism wins my vote', *Financial Times*, 11/12 October 2008 (http://www.ft.com/cms/s/0/35dadeac-9662-11dd-9dce-000077b07658.html).
6. Idem.
7. For a discussion of the cultural significance of Monica-gate see McNair (2002).
8. In 2005 the Nicolas Sarkozy and his first wife, Cecilie, broke the mould in French political journalism when they were reported in the context of an alleged affair she was having. *Paris Match*'s unprecedented front-page coverage of the story that summer changed French political culture forever, bringing it into line with patterns already established in the United States and Britain. For a journalistic account of this episode, see McNair, B., 'Revealed (at last): French politics is a hotbed of sexual scandal', *Sunday Herald*, 28 August 2005.
9. For a recent study of the relationship between politics, media and celebrity, see Michael Higgins' *Media and Their Publics* (2008).
10. See, for example, my *Journalism and Democracy* (2000), and Catharine Lumby's *Gotcha: life in a tabloid world* (1999).
11. Kemp, P., *Sight & Sound*, volume 16, number 3, 2006.
12. *Sight & Sound*, volume 15, number 11, 2005.
13. Jarvis, J., 'Good night to Murrow's legacy of power', *Guardian*, 24 October 2005.
14. Brenner, M., 'The man who knew too much', *Vanity Fair*, May 1996.
15. James, N., 'No smoking gun', *Sight & Sound*, volume 10, number 3, 2000.
16. *Sight & Sound*, volume 10, number 3, 2000.

CHAPTER 6

Witnesses

Coming a close second to the watchdog in the hierarchy of cinematic heroism is the representation of the journalist as *witness* to events, a term which can be viewed as merely descriptive – the journalist monitors and surveys the environment, and thus inevitably witnesses events happening – or as a more symbolic statement of social function, connoting a particular kind of integrity and trustworthiness.

To 'bear witness' is not just to see, but to provide evidence that something has happened, to testify on events in a way that carries conviction and credibility, because of the status of the witness, the scrutiny to which that testimony has been subjected, and the circumstances within which it is delivered. Witnesses testify in court, to judges and juries. Friends and family members bear witness that a couple have been legally married, or divorced, or that a child has been baptised in a particular religious denomination. Journalists testify to the court of public opinion that such-and-such has occurred in the world, furnishing the information, or evidence, upon which publics and their representatives go on to act. To act as a witness is not to judge the rights and wrongs of events – judgement is usually excluded from the practice of objectivity, although journalists bearing witness to some recent conflicts have, as we shall see, challenged this presumption – or to pronounce guilt on the various actors involved in a given situation, but to assist in the process of establishing if indeed a crime (legal or moral) has been committed, after which sanctions and punishments may well be forthcoming.[1]

The role of witness is in the first place purely functional, then, but because information is a weapon the bearer of new information – the witness – becomes also a player in the power games which underpin events. The witness, like the watchdog, may be in possession of information which can threaten others. Some witnesses in some court cases require police protection, because their testimony threatens the powerful, be it a local gangster or a big corporation

(Jeffrey Wigand in *The Insider*, for example). So too the journalist, in his or her capacity as witness, risks the wrath of the powerful as well as those, be they powerful or not, who stand to be damaged by the information which the witness brings to the public domain. In these circumstances the witness is often required to show extraordinary courage, to be heroic, to resist the pressure not to testify.

All journalists are potentially witnesses, in this sense. The investigative journalists of the previous chapter were positioned as witnesses in what were, in effect, media-initiated trials of the Nixon administration, the McCarthy witch hunts and Big Tobacco respectively. Before they can be witnesses, however, investigative journalists are engaged in a particular kind of practice involving discovery and exposure of things which are hidden. There is another kind of journalist – the reporter, or correspondent, and the foreign correspondent in particular, and the foreign correspondent who covers wars and conflict especially, whose status as witness is more direct and literal.

Of all the stories which foreign correspondents routinely cover, stories of death and dying, particularly when they involve the deliberate taking of human life must be ranked as the most important. Part of the function of the journalist-as-witness is to alert us to things happening which we do not know about but should do, in the hope that we will then put pressure on our governments to intervene. Of supreme significance in this context is surely conflict, war, and the associated taking of human life – the tragic, timeless and universal story which it falls upon the war correspondent to deliver.

This book was written at a time of war – the 'war on terror', the 'clash of civilisations', the global jihad and the response to it. This war followed not long after the conclusion of the wars which decimated the former Yugoslavia, which followed in turn the Cold War, or 'New Cold War' of the 1980s, when the US and its allies on the one hand, and the Soviet Union and its allies on the other, pursued a global conflict for ideological, economic and military domination by proxy wars fought in central America, Africa and elsewhere. The new Cold War followed, indeed developed out of, the uneasy peace settlement of the Second World War, and the raising of what Winston Churchill called the Iron Curtain. These conflicts, and the different technological and ideological environments within which they were fought, have presented journalists with very different challenges in their role as witnesses.

As ideologies dissolve and reform, and geo-strategic politics shift, journalists have been required to shift their perspectives in turn.[2] At the same time, journalists have been required to report events overseas – to bear witness to them – against the background of rapidly changing news-gathering and production technologies, on the one hand, and evermore intensive news management practices by the parties to conflict on the other. The former – portable cameras and editing equipment, satellite communications – has tended to expand the zone of journalistic operation in conflict situations, aiding the correspondent's work, while the latter has been the response to that increased freedom by the relevant authorities.

THE FOREIGN CORRESPONDENT IN CINEMA

Films about war correspondents are a prominent sub-genre of journalism movies. Journalists are usually permitted to be present in conflict zones, albeit with conditions attached. Dramas involving foreign and war correspondents thus allow stories about war to be told – they provide a point of view on conflict, not based on actual combat but on its observation and the attempt to translate it into the language of news. This latter element provides a recurring theme of movies about war journalism – the appropriate role of the journalist in conflict situations – to be objective and detached, or subjective and committed? To remain neutral in the matter of who is right and wrong in a given conflict, or to take sides and declare a stance?

Bearing witness to conflict and war was one of the first 'killer applications' of what we now call journalism. Early correspondents wrote home about diplomatic disputes, inter-state relations, wars and battles. This information was crucial to governments as they sought to manage their relations with other states, or to protect their trade interests. Correspondents became the prime source of public information about 'faraway places of which we know little'. The information provided by war correspondents was particularly important, given the high costs of waging war, and the importance of managing public opinion in democratic states. Governments in countries such as the US and the UK have been required to win popular consent before they embark on overseas conflicts. The level of consent extended is dependent on several factors, not least the perception of the legitimacy of the war effort, which in turn is largely informed by the dispatches of correspondents on the scene. The same relationship of cause and effect applies to humanitarian crises such as famine or drought in Africa. It was, famously, the series of heart-breaking TV reports from refugee camps broadcast on the BBC in 1983 by Michael Buerk which triggered the global humanitarian campaign to assist Ethiopia, including Live Aid and all that came after.

The foreign correspondent, like the investigative reporter, often puts him or herself in danger. In conflict situations the reporter may be in the line of fire, or close to it, risking life and limb to bear witness to the progress of the battle or the war. This fact makes the correspondent's role not merely important in the democratic life of a society, but fraught with danger and rich with dramatic potential. The correspondent is thus a glamorous, sometimes sexy figure, ripe for cinematic treatment, and indeed literary. One of the earliest and most famous of fictional journalistic characters is Evelyn Waugh's William Boot, the central protagonist of his satirical novel *Scoop* (1938). Boot is a reluctant foreign correspondent in Africa, believed to have been based on the late Bill Deedes, who covered Africa in the 1930s for the *Daily Express*. Graham Greene's Thomas Fowler in *The Quiet American* (1955) is a foreign correspondent in Vietnam, and the subject of two films to date.[3] In the most recent of these, released not long after the September 11 attacks, Fowler is played by Michael Caine as a cynical observer of American covert action overseas. Reading *The Quiet American*, as this author did for the first time in 2008, one is struck by its resonances with the current era, and the views a journalist based in, say, Baghdad in 2003–8, might hold about the legitimacy of US efforts to impose its will overseas.

The role of the foreign correspondent in time of war is difficult and potentially dangerous, as noted. If a country is at war, do the news media of that country, and the individual correspondent, have a responsibility to the nation state, which may be in mortal peril, or to the principles of objectivity and integrity which normally govern the reporter's work, and which also matter to the health of the democratic state? Can the journalist be simply a reporter of conflict, or is there a requirement to participate, and if the latter, in what ways?

FOREIGN CORRESPONDENT – THE SOLDIERS OF THE PRESS

When a state is engaged in 'total war', as happened twice to the US and the UK in the twentieth century, the expectation is clear: the journalist is part of the war effort, his reportage subordinated to the needs of the state – an unapologetic and enthusiastic propagandist. No British or American journalist was expected (or permitted) to be objective in respect of Nazi Germany in the 1939–45 conflict, and few citizens of those countries would find that surprising or objectionable. To put it another way, objectivity was not considered to be incompatible with willing service for the nation in the face of the fascist threat. In Alfred Hitchcock's *Foreign Correspondent* (1940) Joel McCrae plays Johnny Jones, a crime reporter sent to Europe on the eve of World War Two. In typical Hitchcockian manner the reporter becomes embroiled in espionage and treason, and has to become in effect a combatant in the coming war against nazism.

Commenting on the image of the war correspondent presented in this film, Richard Ness observes that in the decade after the screwball comedies and their assortment of journalistic rogues he [the war correspondent] 'provided a new, more noble image for the screen reporter' (1997: 241). Journalists became the 'soldiers of the press' in the great war effort. In this film the reporter begins

Figure 13 *Foreign Correspondent* (Alfred Hitchcock, 1940). Source: BFI

the story as a classic journalistic hero of the romantic, pre-war type – roguish, somewhat untrustworthy, cynical, but once engaged in his quest for the truth, a reliable and dedicated force for good. He deals only in 'facts', and it is this task which enables the audience to enter into the thriller dimension of the story. The journalist becomes a spy, a licensed investigator whose news-gathering work becomes inseparable from the struggle against the Nazis. The journalist is a hero, fighting against the Nazis and their appeasers.

Not all wars are so consensual as the 1939–45 conflict, of course. In most cases, government decisions to go to war spark debate and opposition from at least some in the public. In this context, where war is a negotiable matter of public policy, the journalist's objectivity must be seen to be applied in the traditional manner, without the taking of sides. Some of the most bitter disputes between the media and political authority have arisen from a difference of view as to how subject to the rules of objective reportage a given conflict is. During the first Gulf War of 1991, western journalists were subject to rigorous controls on where they could go and what they could report. The consequences of the application of these rules structure much of the narrative in David O. Russell's *Three Kings*, where two female journalists use different methods to gain access to good stories – one sleeps with George Clooney's character Archie, the other (reportedly inspired by Christiane Amanpour) appeals to her status as a journalist working for a leading global news organisation.

Similar issues of access and control of media arose in relation to coverage of the invasions of Afghanistan in 2001, and Iraq in 2003. The second Gulf War, launched in March 2003 by a coalition led by the US Bush administration and the New Labour government of Tony Blair, was initially reported in images reminiscent of 1991 – a hi-tech military campaign against a much inferior adversary, leading to swift capitulation by the principal bad guy, Saddam Hussein. As in 1991, although to an even greater degree, war correspondents were managed in such a way as to preserve the illusion of liveness and spontaneity, while ensuring coverage consistent with Coalition military goals. The hundreds of journalists permitted to cover the war on the ground were required to be 'embedded' with active service units, and thus in practice were obliged to see themselves as combatants, in spirit if not in deed.[4]

SALVADOR – THE JOURNALIST AS PROPAGANDIST

The role of the foreign correspondent in time of conflict is potentially controversial, then. And while those in authority have tended to be critical of journalists for a perceived lack of patriotism, for many on the academic side of journalism studies it has been a conservative, propagandistic role. The writings of Noam Chomsky and Ed Herman, for example, implicate the mainstream news media of the US in the propaganda effort of what they term the National Security State, and particularly in the domestic opinion management required by foreign policy.[5] A key case cited in evidence by Chomsky and Herman is the role of the media in the wars of Central and South America which dominated the late 1970s and 1980s. The Chomsky-Herman thesis is that US policy in El Salvador, Nicaragua, Chile and other countries in that region was driven not, as claimed by successive US administrations, by support for democracy and freedom, but by the need to defend US economic interests in the region, which were perceived to be under threat from socialist and communist revolutionaries backed up by the Soviet Union and Cuba. As Steven Soderbergh's *Che* shows (2009), this was not an inaccurate perception, although the scale of poverty and inequality in Latin America may be thought to have more than justified left-wing liberation movements of the type led by Guevara in the late 1960s.

In practical terms, fear of Soviet-led communism meant US support, overt or clandestine, for some of the most unsavoury and brutal regimes ever seen anywhere in the world, which were regularly involved in the organisation of death squads, torture and massacre of their opponents. The US media, in this analysis, acted as the propaganda wing of that effort, playing down the abuses of 'friendly' regimes and exaggerating the threat posed by such as the Sandinistas of Nicaragua. Journalists, editors, proprietors were in effect mobilised as, or volunteered to be, agents of the national security state.

If Chomsky were to write a screenplay based on this perspective, it might well look like *Salvador*, made by Oliver Stone in 1984. Based on the actual experiences of US freelance correspondent Richard Boyle, who co-wrote the screenplay, *Salvador* tells the story of a Gonzo-esque figure with a chaotic personal life and a fondness for substance abuse, who travels to Central America in search of a story he can sell to make some money. It is 1980, and Ronald Reagan has just been elected president. Memories of US intervention in Vietnam and Cambodia are still fresh. While this experience bolsters Boyle's credentials as a war correspondent, his character is also cast as an outlaw – fond of drink and drugs, an unreliable partner for any woman, and someone who sees his work as a route to good times as much as anything else. This stereotype of the war correspondent reflects the danger of the job, and the sense that anyone who would do it has to be a bit crazy. In Michael Winterbottom's *Welcome To Sarajevo* Woody Harrelson's US TV news reporter has a similar, if less extreme persona, which is contrasted at various moments in the movies with the cold detachment of the British journalist Michael Henderson.

El Salvador is also where Boyle's girlfriend lives, and, as we soon learn, his son (whom he has never seen). As the film opens, Boyle is a likeable, if insubstantial figure, a party animal who sees journalism as a means to an end. Heroism

Figure 14 *Salvador* (Oliver Stone, 1984). Source: BFI

is far from his mind as he crosses the border with his hard-drinking buddy (Jim Belushi) into the war-torn country, where he is immediately confronted by the violent realities of an ideologically driven civil war. From here on we observe Boyle lose his naiveté, and his illusions, as he witnesses innocent peasants being brutalised by regime soldiers and death squads, and suspected opposition elements tortured and killed. Boyle takes an existential journey, which we follow as viewers, from apolitical innocence into what Chomsky and Herman would characterise as the cynical realities of US imperialism. Gradually, we are made aware that the atrocities of the fascistic government of El Salvador take place with the covert backing of the US government, despite the presence of a liberal US ambassador in San Salvador.

Two scenes are pivotal, in that they articulate the film-makers' ideal of the journalist's role as witness in such conflicts. In one, Boyle (James Woods) is taken by a photojournalist colleague (John Savage) to El Playon, a site where the death squads dump their victims. The transition from a drunken, jovial Boyle downing tequila shots with his buddies to a man transfixed by the horror of thousands of dead bodies decaying in the tropical sun is chilling, both for him and us, as viewers. The photographer, who has been much longer in the country and will later be killed witnessing a battle, evokes the memory of one of the most distinguished photojournalists, Robert Capa, as he explains to Boyle how he perceives his role.

> You know what made photographers like Robert Capa great, Rich? They weren't after money, they captured the nobility of human suffering. It was more than the bodies, Richie, he got *why* they died. You got to get close, Rich, to get the truth. You get too close, you die.

Within the notion of journalist-as-witness, the photojournalist is an especially compelling figure. He (or, rarely, she – see Chapter 7) takes the photograph, which becomes the silent, permanent testimony of what has occurred, usually without editorialising or literary embellishment. Capa's famous photograph of the Spanish Civil War combatant at the moment of death, head pushed back by the impact of a bullet, is iconic. Savage's character references it here, as he photographs the birds of prey picking on the corpses of the dead. He is the witness to this atrocity, and Boyle is humbled. From here on in, he knows that it is time to get serious about his job.

Later in the film Boyle bears witness to the deaths of four US nuns who have been doing humanitarian work in El Salvador. We have seen them raped and murdered by men we presume to be linked to the right-wing death squads, but US officials and journalists are happy to agree that this is the work of left-wing insurgents, thus reinforcing the US government line that this is a legitimate war about resisting the communist threat in America's backyard.

Boyle angrily rejects this whitewash, and launches into a tirade against the complicity of the US. This occurs after a scene in which we see him argue with representatives of the 'official' US media at a party. This scene, contextualised by newsreel footage of president-elect Ronald Reagan warning about the danger of communism in Central America, functions to present a Chomskyan analysis of mainstream media coverage to a group of sinister, or merely stupid US embassy officials, CIA agents and journalists. As the pro-regime journalists sip their cocktails and praise Salvadorean democracy, Boyle launches into an attack on their complacency.

> Democracy! What kind of democracy is it when you have to vote, and if you don't vote you're branded a commie subversivo. People would vote for Donald Duck, or Genghis Khan, or whoever the local cop tells them to, because if they don't [throws a photograph of a torture victim on the table] this is what happens.

Salvador was financed by Hemdale Film Corporation and shown in mainstream cinemas throughout the world. Although it made only $1.5 million at the US box office on initial release, it was nominated for two Oscars and stands to this day as the most radical indictment ever made of the performance of the US media in 1970s and 1980s Central America.

The film also captures a period in the history of foreign correspondence which would shortly end – the era of the New Cold War (as Chomsky called it, in reference to its similarities to the original Cold War depicted in *Good Night, and Good Luck*). This was a period in post-war geopolitical history when heroes and villains were easily identifiable, from whatever position one took. Reagan's America was a world where good and evil were concepts equating to the US and the USSR ('the evil empire'), capitalism and communism, west and east, democracy and dictatorship. From the opposite perspective, America was cast as the force for evil in Central America, Africa, Asia and elsewhere, and the forces of the left, such as the guerillas of El Salvador and Nicaragua, viewed as progressive radicals. *Salvador* reflects that bi-polarity, and dares to endorse the left-wing analysis by portraying the US as unambiguously wrong, and as complicit in the most atrocious acts imaginable. Boyle's correspondent bears witness to these atrocities, and then comes to the conclusion that it is his side – Us (i.e., the US government), and not Them – which is in the wrong.[6]

WELCOME TO SARAJEVO – NEW WORLD DISORDER AND THE JOURNALIST AS BYSTANDER

The Chomsky-Herman propaganda model underpinned a critique of US news coverage of foreign affairs in the 1970s. It served well in the 1980s when the world was divided into two monolithic blocs, and journalists were under pressure to endorse a view of global politics structured around and by clearly distinguishable, and mutually incompatible ideological positions. Even if it was very possible for some rebellious and maverick journalists such as Richard Boyle to challenge the Cold War paradigm, the mainstream media and their employees were much more likely to internalise and work within it, as were journalists on the other side. Foreign news in those days *was*, often, propaganda, whether by journalistic intention or not. News was selective and slanted, with a view to portraying the other side in the worst possible light, not least because this was what journalists on both sides believed to correspond to the objective truth. Journalists both east and west believed in the Enemy other.

The propaganda model is less helpful, however, when reviewing the performance of the media in the post-Cold War world, not just in countries such as the UK with strong public service journalism traditions (and where, as a consequence, the propaganda model's assertion of straightforward ideological domination of news by self-interested economic elites was never adequate) but also in the US itself. After the fall of the Berlin Wall in 1989, and acknowledgement by the communist parties of the Warsaw Pact that the game was up, what President Bush the first declared as a 'new world order' came into being.

This period lasted nearly twelve years, between the fall of the Wall in November 1989 and the World Trade Center attacks of September 11 2001, during which the east-west bipolarity of the cold war was replaced with something altogether more confusing and blurred. Marxism-Leninism as practised in the Soviet Union and its allied states was exposed as bankrupt, and Marxism itself, in so far as it predicted or called for the replacement of capitalism by something called communism (or even socialism), fell out of favour with all but a marginalised minority of leftist 'radicals', who now looked quaintly old-fashioned. Fukuyama called it 'the end of history' (1992), which it clearly was not, but it was certainly the end of a particular phase in human history, which had dominated all political and cultural formations, including those of the news media, since the end of the First World War.

The positive dimension of the new world order was seen in the global response to Saddam Hussein's invasion of Kuwait in 1990, when a broad coalition of countries – including Arab and muslim states, those of Europe and Asia, both capitalist and communist, right and left – united under the UN banner to intervene against Iraq. Here, for the first time since World War Two, dictatorship was resisted with effective international force. Saddam Hussein had virtually no defenders, and governments of all ideological and theological stripes endorsed the action of the US and its allies to eject him from Kuwait.

As the 1990s progressed, however, and the unforeseen consequences of the collapse of Soviet power began to be felt, a less welcome feature of the post-Cold War era emerged – new world *disorder*. Marxism-Leninism, for all its negative features, had contained a number of primitive forces in the countries over which it gained sway, in particular racism and ethnic conflict. Yes, it took totalitarian control to suppress these impulses (which were never seriously tackled at the ideological level), but suppressed they were, in the USSR, Central and Eastern Europe, and Yugoslavia.[7] With the end of state socialism, the ugliest forms of nationalism and ethnic hatred were unleashed, leading to conflict and war. The violence reached its greatest intensity in former Yugoslavia, where Serb and Croat nationalists fought with muslims, introducing the term 'ethnic cleansing' to describe their policy of intimidating, evicting and massacring those whom they saw as ethnically incompatible with a 'greater Serbia'. War correspondents were called upon to witness these conflicts, and arrived in numbers in the Balkan region in the early 1990s. What they found was very different from the relative clarity of the Cold War, but a replaying of more ancient enmities, when friends and enemies were indistinct, atrocity and amorality were everywhere, and no-one, least of all journalists, really knew why it was happening. The films made about the conflicts in former Yugoslavia depict journalists lost in ideological confusion, forced into the position of bemused bystanders.

In Danis Tanisovic's *No Man's Land* (2001) the late Karin Cartlidge plays a courageous if somewhat arrogant TV news presenter caught up in the fratricidal absurdity of the Bosnian civil war. Its black comedy uses satire to make its points, but the themes are deeply serious, as one would expect from a Bosnian director himself forced to curtail his studies in 1992 due to the civil war. *No Man's Land* won the 2001 Oscar for Best Foreign Language film. Satire and cynicism towards the UN and other international bodies also infuses Michael Shepard's *The Hunting Party* (2007), about three journalists who set out to capture a fugitive Serbian war criminal.

Made five years earlier, Michael Winterbottom's *Welcome To Sarajevo* covers the same period as Danovic's film, focusing on the 1992 siege of Sarajevo. Winterbottom's film takes the true story of ITN correspondent Michael Nicholson, who covered the Bosnian conflict and went on to adopt an orphan, Natasha. This, like *No Man's Land*, is a film about the journalism of conflict, but also (and perhaps principally) the dilemma faced by journalist-as-witness to the human impact of civil war and, in this particular case, ethnic cleansing. The majority of the film's running time is concerned with the human cost of war. *Welcome To Sarajevo* is a cinematic howl of rage at the horrors of the wars in former Yugoslavia, and the inability or reluctance of the international community to stop them. Winterbottom presents a polemic against the abuse

Figure 15   *Welcome to Sarajevo* (Michael Winterbottom, 1997). Source: BFI

of human rights, and our collective complicity in permitting such abuse at the heart of 'civilised' Europe. Soundtrack music by late 1980s 'Madchester' bands such as the Happy Mondays and the Stone Roses reminds us that Sarajevo is, or was, a modern industrial city not very different from what one would find in the north of England in the early 1990s. At the end of the film, as some normality begins to return to the traumatised city, we see a 'Miss World – Siege of Sarajevo Heat' played out before the assembled media. These are people like you and I, the film says. Girls in bikinis, guys trying to catch their eye. Help them be normal again.

   Like *Salvador*, the film raises the issue of the journalist's role in such circumstances. Can he – should he – report on these abuses inflicted against civilians, under the noses of UN troops and western leaders, with objectivity and professional detachment? Or should he get involved, not necessarily in the ideological struggle, which is confused and impenetrable to the outside observer in any case (unlike the situation in El Salvador a decade earlier), but in the lives of the people he is covering? BBC war correspondent Martin Bell was compelled by his experiences reporting the siege of Sarajevo (in the course of which he was wounded by shrapnel from a Serbian grenade) to write a book challenging the normative ideal of journalistic detachment in coverage of wars where civilians are the victims of atrocities (1996). In Winterbottom's film, inspired by Michael Nicholson's real-life adoption of Natasha, Michael is in bed with his wife at home, reflecting on how he has ended up bringing Emira back to the UK with him: 'She [Emira] thought I should help. I realised I could, and there didn't seem to be any reason not to.'

With reference to this simple logic, backed up by the scenes we have seen of atrocity and terror directed against the children of Sarajevo, reportorial objectivity and detachment are cast aside. Later, Michael insists on filling his reports with footage of orphans under fire as a means of attracting viewers' and policymakers' attention to *his* priority – getting the children out of the besieged city. The manipulation of the visual power of TV news media is justified in some circumstances.

This alerts us to the film's main issue: the extent to which the war correspondent's status as witness can be exploited to make tragic events visible, first on the news agenda, then in public debate and governmental priorities. Michael is witness to an unfolding human tragedy – the plight of the orphaned children – and uses the agenda-setting power of ITN to bring it to the attention of the world. As with Michael Buerk's famous reports from Ethiopia, the journalist in this case alerts us to a wrong about which we might otherwise be ignorant, and is an essential first step in prompting governmental intervention. To perform this role in Sarajevo (as in other war zones), where snipers lurk and drunken paramilitaries are never far away, is indisputably *heroic*. And if it requires graphic TV news images to be effective, then this is, we might conclude, a justification for their inclusion. Susan Moeller's *Compassion Fatigue* (1999), which reflects in its title a 1990s debate about the allegedly negative impact on western public opinion of graphic images of war, famine and catastrophe, argued that:

> TV audiences have in general very little understanding of events in the developing world or of major institutions or relationships. This is in part the result of TV coverage which tends to focus on dramatic, violent and tragic images while giving very little context or explanation to the events which are being portrayed. (1999: 17)

In *Welcome To Sarajevo*, Michael begins the film with a position close to this, and a sneery disregard for the values of 'news as entertainment', even as he searches for the right shot of tragedy to frame his story. In the end, however, it is the unique power of the television image which he enlists to help him help the victims of the siege.

9/11 AND AFTER

Already in the 1990s war correspondence was being transformed by the emergence of globalised, always-on media. The launch of Cable News Network in 1980 and its subsequent expansion had, by the mid-1990s, already produced the phenomenon of 'real-time news', as seen in the first Gulf War of 1991. There and then, for the first time, it was possible for TV viewers sitting at home, or in their hotel room, or anywhere that had access to CNN, to watch events in Kuwait, Iraq, Israel and elsewhere unfolding live. Real-time news was literally that – news as a representation of something that was happening at that moment, as opposed to the report of an event which *had* happened at some time in the past.

Jean Baudrillard provoked intellectual and public ridicule when he proclaimed in a book of that name that *The Gulf War Did Not Take Place* (1991). He meant, of course, not that people did not die in the expulsion of Saddam Hussein from Kuwait, nor that violence was not used, but that the war was experienced by hundreds of millions of people all over the world in a manner more akin to a simulation in a video game than an actual war – that the Gulf 'war' was experienced by those who fought it, and by those who watched it on TV, as a virtual conflict, fought largely with the aid of computers, satellites and public communication channels such as CNN.

Postmodern philosophy aside, the Gulf War of 1991 was the first to be globally consumed through live TV news coverage of everything from Cruise missiles in flight to civilians being dug out of bombed buildings. The arrival of this means of reporting warfare produced a major new challenge for governments in democracy: assuming that one did not wish to censor CNN and the other real-time news channels which followed it, how could decision-makers make policy and implement it in conditions where every casualty of war was potentially a presence on TV screens in every home in the land? War has always been hellish. Only in the 1990s did the nature of that hell enter our comfortable late capitalist homes, through our TV screens, and thus have the capacity to shape how citizens viewed the decisions of their governments to wage war. After 1991 the genie of real-time news coverage was released, changing audience expectations of what could be reported, and what *should* be reported, forever.

Few films were made for the cinema about the 1991 Gulf War, and only one made in English featured the role of the correspondent in the conflict. *Three Kings* (David O. Russell, 1999) starred George Clooney and was notable for its engagement with the impact of a new kind of globalised, real-time media presence. As noted above, the film contains what one reviewer rather ungenerously called 'a misfired parody of CNN reporter Christiane Amanpour'.[8]

By September 11 2001, a decade after the first Gulf War, real-time news had been joined by the internet, and the early manifestations of a globalised news culture characterised by interactivity and participation. Although numbers of users remained small at the start of the millenium, there were 'bloggers' and an expanding blogosphere of linked commentators and reporters. People were growing used to taking digital photographs on their cell phones and cameras, and learning how to upload them to the internet, where they became accessible to the global internet community. The communication environment had changed radically, and the first organisation to weaponise the new technology and the networks it brought into being was al-Qaida.

The attacks of September 11 on New York and Washington represented a dramatic escalation of a terrorist tactic first seen in the 1970s and 1980s, when groups such as the IRA and the PLO mounted 'spectacular' acts of terrorism designed to seize the attention of TV news organisations and shape the news agenda in their favour. What al-Qaida did on September 11 was to raise the global impact of such tactics to unprecedented levels by a combination of astutely symbolic targeting and a sophisticated awareness of how the media operated in the twenty-first century. The 9/11 attacks were captured live on camera by professional news organisations based in New York, as well as by onlookers with cameras. The resulting footage went on twenty-four-hour news channels, as well as terrestrial bulletins the world over, and also the internet. As a result, 9/11 presented to billions of people all over the world something they had never seen before – thousands of people, dying in real time, before their eyes; a real-life snuff movie, on a scale never imagined. Many more people had perished in previous conflicts, but never had their death agonies been accessible to TV and internet users, live and uncensored. Oliver Stone's *World Trade Center* (2007) was, in comparison to the actual news coverage of the day, pallid.

The main impact of the September 11 attacks was a consequence of their mediated nature – to instil fear and panic, not merely in the citizens of the United States and elsewhere, but in their governments, leading to the 'war on terror', the invasions of Afghanistan and Iraq, the human rights abuses of Abu Ghraib and Guantanamo, and much more that has been criticised, such as the US Patriot Act and the mooted introduction of identity cards in the UK. For the islamists, however, the success of the attack demonstrated the potential for using emerging globalised communication networks as weapons in their global jihad. Thereafter, we were all the potential targets of islamic terrorism – ordinary people going about their business in Bali, Madrid, London, Glasgow, Mumbai, and journalists as they reported on these events. The immediate damage done by an attack was magnified exponentially by the psychological impact of watching news about them on news and internet channels. In this context, no-one was exempt from the effects of televised atrocity. Atrocity, moreover, carried out in such a way as to maximise news coverage and audience horror – grisly decapitations and tortures worthy of any medieval inquisitor, captured on film and then uploaded to Al Jazeera or some other outlet, where the images would be transmitted in whole or in part. So common did the tactic become that by 2004 media organisations and commentators in the UK were publicly debating the ethics of showing the material, even edited. Did it encourage further such killings, if they were shown even in heavily censored form? Did it amount to providing terrorists with the 'oxygen of publicity'?

A MIGHTY HEART – THE JOURNALIST AS TARGET

The film which best captures the new status of the journalist-as-target is *A Mighty Heart*, directed by Michael Winterbottom and released to critical acclaim in 2007. Five years after the first case of a western journalist being targeted for ritual execution by jihadis – that of *Wall Street Journal* reporter Daniel Pearl – Winterbottom's film seeks to emphasise what it is that the foreign or war correspondent does, or should be doing, and why he (or she) should be considered above the conflict by all combatants. In a scene at the beginning of the film, Pearl (Dan Futterman) explains to someone who is questioning his motives for reporting islamist groups in Pakistan: 'That's why I'm a journalist, to let people know.'

When, after Daniel's kidnapping, his wife Mariane (also a journalist, played by Angelina Jolie) goes to meet a Pakistani government minister, the latter blames Pearl for what has happened.

> *Minister:* Why does he want to meet these people? This isn't the business of a journalist.
> *Mariane Pearl:* Forgive me for correcting you, but it is absolutely the business of a journalist.

The journalist is a witness, and thus should not be a target. At various points in the film, including in the course of a televised interview, she undertakes to try to secure the release of her husband, Mariane stresses Daniel's honesty in his journalism – 'I never saw him tell a lie' – and his desire merely to discover and report the truth, including the truth about radical islamism. These efforts to engage the kidnappers with an appeal to liberal journalistic values were, of course, unsuccessful, and Daniel Pearl was beheaded on camera in early February 2002. On the other hand, Mariane Pearl was not to know the nature of the enemy she was dealing with, and such tactics had never been used on a western journalist before.

The central role in *A Mighty Heart* is not Daniel Pearl's but Mariane's, and Angelina Jolie's performance was widely praised for its authenticity and realism. According to UK film critic Mark Kermode (not an easy man to please), in a BBC documentary about Jolie screened in 2008, 'I believed so completely in her portrayal of Mariane Pearl that I forgot I was watching Angelina Jolie'.[9] In the same programme Jolie explained her attraction to the figure of Mariane Pearl.

Figure 16 *A Mighty Heart* (Michael Winterbottom: 2007). Source: BFI

I admire her so much as a woman, and how she handled that situation, with so much that was going on in the world, and the still continuing threat of terrorism, this woman went through the worst of it, but still has this tolerance and this understanding.

In the film, her professional status as a foreign correspondent is significant, since it falls on her to define in some key speeches the nature of that role to the Pakistani minister and others, and to defend it despite the trouble it has brought upon her and her family. It is less important to the human story which dominates the narrative, however, than her role as wife to the kidnapped Daniel.

CONCLUSION – A SALUTE TO THE WAR CORRESPONDENT

If the period of 'new world disorder' – 1989–2001 – can be seen as one of ideological re-alignment and blurred boundaries in which the journalist is positioned as a bemused bystander, the post-9/11 years have seen a re-assertion, if in different form, of the Cold War notions of good and evil, and the idea that there is a clear and unambiguous enemy against which we should unite. This enemy is not defined in terms of left/right, or socialism/capitalism, but medieval theology against liberal modernity. And since liberal journalism, as we are discussing it in this book, is very much both a product and a condition of modernity and the Enlightenment project, reporting militant islamism within a framework of objectivity has not been possible. As *A Mighty Heart* shows, and despite the efforts of courageous figures such as Daniel and Mariane Pearl, the extension of objectivity and balance to islamic fascism is no more appropriate or practical than it would have been to the Nazis. The journalist, especially if he is jewish and American, as Pearl was, cannot appeal to a jihadi's sense of self-interest, far less fairness, in seeking reliable information for a story which will then present the jihadi case to the world. The post-9/11 era is, in this sense, closer to the context within which war correspondents did their job in 1939–45. Radical islam has not the firepower or strategic capability of Hitler's Reich, but it is equally offensive to the liberal democratic world-view and mindset, and has tended to be treated that way by all except a few maverick reporters. Attempts to portray the 'positives' of islamism have not been persuasive, and are regularly undermined by appalling tales such as that of the two boys publicly hanged in the Iranian city of Masshad for homosexuality in July 2005, or that of the sixteen-year-old girl stoned to death in Somalia in October 2008 for alleged adultery.

This is not to say that there are not many journalists who aspire to report the war on terror with a degree of detachment and critical scrutiny of both sides. Everyone knows about Abu Ghraib, and movies have been made (and widely seen) about events there and elsewhere. Such coverage is never without risk, even in a liberal democracy, and I will end this chapter with the sobering statistic, cited in *A Mighty Heart*, that more western journalists died during the invasion of Afghanistan than did Coalition troops. In November 2008, newspapers in the UK were reporting on the circumstances behind the death in Somalia of BBC news producer Kate Peyton, killed by gun fire in the streets of Mogadishu as she was preparing to go on an assignment. The inquiry investigated the performance of her employer in taking the necessary steps to maximise her safety, and it made a number of criticisms. But like foreign correspondents down the years, Kate appears to have understood that her's was a particularly dangerous occupation. She, like so many foreign correspondents, was an exceptionally brave individual who gave her life in the service of her role as witness to an inhuman war. Whether in Somalia, Afghanistan, Iraq or anywhere else, the days when mainstream journalists could be depicted, as in *Salvador*, as submissive propagandists, were over.

POSTSCRIPT – THE CITIZEN WITNESS

Recent years have seen the rise of the 'citizen journalist', and the role of user-generated content in news coverage of stories such as the Mumbai terror attacks of November 2008. This trend had not, as of this writing, produced a feature-length film in the cinemas. That it would in due course was, given the movie-makers' desire for new and exciting stories of heroism, probably inevitable. Perhaps a future edition of this chapter would have to include reference to dramas about the increasingly important role of the non-journalist, the amateur news-maker who Twitters and flickrs and blogs and emails text and pictures about events going on to the globalised public sphere, events in which he or she is personally involved. Perhaps the next conflict story, as commentator Jeff Jarvis predicted in the aftermath of the Mumbai events, 'will be seen live and at eye level' by millions, even billions of people. Increasingly, it is the civilians who report on what is being done to them, as it is being done.

NOTES

1. For a recent scholarly discussion of the nature of the witness in the age of mass communication, see the essays assembled in Frosh and Pinchevsky (eds), *Media Witnessing* (2008).
2. For a study of the role of the foreign correspondent in the post-Soviet 1990s, see McLaughlin's *The War Correspondent* (2002). Allan and Zelizer's edited collection on *Journalism After September 11* (2002) explores the challenges faced by journalists in an environment defined as 'war on terror'. Maltby and Keeble's *Communicating War* (2007) incorporates the experience of conflict in Iraq and Afghanistan.
3. The first directed by Joseph L. Mankiewicz in 1958, the second by Philip Noyce in 2002.
4. See Seib (2004) for a discussion of coverage of the invasion of Iraq.
5. See volumes one and two of their *Political Economy of Human Rights* (1979) for the evidence which they present to support the 'propaganda model', as they call it. Chomsky's *Manufacturing Consent* (1988) summarises the argument.
6. Roger Spottiswoode's *Under Fire* (1983) told a similar tale in relation to Nicaragua, this time with wholly fictionalised journalists. Stone's film is the more visceral and uncompromising, however.
7. Sasha Baron-Cohen's screen journalist, *Borat*, with his parody of Soviet-era attitudes to sexuality, ethnicity and disability in post-Soviet Kazakhstan, is not far off the mark.
8. Hoberman, J., 'Burn, blast, bomb, cut', *Sight & Sound*, volume 10, number 2. The Amanpour character is 'hardboiled yet overemotional ... [she] swears like a drill sergeant but can be reduced to tears by the sight of oil-soaked birds. She is regularly confounded by Clooney yet, as immediately recognised by both Iraqis and American brass, several times saves the day. Her compassion is crucial.'
9. *The Culture Show*, BBC2, 27 November 2008.

CHAPTER 7

Heroines

W omen journalists feature in several chapters of this book, as investigative reporters, foreign and war correspondents, editors, tabloid hacks (or hackesses, if such a term exists), producers and media executives. By devoting an entire chapter at this point to the representation of women in journalism, I have no desire to separate them off from the more general issues I am concerned with, or to ghettoise them. Such a chapter is justified simply because women themselves – as practitioners, scholarly observers and consumers of journalism – have for a long time discussed the place of their sex in the news media, often critically.[1] Women present a distinct category of movie journalist who, if not necessarily or always heroic, are generally accepted to have been stereotyped and marginalised in the history of cinema.

One consequence of women's improved socio-economic status within advanced capitalism is that women are more often represented in the media in ways which reflect feminist ideas about sexual equality in the workplace, in the domestic environment, in the bedroom, in the culture. From the post-feminist perspective of the times in which we live, moreover, cultural producers (male and female) can also acknowledge without being accused of sexism the capacity of women, shared with men, for badness and villainy. I will consider villainous images of female journalists in this chapter, within an examination of how their representation has become at one and the same time more numerous, more diverse and, I will argue, more positive. In particular, I will explore what cinema has to say about femininity and its articulation within a sub-sector of the media industry which has traditionally been downgraded as a journalistic variant of 'women's work' but is now taken with increasing seriousness both in commercial and cultural terms. I refer to the rise of style journalism – a term often used in conjunction with 'dumbing down', 'infotainment' and 'middlebrow'.[2] In a context where more and more women are starring in the movies as crime reporters, foreign correspondents and other once-male preserves of the profession, I will argue that the growing visibility of style journalism in films such as *The Devil Wears Prada* (David Frankel, 2006) and *Sex and the City* (Michael Patrick King, 2008) is evidence not of journalism's decline into infotainment but a reflection of the enhanced socio-economic status of women within the cultural economy, and the associated elevation of female tastes and desires within the industry.

WOMEN IN JOURNALISM

The conventional narrative about women in liberal journalism goes something like this: historically, women have been subordinated in art and culture, and in journalism especially, which has been a male-dominated profession from the beginning. The reason for this is that patriarchal societies have, as a condition of their existence, until very recently (and in some societies more recently than others) excluded women from full and active participation in most areas of public life, including the production of art and culture.[3] Journalism is a form of writing, and also of artistic production, but its accessibility to women living in patriarchy has been limited by the fact that it often requires access to the corridors of political, corporate and cultural power, and the power elites who make key decisions. Political journalists must be able to mix and mingle freely with (largely male) politicians, whenever and wherever they do their networking. In the film *Rag Tale* (Mary McGuckian, 2005) there is a scene in which media baron Richard Morton and his wife, deputy editor M. J. (Jennifer Jason Leigh), host a dinner for a group of the Prince of Wales' advisers. Morton wishes to impress them in his drive to win a peerage. The protocol sent to Morton in advance instructs women to leave the table before the business discussion begins. This may be satirical exaggeration of the sexism which structures the ultra-conservative monarchy, but the point is valid – in many circles of the establishment in Britain and elsewhere, women are still regarded as less than equal.

War correspondents must be able to mix and mingle freely with (largely male) soldiers, in a culture where women are, even in the twenty-first century, prevented by most armies from taking front-line roles. Crime reporters must be able to associate with the low life of a city which, given the masculine nature of most criminal sub-cultures, is easier for men than for women. Joel Schumacher's *Veronica Guerin* (2003) tells the true story of how one female crime reporter paid the ultimate price for persisting with her investigation in a brutish world of male gangsters.

For these reasons journalism has been less accessible to women within patriarchy than, say, the art of poetry or novel-writing. Deborah Chambers and her co-authors observe that 'during the nineteenth century societal attitudes in the United States and Britain discouraged women from journalism. Generally regarded as a "craft", even a rough and tough craft, journalism was deemed usuitable for educated ladies' (2004: 16). Joseph Saltzman notes that in the nineteenth century 'most female journalists were not permitted to write on important topics. Front-page assignments, politics, finance and sports were not usually given to women. Top newsroom positions were for men only'.[4] Of Sweden, Marlene Djerf-Pierre writes that 'newspaper journalism was clearly gendered in the early years of the twentieth century, with certain positions and areas of coverage designated for men and women, respectively' (2007: 84).

As late as the 1950s very few women indeed worked as journalists in the mainstream news media, as opposed to the recognised female realms of magazines such as, well, *Women's Realm*. Women journalists majored in areas of social life where they could legitimately be dominant, or at least authoritative, *as women* – in general, matters to do with child-rearing and the domestic, as well as fashion and the decorative arts. Women were accepted in newspapers and periodicals as long as they were content to be domestic correspondents and 'agony aunts', dispensing words of wisdom to the female readers of magazines.

There were, of course, a few – very few – exceptions: Lee Miller, one-time model and muse of surrealist photographer Man Ray, was a photo-journalist in wartime Europe, famously photographing herself in Hitler's derelict bathroom; travel writer Freya Stark; and Sara Jeanette Duncan, who wrote for the Canadian press in the early twentieth century.[5] But the significant erosion of patriarchal structures in western journalism began only some time after World War Two, with the onset of second-wave feminism and the sexual revolution. In the 1960s British journalist Katharine Whitehorn became one of the first women to break out of the domestic zone of competence and report and comment in depth on the male worlds of politics and business. Whitehorn's interviews, columns and features were a key attraction of the *Observer* until 1996, and she is now acknowledged as a pioneering figure.

Further landmarks in the advance of women in journalism include the first female TV news reader in the UK, Angela Rippon, for the BBC in 1975; the rise of Anna Ford, who became ITV's first regular female anchorwoman in 1978; the appointment of the first female editor to a UK national newspaper in 1988. In 1983, young BA Journalism graduate Christiane Amanpour joined CNN as an assistant, going on to become one of the world's leading foreign reporters just as real-time news was becoming established. Today Amanpour is a world-renowned figure, perhaps the most famous of celebrity journalists, male or female. As a recent profile put it,

with the rich timbre of her voice and her accent – Amanpour has an Iranian father and grew up in Tehran and London – when the CNN journalist arrived on screen, she was decidedly different from the journalists Americans were used to seeing on television. She was a woman, for a start, and not a bland midwestern blonde. She was the first big star to come out of CNN.[6]

But certainly not the last. Amanpour's success signalled the emergence of a generation of female journalists working at the top of their profession, including – indeed especially – in traditionally male sub-sectors of the business such as war and foreign correspondence. While Amanpour strode the world for CNN, Kate Adie became a celebrity foreign and war correspondent for the BBC, placing herself at the scene of the US bombing of Libya in 1986, and the Tien An Mien Square massacre in 1989. Adie, like Amanpour, suffered a certain amount of backlash from commentators who criticised the 'parachuting in' of such celebrities to war zones. This view informs the character of Jane Livingstone in Danis Tanovich's *No Man's Land* (2002), played by Karin Cartlidge as a posh, pucker, but extremely tough and determined reporter.

Since Adie and Amanpour there have been many more female foreign correspondents, some of whom have paid dearly for their dedication to the job. The fates of such as Kate Peyton, Anna Politkovskaya and Veronica Guerin confirm that, in some things at least, women are now equal to men in the journalistic profession, and that gender is no predictor of who lives and who dies in the zone of conflict.

The extent of progressive change in the status of women in journalism is a matter for debate, but that there have been at least some advances on a number of indicators is beyond dispute. Female students in my journalism classes can today be encouraged by the example of women editors, present and past, in several UK national newspapers, from the red-top *Sun* and *News of the World* to mid-market and elite titles such as the *Express* and the *Sunday Telegraph*, women news executives and senior producers in broadcast outlets such as the BBC, women who are internationally respected foreign and business correspondents, political columnists and broadcast anchors. Not sufficient, some will argue, and they may be right in so far as news rooms are still far from female- and mother-friendly working environments. Some professional specialisms, such as political reporting and photojournalism, particularly in conflict zones,[7] are still dominated by men. There is still, one might say, institutional sexism deeply ingrained within journalism. There can be no serious cause for doubt that the trends are on balance progressive, however, and that given the numbers of female students of journalism one now sees in universities, this will continue.[8]

SOB SISTERS OR SUPER BITCHES? WOMEN, JOURNALISM AND THE MOVIES

Women have been the victims of sexual discrimination in the journalistic profession. Female journalists, it is further argued by students of the journalism movie, have generally been represented in cinema in ways which reflect and reinforce the ideological assumptions underlying that discrimination. These assumptions mainly concern the appropriate field of competence, or news-gathering remit, of the female journalist – the domestic realm, as noted above, and the human interest-oriented, emotionally fraught, 'soft' news agenda. Within journalism there has traditionally been a zone of 'women's work', and films about journalism have reflected this.

Second, films have reflected assumptions about the qualities a woman needs to have if she is to be successful in the overwhelmingly masculine world of journalism. She must be more manly than the men, tougher and more ruthless. In being so, however, she is somehow less than a 'real' woman. This, for Joe Saltzman, is the 'dichotomy never quite resolved' in representations of women journalists.[9] 'How to incorporate the masculine traits of journalism essential for success – being aggressive, self-reliant, curious, tough, ambitious, cynical, cocky, unsympathetic – while still being the woman society would like her to be – compassionate, caring, loving, maternal, sympathetic'.

The impact of these assumptions is that women until quite recently have been largely absent from movies about those types of journalism deemed most worthy and important to a democratic society, such as political journalism, foreign correspondence and investigative reporting – what one might call the commanding heights of the public sphere, where prestige and power are concentrated, and from which women have historically been excluded.

Similarly, they have rarely been represented as editors or news room managers, reflecting their subordinate positions within professional struc-tures. Where women *have* been visible in films about journalism, it has usually been as secretaries and other types of minion, supporting their male colleagues in the news room. In *Sweet Smell of Success*, for example, J. J. Hunsecker's secretary faithfully types his slander-mongering columns (until the point comes when she has had enough, and rebels). In Mary McGuckian's *Rag Tale*, which *does* contain three substantial roles for women journalists, a clutch of female secretaries form the chorus to the largely male editorial team. None of this could be said to misrepresent the facts of office life in an average twentieth or indeed twenty-first century news room. Nor could the relative absence of women war correspondents in movies of the pre-feminist era be read as 'bias'. This *is* how things were.

Where women *have* been represented as journalists in the movies they have often been portrayed in ways consistent with tendencies found in other cultural spheres: as highly sexualised, beautiful bodies, preferably with blonde hair, covering human interest stories and 'fluff' (see Angelina Jolie in *Life or Something Like It*, for example; or Christina Applegate in the comedy *Anchorman*, which subverts the stereotype). Women are often represented as beautiful but hyper-ambitious, toxic *femme fatales* who have sacrificed their femininity for professional advancement, as in the case of *To Die For* (Gus Van Zant, 1995) where Nicole Kidman plays an amoral career climber who stops at nothing, even the murder of her own husband, to achieve her professional goals. Joe Saltzman observes that 'female journalists in popular culture are seldom shown as fully developed human beings'.[10] Loren Ghighlione agrees that 'the contemporary news woman, while regularly cast as a tough, talented pro, often bears the burden of being depicted as an emotionally empty Super Bitch or Super Whore'.[11]

These are stereotypes, yes, but have they any foundation in reality? Yes again, in so far as women in journalism, like women in politics, women in law enforcement and women in science have, in order to be successful, often had to go against the grain of what patriarchal society expects a 'good' woman to be – that is, a mother and home-maker. A woman cannot 'have it all', it is often said – career *and* family, satisfying job *and* home life with children. Something has to give. Feminists in recent times have acknowledged the genuine dilemmas women face in reconciling the public world of work, which they have fought for and gained steadily increasing access to, with the private world of family and child rearing. Movies about journalism have often explored those questions, if usually through the lens of male script writers and directors, and without any overt engagement with feminist discourse, which did not really become a feature of mainstream culture until at least the 1980s. When Rosalind Russell in Howard Hawks' *His Girl Friday* struggles with the choice between a life of cosy domesticity with her new fiancé and a resumption of her career as a reporter she dramatises a real issue for women in journalism, as relevant in the late 1930s when the film was made as it is now.

FEMALE JOURNALISTS IN FILM: FEMININE OR FEMINIST?

Cinema *has* been part of the cultural apparatus of patriarchal oppression, then, representing women in journalism not only as they have been and are (discriminated against and structurally subordinate to men), but as they are perceived to be by wider society and, recalling the function of film as myth, as it is perceived that they *should* be. Representations of strong female journalists often end with the woman's acceptance of and return to 'proper' femininity. But not always. If film has been, overall and on balance, a conservative medium in relation to sexual politics it is now possible, precisely *because* of the achievements of those politics, to undertake a more nuanced, post-feminist reading of how women are represented in journalism.

By 'post-feminist' I do not mean a period after feminism, but an ideological environment in which there is, first, recognition, implicit or explicit, of the genuine advances which women have made in journalism in recent times, as in other traditionally male-dominated professions; and second, that the images of women journalism produced for cinema in the past can be re-read as more than sexist stereotypes and caricatures. That said, stereotypes and caricatures are at the heart of all story-telling, and we should not be surprised that women are victims of the compressions made by film-makers in their efforts to reduce complex reality to ninety minutes of engaging celluloid. Male journalists too are often reduced to stereotypes in film – the drunken hack about which Howard Good wrote an entire book (2000); the unprincipled tabloid reptile documented by many of the US scholars in this field; the noble heroes of Watergate.

Saltzman, Ghiglione and others who have specialised in this area note throughout their writings the paradox that, sob sisters, super bitches and sexist assumptions notwithstanding, female journalists have often been depicted as strong, tough, assertive, intelligent and independent. Rosalind Russell's Hildy in *His Girl Friday*, one of the earliest and most highly regarded examples of the women-in-journalism sub-genre, displays many strengths (as well as some stereotypical traits expressive of the times in which it was made) which a modern-day feminist in a contemporary newsroom would not be ashamed to emulate.

These qualities are only 'manly' if it is assumed that masculinity has a monopoly on them. Once the feminist idea that women and men are equal (if different) is accepted, along with the idea that women can be just as strong, tough and determined as men when it comes to work and life, then we are free to judge characters such as Hildy Johnson for what they are – feminist icons ahead of their time, bestriding the silver screen long before the discourse of feminism became widespread in western culture. We can suggest that at least some examples of the female journalist in film can be read as progressive, spearheading a feminist view of women in work which would much later become mainstream. There were always strong, powerful women working in journalism, notwithstanding the deep-rooted sexism of the profession. More often than might be expected, the movies took these women and placed them at the heart of popular culture.

Saltzman explains why this should have been so: just as the leading men of the movie industry have always been drawn to journalistic roles for their perceived importance and glamour, as well as the richness of the parts which journalistic stories often generate, women have found the portrayal of journalists working in a largely man's world challenging and satisfying. Precisely because the news room and other arenas where journalism has been practised, such as the front line in a war zone, are such masculine environments (and a recent film like *Rag Tale* has us believe that this is still the case, at least at the more popular end of the newspaper market) women have risen to the challenge of playing characters who can compete within them and win. Notes Saltzman, 'motion pictures offered the meatiest roles for female actors and created the perfect battleground of the sexes'.[12]

HIS GIRL FRIDAY AND THE STRONG FEMALE REPORTER

One of the earliest acknowledged classics in the genre of movies about journalism features a woman reporter, Hildy Johnson. Hawks' film is based on Ben Hecht's successful stage play of 1928, *The Front Page*, which established the romantic rogue stereotype of the journalist (see Chapter 9). *His Girl Friday* turns one of the play's two leading male characters into a woman, and sets her against editor and former husband Walter Burns (Cary Grant) in a battle of verbal wit and competing journalistic ethics. At the beginning of the film Hildy arrives in the news room, having retired from journalism, to introduce Walter to her new fiancé, Bruce Baldwin, an insurance salesman from Albany, New

Figure 17 *His Girl Friday* (Howard Hawks, 1940). Source: BFI

York. The story then focuses on Walter's struggle to win Hildy back as a staff reporter, in the face of her disgust at what she sees as his corrupt and cynical tabloid news values. This is not a struggle in which the male editor has it easy.

Hildy Johnson provides evidence from popular culture of Loren Ghiglione's assertion that 'news women of the 1920s and 1930s were not only as talented but just as tough as their male counterparts'.[13] Ness agrees that 'the journalistic profession provided one of the few working environments where a battle of the sexes could be waged on nearly equal terms. While women were only rarely afforded positions of power as editors or publishers, on the level of basic reporters they were able to hold their own against their male counterparts' (1997: 72). That said, she was represented as a woman working reluctantly, if courageously, in a man's world, experiencing the tension of 'achieving journalistic success by denying her womanhood'. In *His Girl Friday* Hildy seeks Walter's blessing for her intended new life of domesticity with Bruce in Albany but the narrative trajectory makes it clear that, deep down, as Walter puts it, 'you're a newspaper man'.

Hildy Johnson was modelled on Adela Rogers St Johns, a reporter for the Hearst organisation. She was of a screen type labelled the 'sob sister' by some cultural historians, referring to the fact that female reporters in the early twentieth century tended to be given the 'sob stories' – stories which had strongly emotional angles judged appropriate for a woman to report.[14] In American popular cinema the most prominent early representation of a female journalist was the character of Torchy Blane, played by Glenda Farrell, who featured in eight successful films of the 1930s.[15] For Saltzman the term 'sob sister' is not appropriate to Blane, however, or indeed Hildy Johnson. Blane, he notes, 'went after fast-breaking, sensational stories as aggressively as any newsman. She was no sob sister, no gushy old maid, no masculine-looking lady'.[16] A more contemporary, and comic reference to the notion of the 'sob sister' is contained in *Anchorman* (Adam McKay, 2004), the Judd Apatow-produced retro-chic pastiche of 1970s TV news. When Veronica Corningstone, 'the little lady of the news desk' played by Christina Applegate, arrives at Ron Burgundy's San Diego news room expecting to be taken seriously she is immediately assigned the soppy human interest stories, such as the story of a cat fashion show (she has her revenge, it should be noted, at Ron's expense. This is a post-feminist film set in a pre-feminist world, fully aware of the sexist limitations of the stereotype Veronica represents, and prepared to have fun subverting it).

Women journalists have sometimes been viewed as 'sob sisters', then (and there will probably be some news rooms, even in the second decade of the twenty-first century where they still are), and represented in this way in film. But they have also been portrayed in film as tough and determined. The strength and sassiness of Hildy Johnson is, decades after she first graced the silver screen, a radical and empowering posture. And she is not alone. Women *in* the media have frequently been represented *by* the media as strong and powerful figures.

WOMEN JOURNALISTS IN THE POST-WAR ERA

Ness observes that the dominance of war films in the 1940s produced

> a shift in the role of women in journalism films. While they had [during the war] been on a nearly equal level with men, the era of *Rosie the Riveter* relegated them to more domestic tasks. Those few female war correspondents who appeared on screen were forced into domestic roles ... The ground lost by women in the journalism genre during this period would not be regained for several decades. (1997: 241)

The female journalist re-emerged as a major figure only in the 1980s, reflecting the slow but steady progression of women within the journalistic profession in the wake of second-wave feminism.

In the period from the 1980s up to 1996 women played a number of notable lead roles in films about journalism, including both heroic and villainous representations, and some that were somewhere in between. In *Absence of Malice* (Sydney Pollack, 1981), Sally Field played an investigative reporter whose ethical laziness leads to a life-threatening crisis for the subject of one of her stories, a small businessman played by Paul Newman. In *To Die For*, by contrast, possibly the most villainous journalist ever presented in cinema, male or female, Nicole Kidman is ferociously ambitious local TV weather girl Suzanne Stone. So desperate is she for success in network TV that she engineers the murder of her own husband at the hands of a besotted teenager. Directed by Gus Van Zant, whose progressive sexual politics are well known, *To Die For* has not generally been read as a misogynistic work, but does exemplify a negative stereotype of the female journalist (and the female media worker more broadly) as a super-bitch lacking in scruples, prepared to sleep with anyone and do anything to get to the top.

Faye Dunaway plays another kind of frequently seen media bitch in *Network* (Sydney Lumet, 1976) – a network executive determined to turn the 'quality' TV news show presented by anchor Howard Beale (Peter Finch) into infotainment. In *The Insider* the company lawyer who prevents the transmission of Jeffrey Wigand's whistle-blowing interview on *60 Minutes* is a woman (Gina Gershon), and clearly signalled as a key villain of the piece (although male executives at CBS are also singled out). Jennifer Jason Leigh's M. J. in *Rag Tale* belongs to the same sub-species, although she becomes a tragically sympathetic character in the end.

Less toxic women feature in *Broadcast News* (James L. Brooks, 1987), where Holly Hunter and Joan Cusack play TV news producers working hard to maintain journalistic integrity in the face of company pressure to 'dumb down' the news and make it more human interest-oriented. Here, interestingly, the traditional association of journalistic dumbing-down with the feminine is subverted by the fact that it is William Hurt's new boy in the newsroom, photogenic and handsome, who cries the fake tears which symbolise the corruption of news with commercial values.

WOMEN IN JOURNALISM, 1997–2008

In the period 1997–2008, women were depicted as war correspondents in *Three Kings* and *No Man's Land*; as investigative reporters in *Veronica Guerin* and *The Life of David Gale*; and as a political journalist in *Lions for Lambs*. In *The Life of David Gale* (Alan Parker, 2002) Kate Winslet plays Bitsey Bloom, a 'hard-nosed reporter turned crusader'.[17] Cate Blanchett is a features writer in *The Life Aquatic with Steve Vissou* (Wes Anderson, 2004).

Women, as we have seen, have in the past been represented on occasion as serious journalists, as exemplified by the sassy intelligence of Rosalind Russell (who so easily outmanouevres Cary Grant's Walter). The number of these heroines has increased, however, as the content of their representation has changed to reflect an evolving sex-political environment and culture. Lois Lane in *Superman Returns* is not the Lois Lane played by Margot Kidder opposite Christopher Reeves. She is a Pulitzer-prize winning single mother, tough and resourceful, no pushover to be whisked away on the night air by a masterful man of steel. She is, in short, a particular kind of feminist, and an expression in representations of journalism of the positive changes which have affected the lives of real women. Young women in the multiplex audience expect to see young women who embody their aspirations in the fictional newsrooms of Hollywood, and Hollywood has met that expectation.

Mainstream movie-makers have also internalised the feminist critique of journalism's sexism, in films such as *Anchorman* (2004) which immersed themselves in the clothes, sexual politics and social attitudes of the 1970s, replaying their politically incorrect attitudes to sexism, racism and life in general in a manner that was affectionate and nostalgic, but from a position three decades later in which it is acknowledged that such attitudes are unacceptable (at least in polite company). In *Anchorman* Will Ferrell plays anchorman Ron Burgundy, a self-styled 'lover of the ladies' who drinks large whiskies just before his show commences, has a wide range of amazing abilities in all walks of life, such as playing jazz clarinet, and who regards women as accessories and potential bed partners rather than colleagues. He is the caricature of the male celebrity journalist, in love with himself and his own importance, and ruthless in his determination to maintain his position. The arrival in his news room of a new female colleague – blonde, beautiful and talented Veronica Corning-stone, played by Christina Applegate – is thus a threat to Ron, and he responds accordingly. But this is a post-feminist text, in that after all the ribbing endured by Christina Applegate's character, it is she who emerges triumphant and Ron who is exposed as a failure.

A GLASS CEILING?

On the basis of the films released since 1997 the world as represented in movies about journalism can be argued to be reflective both of the advances women have made, and the lingering stereotypes and assumptions which constitute, as some critics have asserted, a kind of glass ceiling. In some films, female news readers are pretty and blonde (although Angelina Jolie's somewhat stereotypical role in *Life or Something Like It* is more than redeemed by her performance as Mariane Pearl in *A Mighty Heart*). On the other hand, the equation of 'pretty and blonde' with subordinate and stupid can no longer, if it ever could, be assumed. Both Kate Winslet and Cate Blanchett are blonde and (in the opinion of most cinema-goers) pretty in their movies, but they are certainly not weak, or inferior to the men around them. If anything (and this is certainly true of Blanchett's Veronica Guerin) they are tougher than some men would like them to be. Kirsten Dunst's demure and deferential sub-editor in *How To Lose Friends and Alienate People* (see below) is in this context an exception to the pattern of strong women journalists visible in the movies since 1997.

The enduring sexist assumptions which act as a kind of 'glass ceiling' limiting the progress of women in journalism can be seen in Joel Schum-acher's *Veronica Guerin*. Based on a true story which has come to symbolise the heroism of journalists in general Cate Blanchett plays Guerin, who was murdered by organised crime elements in Dublin in 1996, as a courageous and determined investigator. Guerin takes beatings and abuse as well as her fair share of obfuscation from the police, in order to get the story she believes has to be told. She is in the best tradition of the journalist-as-watchdog, and pays for this dedication with her life. She is unmistakeably a heroine. Throughout the film, though, there are references to the family in the background – her husband and her son, who are also threatened by the criminals. At one point, shots are fired at her house. Viewing these scenes the viewer finds himself asking (or this viewer did): what right does this woman have to put her loved ones at risk in this way, and her young son in particular? She can be as brave as she likes, and take any risks, because she is an adult and has the right to choose, but her family are unwilling participants in the drama. She puts their happiness and well-being at risk, as much as her own. In short, her character is consistent with that stereotype of the female journalist which portrays her as more ruthless and self-determined than any man.

This is one reading of the film, and notable because it is unlikely that Michael in *Welcome To Sarajevo* or any of the male journalists portrayed in similarly heroic circumstances would have their apparent disregard for their family responsibilities framed in this way, and made to seem like individual selfishness. When Michael brings Emira home to stay with him and his wife, the latter expresses some surprise, perhaps mild hesitation, but then there is nothing but serene acceptance of the potential impact of his decision on a family. One cannot help but admire Veronica Guerin in the film, and nor can one help but ask was it worth it, not just to her, but to the son who lost a mother, and the husband who lost a wife?

Daniel Pearl's actions in *A Mighty Heart*, which also lead to the loss of a husband and a father in circumstances which might reasonably be seen as reckless, are never subject to this kind of moral judgement. Jolie plays Mariane Pearl's deepening sense of desolation at the loss of her unborn child's father with skill, but there is barely a hint of reproach that she should have been placed in this position by her husband's hunger for the story which will kill him. We have progress, then, in that Guerin exists and is immortalised on film for her courage, but reaction too, in so far as the director seems to be asking if this is really the appropriate work for a woman in Guerin's position.

THE RISE OF STYLE JOURNALISM IN THE MOVIES

Recent decades have seen significant progressive changes in the structural position of women within society, and within the journalistic profession. These have been reflected in cinema where there have been more portrayals than ever before of women performing traditionally masculine journalistic roles – war correspondent, investigative journalist, and so on. But feminism has also meant a re-evaluation and re-assertion of femininity, and what used to be dismissively referred to as the journalism of 'women's issues' – that is, coverage in magazines and newspapers of domestic matters, fashion and human interest. Recent films about journalism, such as *The Devil Wears Prada* and *Sex and the City*, have reflected these changes.

Traditionally, as noted above, the writing and reporting which women do has been viewed as less important than that of men, precisely because it has dealt with the (presumed) feminine realms of the domestic and the emotional. That prejudice has eroded as the socio-economic and political status of women has advanced and their particular concerns have been elevated in importance.

The public sphere has been privatised, bringing with it a progressive recognition that the concerns of the individual and the family – the personal – are indeed political, and worthy of journalistic effort and attention.

In the late nineteenth and early twentieth centuries, as women became more literate and emerged into the consumer market in greater numbers, a women's version of the 'New Journalism' became visible in the mainstream news media. Mass, popular journalism was being born at this time in newspapers such as the *Daily Mail* in the UK, and part of that trend was a journalism specifically addressed to and written by women in their capacity as home-makers and emerging consumers. In the US, by 1900 around 7 per cent of journalists were women (2,193).[18] Anne Varty's anthology, *Eve's Century*, makes available some of the journalism written by women in that period (2004).

The satirist Dorothy Parker pioneered a more recognisably 'feminine' journalism of fashion and style, at the same time as presenting her work as having aesthetic value.[19] Born in 1893, Dorothy Parker wrote essays and columns for the first incarnation of style magazine *Vanity Fair* in the 1920s, and is today recognised as a pioneer of style or celebrity culture. While sticking with sterotypically 'feminine' subjects in her writing, Parker developed a public persona which was rare for a female writer and which 'evolved through her journalism and was disseminated through the sophisticated style magazines of New York' (Hammill 2007: 3). Parker 'used her petite, pretty, feminine appearance to disarm, and to lend additional impact to her satire' (Ibid.: 5), which was so biting and sharp that it survives to this day in the form of numerous aphorisms.[20] With her maverick, left-of-centre politics, she anticipates the persona of contemporary columnist Julie Burchill, also renowned for her sharp wit and take-no-prisoners approach to her subjects. But as Hammill observes, even although Parker was a best-selling writer of plays and essays, she remained a marginalised, cultish figure in American literary life until the late twentieth century. In 1994 she was played on screen by Jennifer Jason Leigh in Alan Rudolph's film, *Mrs Parker and the Vicious Circle*.[21]

Women have continued to write in women's magazines, of course, which since Helen Gurley Brown invented 'Cosmo' girl in the 1960s have steadily become more 'frank' in their treatment of female sexuality, and more reflective of woman's changing position within the workforce. The domestic realm, matters of the heart and sexuality remain important dimensions of women's journalism, increasing their visibility within the public sphere as women have ascended the socio-economic hierarchies of liberal capitalism. The journalism of style, be it addressed to matters of fashion, sexual manners, or health and fitness, has acquired respectability and prominence. Style journalism is still viewed as part of the feminine, but its status has radically altered. Today, to work on a magazine such as *Vogue* is regarded as evidence of professional journalistic success – still glamorous and sexy, yes, but also now worthy of a serious woman's efforts. In the post-feminist world the stigma which once attached to such journalism and to those who wrote it is over-written with an appreciation of its cultural value.

THE DEVIL WEARS PRADA

This trend has been reflected in a wave of films about 'style' journalism – the journalism of fashion, culture and celebrity exemplified by the contents of magazines such as *Vogue* and *Vanity Fair*. Such films frequently contain within them debates about the relative worthiness of gossip columns, or fashion spreads, or celebrity interviews, and they are often critical, but such journalism is no longer presented as laughable, even when it is portrayed in teen comedies such as *13 Going On 30* (Gary Winnick, 2004), and *How To Lose a Guy in 10 Days* (Donald Petrie, 2003). The position of women in late patriarchy has changed, and with it the status of women working within the lifestyle and entertainment spheres of the media.

Even in films such as *Sex and the City*, *The Devil Wears Prada* and *How To Lose Friends and Alienate People*, men are still a powerful, sometimes dominant presence. In the latter, Jeff Bridges' portrayal of Claydon Harding, modelled on Graydon Carter of *Vanity Fair*, reproduces the unquestioned authority of the male editor over a largely female staff. The women do much of the work, but in this case, as in many others, a man takes the key decisions. Claydon is the undisputed boss at *Sparks*, although his magazine is targeted at a female audience obsessed with fashion and film stars such as the airhead-ish Sophie Maes. Claydon has a dutiful wife, who appears from time to time, dressed in pink and with two adorable girl children in tow.

The lead character in *How To Lose Friends* ... is a male journalist, Sydney Young, loosely based on the author of the book on which the film is based, Toby Young. He it is who joins *Sparks* as an unknown and a novice, who locks horns with his immediate boss, Laurence, and then succeeds to his senior job as Culture Editor, all with the apparent minimum of effort. The lead female role, played by Kirsten Dunst, is presented as an aspiring, intelligent, would-be novelist who has somehow, by her own account, allowed herself to be diverted from her 'real' vocation in life – to be a writer – by this trivia. She has her status and integrity undermined by falling for the aforementioned Laurence, whose wife, meantime, is only seen from the rear, in two brief scenes where she too is the foil for the joke. In the end, Dunst's character has to be rescued by Sydney who finds her at an open-air screening of her favourite film, *La Dolce Vita*. Even in *How To Lose Friends* ..., however, among the more conservative of recent films about journalism in its adherence to sexist stereotypes, the traditionally stigmatised zone of style and celebrity is re-evaluated,

Figure 18 *The Devil Wears Prada* (David Frankel, 2006). Source: BFI

rehabilitated and intellectualised. The film is not a 'feminist' text, then, or even a post-feminist one, but it embraces one of the lessons of the post-feminist era – that style journalism is a valid object of interest, a fascinating subject, an honourable trade.

The Devil Wears Prada also contains this meaning, although it addresses the subject of style journalism from a much more female-centred and feminist-informed perspective. Here, the fictional editor played by Meryl Streep is reportedly modelled on Anna Wintour, editor of *Vogue* magazine and by reputation a towering figure. Andy Sachs, a novice entering a world of which she knows little is played by Anne Hathaway. Like Sydney in *How To Lose Friends* ..., she is at first dismissive of the legitimacy of style journalism, which she sees as a mere stepping stone to something more serious. Before long, however, she is forced to engage in an internal debate about the validity of her job.

Miranda Priestley is the advocate of the value of fashion and style journalism, as in a scene where she berates Andy for laughing off the seriousness with which she is asked to judge which colour of blue belt to accompany a designer dress.

Miranda: Something funny?

Andy: No, no, nothing, it's just, you know, both of those belts look exactly the same, and I'm still learning about this stuff, and eh ...

Miranda: This, stuff? Oh, I see. You think this has nothing to do with you. You go to your closet, and you select, I don't know, that lumpy blue sweater [you're wearing] because you're trying to tell the world that you take yourself too seriously to care what you put on your back, but what you don't know is that that sweater is not just blue, it's not turquoise, it's not lapis, it's actually cerillion. You're also blithely unaware of the fact that in 2002 Oscar Lorenzo did a collection of cerillion gowns, and then – I think it was Yves St Laurent, wasn't it – who showed cerillion military jackets? And then cerillion quickly showed up in the collections of the major designers, and then filtered down through the department stores, and then trickled on down to some tragic casuals corner where you no doubt fished it out of some clearance bin. However, that blue represents millions of dollars and countless jobs, and it's sort of comical how you think that you've made a choice that exempts you from the fashion industry, when in fact you're wearing a sweater that was selected for you by the people in this room, from a pile of stuff.

CONCLUSION

As this book went to press, cultural commentators were observing the huge success of movies marketed for women, such as *Mamma Mia* (Phyllida Lloyd, 2008) and *Sex and the City*, and predicting more of the same in years to come. These were not feminist movies in a directly political sense, and were criticised by some feminists for their endorsement of certain stereotypes traditionally deemed sexist. *Sex and the City*, for example, is essentially a film about finding your man and getting him to buy you things. Other critics, however, claimed these movies as evidence of a cultural landscape in which women had now, and not before many years of radical campaigning had prepared the ground, advanced sufficiently in the struggle to reform and even abolish patriarchy that they were now able to sit back and allow themselves to be pampered a little (I simplify, of course, but this is the essence of the case for a feminist reading of *Mamma Mia* and the like – we've done the politics and won, now let's wear the frocks and sing along to *Dancing Queen* – you know we want to!).

Sex and the City is a film about a female journalist, and the vehicle for the story of four professional women living and working in New York. Carrie's journalism is of the confessional type which has become more prominent in recent years, written by and for women (though men are by no means excluded from enjoying it). It deals with love and sex and fashion, as does the TV series. The movie version succeeds as cinematic entertainment, and although it has little to say about the practice of style journalism, or the role of women within the journalistic profession, that the film was made at all, and its huge success (nearly $0.5 billion at the box office), confirm the trend established by the *Devil Wears Prada*. 'Women's journalism' has acquired a cultural significance which reflects the raised status and spending power of its core market, the post-feminist generation of working women with money to spend, time to play, and the confidence to celebrate their femininity through guilt-free conspicuous consumption. In the hierarchy of taste within which the journalism of fashion and style has traditionally been subordinate to that of manly subjects like war and economics, journalism by and for women has been elevated.

The feminist movement remains divided around how to interpret this turn in the culture, just as it is divided over how to interpret the rise of style journalism. One of the leading scholarly works on women's journalism, acknowledges that there has been progress on the position of women within the journalistic profession, while cautioning that this 'does not necessarily indicate their empowerment within media structures' (Chambers et al., 2004: 10). Indeed not, but these authors go on to make the more problematic (it seems to me) argument that the rise of women in journalism has coincided with 'a market-led, depoliticised "post-feminist" redefinition of news ...

a post-feminist discourse is linked to a devaluation of serious news, such as foreign affairs' (Ibid.: 13).

This is precisely the criticism made of talk shows, lifestyle journalism and other categories of public media seen as 'women's work' by male commentators. It endorses that patriarchal narrative of cultural decline (where decline equals feminisation) when it explicitly condemns the 'new girl' writing of such as Candace Bushnell *(Sex and the City)*, who are blamed for failing

> to bolster the professional credibility of the female columnist. This 'new girl writing' has inspired and sanctioned the rise of a whole new feminine, but covertly anti-feminist, journalistic form in the twenty-first century in which it is now permissible for women to expose their own and other women's personal insecurities and vulgar habits, sexual conquests and defeats, and abuses of substances and people. (2004: 217)

This cultural pessimism misreads the trends and understates the political progress of which they are an index. Just as the success of the film *Mamma Mia* is a celebration of girlie things in which the most radical feminist can now safely indulge, so *Sex and the City* and *The Devil Wears Prada* represent in cinematic terms a feminised culture which recognises the importance of clothes, fashion and romance to the modern woman, who works but also wants to shop and look sexy. Both films speak to a cultural environment in which what women want matters more than it ever did, commercially and politically, and which a high-powered women's journalism has developed to service.

NOTES

1. The most recent and comprehensive study is contained in *Women and Journalism*, edited by Deborah Chambers et al. This collection reviews the history of women in the profession, and then addresses themes such as 'Women war correspondents' and confessional journalism. The website of the Institute for the *Study of Journalism in Popular Culture* (*www.ijpc.org*) contains Joe Saltzman's essay on 'Sob sisters'. M. Djerf-Pierre's 2008 essay in *Nordicom Review* discusses the position of women journalists in Scandinavia.

2. Faye Hammill's *Women, Celebrity and Literary Culture Between the Wars* is a recent and rare book-length study of the 'middlebrow', and includes chapters on the journalistic work of Dorothy Parker, Anita Loos and other women who struggled to be taken seriously as writers because of their gender and subject matter.

3. Germaine Greer's 1981 book *The Obstacle Race* traces the marginalisation of women within visual culture (marginalised in every capacity except that of models and muses, of course), and notes that the resources required to design and construct signature buildings, or to stage the elaborate sets used by Renaissance sculptors and painters, were denied to female artists such as Artemisia Gentileschi, who were thereby 'hidden from history' until late twentieth-century feminist historians such as Greer rediscovered them.

4. Saltzman, J., 'Sob sisters: the image of the female journalist in popular culture', *IJPC*, 2003.

5. For an essay on Duncan's work, see Hammill 2004.

6. Goldenberg, S., "'Somehow I don't feel it in my gut'", *Guardian*, 1 December 2008.

7. Coverage of a 2008 exhibition of work by female photojournalist Susan Meiselas observed that 'ever since [the 1930s, when Robert Capa defined the sub-genre with his images of the Spanish Civil War] conflict photography has been seen, essentially, as a man's job' (Abrams, Melanie, 'From the fringes to the frontline', *Guardian*, 17 April 2008). The report noted that even then, in the early twenty-first century, seventy years after Lee Miller blazed the trail, only seven of seventy-nine Magnum reporters were women.

8. Research data and other material on the status of women in journalism is contained on the website of the Fawcett Society (*www.fawcettsociety.org.uk*). Chambers et al. argue that 'women are still concentrated in sectors considered to be "soft" news, such as those with an emphasis on "human interest" stories, features and the delivery of a magazine-style of journalism. In television – where spectacle counts – emphasis on the decorative value and even the sexualisation of women journalists is overt' (2004: 1). This is true, in respect of figures such as Kirsty Young in the United Kingdom and her equivalents (young, attractive, frequently blonde women) in other countries. To this day, the news media frequently run articles alleging that female presenters and journalists are selected not for their professional ability but for their looks, often at the expense of less photogenic men. The 'sexualisation' of TV news in particular is linked with a broader marketisation of news, in which appearance and presentation are considered to be more important than content.

9. Saltzman, J., 'Sob sisters: the image of the female journalist in popular culture', *IJPC*, 2003.

10. Idem.

11. Ghiglione, L., 'The American Journalist: fiction versus fact', unpublished essay on *IJPC*, *www.ijpc.org/ghigline.htm*. See also Ghiglione, L., Saltzman, J., 'Fact or fiction: Hollywood looks at the news', www.ijpc.org/hollywoodlooksatthenews2.pdf.

12. Saltzman, J., 'Sob sisters: the image of the female journalist in popular culture', *IJPC*, 2003.

13. Ghiglione, L., 'The American Journalist: fiction versus fact', unpublished essay on *IJPC*, *www.ijpc.org/ghigline.htm*. See also Ghiglione, L., Saltzman, J., 'Fact or fiction: Hollywood looks at the news', *www.ijpc.org/hollywoodlooksatthenews2.pdf*.

14. Saltzman, J., 'Sob sisters: the image of the female journalist in popular culture', *IJPC*, 2003. Saltzman records that the term 'sob sister' dates back to 1907 and the trial of millionaire Harry K. Thaw for a crime of passion. The trial was reported by four female reporters, who became known as the 'sob sisters', meaning 'big-hearted but soft-minded, emotionally generous but intellectually sloppy' (2003: 2).

15. Howard Good has written a book-length study of Torchy Blane in *Girl Reporter* (1998).

16. Saltzman, J., 'Sob sisters: the image of the female journalist in popular culture', *IJPC*, 2003.

17. She is compared to James Stewart's campaigning journalist in *Call Northside 777* (Henry Hathaway, 1947) in a review by Richard Kelly, *Sight & Sound*, volume 13, number 4, 2003.

18. Cited in Saltzman, J., 'Sob sisters: the image of the female journalist in popular culture', *IJPC*, 2003.

19. Faye Hammill's study observes that Parker's writing negotiated the tensions between femininity and public display in early celebrity culture, and that 'her journalism mediates the discourses of sophistication, sentiment and Modern Love' (2007: 29).

20. For example, when asked to make up a sentence with the word 'horticulture' in it, she replied after some thought, 'You can drag a horticulture, but you can't make her think'.

21. Leigh played a Parker-esque journalist in another film made around the same time, *The Hudsucker Proxy* (Coen Brothers, 1994).

CHAPTER 8

Artists

It is part of the mythology of journalism that every journalist secretly wishes to be a novelist, and has an unpublished typescript or two in his or her desk drawer. There is some truth in this notion, which arises from the fact that so many journalists perceive their profession to be in some sense less worthy than that of the true man or woman of letters, the genuine artist. Journalists often harbour inferiority complexes, and even those who have succeeded in rising to the upper ranks of the profession may see themselves as under-achievers who have missed their true calling in life. In the hierarchy of cultural distinction, journalism lies below literature in the minds of many of those who practise either or both.

The rise of New Journalism in the 1960s, Tom Wolfe persuasively argued, was a product not least of the ambition of some journalists to be regarded by their peers and their publics as more than hacks, and to acquire the status of literary figures in a cultural marketplace where literature was annointed as Art and journalism was so often regarded as Trash. Hunter S. Thompson is described in one recent profile as 'a writer who wanted to be a novelist but wound up revitalising journalism while simultaneously despising it'.[1] His *Fear and Loathing in Las Vegas* is perhaps the best example of the ambivalence created by the status gap which exists between journalism and creative writing, the lingering sense even amongst the greatest of journalists that what they are doing is less worthwhile as cultural practice than the work of the novelist or poet. Is it a novel, or a work of reportage? Is it both, and does it matter?

By the 'art' of journalism I refer to the literary (or 'New') journalism of Wolfe, Capote, Didion and Kapuscinski, and before them, to the book-length reportage of George Orwell, John Reed and John Hershey. More recently, we have seen the emergence of the Norwegian Asne Sierstad, whose books on Afghanistan and Chechnya have achieved bestseller status all over the world. Indeed, non-fiction publishing in general, including forms which may cross over into journalism but are regarded as distinct genres, such as autobiography and memoir, has risen in the best seller lists. This is part of what one might call a 'cult of factuality', or reality, by which I mean a widespread public interest in the real, as opposed to the made-up, the imagined, the fictional, which characterised late twentieth and early twenty-first century capitalist culture.

Linked to that trend has been a public debate pursued in literary supplements, culture shows on TV and radio, and even in self-consciously postmodern comedy shows such as *The Simpsons*, about the nature of the real and its representation in culture. In the past it was generally accepted that journalists deployed facts to write news, while fiction writers called on their sensibilities and aesthetic skills to create art. Both journalist and artist addressed the real on some level, but there was generally recognised to be a clear separation of the two. The rise of a cult of factuality (seen also in the reality-TV phenomenon) has highlighted the status of Truth, and what kind of representation is required, and best suited, to access it. The question 'Is it Art, or is it Journalism?', similarly, has been the subject of more than one of the films made about journalism since 1997.

THE ART OF JOURNALISM

Although journalism and art have always been linked, albeit uneasily, the late twentieth and early twenty-first centuries have seen the subjective and creative dimensions of journalism given much greater recognition and legitimacy than ever before. In a world where the limits of objectivity and related concepts such as journalistic detachment are widely acknowledged both by professionals and the critical community, the idea of journalism-as-art is no longer controversial, be it in the context of a feature-length documentary by Scottish director Kevin Macdonald (*One Day in September*, 1999; *Touching the Void*, 2003),[2] or a big-budget Hollywood exploration of the journalistic writing of Truman Capote (*Capote*, Bennett Miller, 2005; *Infamous*, Douglas McGrath, 2006).

This chapter sits here in the 'Heroes' section of the book because journalistic artists are often celebrated cultural figures, even celebrities. 2008 saw the cinema release of a feature-length documentary about Hunter S. Thompson, one of the greatest journalistic celebrities of the late twentieth century. This followed Terry Gilliam's 1998 adaptation of Thompson's *Fear and Loathing in Las Vegas* (1998), and not one but two films about Truman Capote released in the same twelve-month period in 2005–6.

These journalists were celebrities, yes, but were they characters to be admired and emulated? I would answer yes, if only on the basis of those of my students, colleagues and friends over the years who have advanced their names as examples and role models, despite the alcoholism, the drug problems, their unlikableness as human beings, their premature deaths. Those journalists who have been recognised as artists have often been *anti*-heroes. Just as Eastwood's Man With No Name was such an anti-hero, I will claim the likes of Thompson, Capote and their journalist-artist peers as cultural icons signifying, on balance, positive rather than negative characteristics.

The notion of journalism-as-art inevitably requires engagement with the interplay between objectivity and subjectivity, and problematises the status of the journalist as a detached, reliable observer of fact-based reality. What is true, and what is invented in the book-length journalistic texts of Thompson and Capote? That such questions have even to be asked makes some question the integrity of such journalists, and of those like Michael Moore who present themselves as journalists but are then accused of producing mere polemic, or worse, propaganda for their favoured causes. Journalists who lay claim to the status of auteurs and artists are often, for that very reason, controversial figures and, if not quite villains, less than heroes of the type who populate *The Insider* or *Good Night, and Good Luck*. They *are* inspirational figures, however, attractive and compelling, even as their personal behaviour may appal (this is certainly the case with Capote and Thompson).

Then again, heroes in any walk of life are usually more complex and ambivalent characters than their public profiles suggest. And that, often, is precisely the point of what these journalists write – to question the viewpoint which sees the world in black and white, and Reality and Truth as easily accessible phenomena. To bring this idea to the heart of the public sphere is transgressive and boundary-breaking, and thus might in itself be judged an heroic act.

ART FOR JOURNALISM'S SAKE

Christopher Hitchen's foreword to a collection of the journalism of Karl Marx (2007) begins with an anecdote encapsulating the tension that has always existed between the practices of journalism and Art (where art has a capital 'A').

Commenting acidly on a writer whom I perhaps too naively admired, my old classics teacher put on his best sneer to ask: 'Wouldn't you say, Hitchens, that his writing was somewhat journalistic?' This lofty schoolmaster stressed the last term as he meant it to sting, and it rankled even more than he had intended. Later on in life, I found that I still used to mutter and improve my long-meditated reply. Emile Zola – a journalist. Charles Dickens – a journalist. Thomas Paine – another journalist. Mark Twain. Rudyard Kipling. George Orwell – a journalist par excellence.

Somewhere in my cortex was the idea to which Orwell himself once gave explicit shape: the idea that 'mere' writing of this sort could aspire to become an art, and that the word 'journalist' – like the ironic modern English usage of the word 'hack' – could lose its association with the trivial and the evanescent.[3]

Hitchens was not the first, nor the last, to find the commonplace critical dismissal of journalistic writing troubling. From very early in the cultural history of capitalism a divide opens up – a taste distinction, to use Bourdieu's term – between writing which is regarded as aesthetically worthy, and that which is viewed as mechanical and workmanlike – as 'hack work', lacking in literary merit. As John Carey persuasively argued in *The Intellectuals and the Masses* (1992), the establishment of this hierarchy of literary value may be viewed as a response to the growth of a mass reading public following the educational reforms of the nineteenth century, and the subsequent need to wall off the tastes and interests of the great unwashed from those of the educated and monied elites who had hitherto monopolised both the production and the consumption of writing. Buying into this view, and aspiring to the social cachet associated with being an artist rather than a mere producer of news, many journalists came to despise and devalue their own work, and to see it as much less important and worthwhile than the writing of 'literature', especially of novels, which by the late nineteenth century had become the dominant literary form. Journalism came to be viewed not as a respectable pursuit in itself, but a stepping stone, a bridge to something better than hack work. Michael Wolff's 2008 biography of Rupert Murdoch recounts how the Australian media baron's father, Keith, having been expected to become a clergyman in late nineteenth century Melbourne, 'instead becomes a journalist' and thereby turns himself into something of a social outsider. This because 'at the turn of the century, journalism is nobody's idea of a profession' (2008: 64).

The widespread perception has been and remains (if it is now in decline, not least thanks to films such as *Capote* and *Infamous*) that journalism is of intrinsically lesser value than literature, and no group has held that view more strongly than journalists themselves. In explaining the rise of what he termed New Journalism in the latter half of the twentieth century, Tom Wolfe argued that many journalists harboured an inferiority complex about their status, and wished for nothing more than to be thought of as 'real' writers (Wolfe and Johnson 1975). This crisis of literary identity, he observed, was one of the driving forces in the emergence in the twentieth century of a form of journalism which explicitly united reportorial and literary techniques in pursuit of truth.

Wolfe's essay on 'The New Journalism' is rightly seen as a key moment in the development of what we might characterise as the fight back, since it both recognised and championed the growing number of journalists who applied the techniques of creative writing to their reportage. Wolfe and others had been doing it since the 1960s; Gay Talese, Jimmy Breslin and others from the 1950s. But as Hitchens' examples remind us, the links between journalism and fiction writing were already established long before that, in the nineteenth century, in the work of Charles Dickens for example. In addition to his prolific fiction output, Dickens wrote more than 350 articles comprising over a million words of journalism in the form of reportage, columns and other short pieces (Tulloch, 2007).

Dickens was himself one of those who regarded journalism as of lesser value. John Tulloch notes with reference to Dickens that 'one obvious reason for the low status of English journalism has been its perceived lack of creative control by the author compared to the control allegedly associated with the "artist"' (2007: 61). The journalist typically contributes material to a content brief usually set by an editor, and to a style, length and general format determined by the publication in question. He or she lacks creative autonomy, certainly by comparison with the novelist holed up in his garret somewhere, penning the great book. And of course there is truth in this comparison. The journalist is an employee, a wage slave, at least until s/he acquires the status to initiate his or her own ideas for articles, to write or speak in his or her own voice, and to be paid a salary in excess of the norm for his or her colleagues of a similar age.

It was, of course, always inaccurate to juxtapose all journalists as publishing's proletarians selling words by the bushel, and literary writers as artists with absolute freedom. These are stereotypes which mask the huge variety of potential statuses accessible to a writer of either fact or fiction (or both, as the literary journalists sought to become). All writers must sell their work if they are to make a living from it, and all publishing has, since the invention of the commercial printing press in late medieval Europe, had the character of a marketplace within which the writer must operate, selling a literary persona, and the books and pamphlets within which it is contained.[4] Within both journalism and literature there are gradations of status, levels of autonomy to which the writer may aspire, based on qualitative judgements of his or her artistry as a writer, or marketability as an author (not always the same thing, as in the autobiographical memoirs of TV and sports stars who employ ghost writers to translate their anecdotes into book-length narratives).

Key to both practices is facility with the written word, the ability to communicate meaning through language, to convey truth not merely through the accurate reportage of key facts, but in the evocation of atmosphere, feeling and mood. Journalists tell 'stories', just like novelists and playwrights. News stories can be analysed in terms of their narrative structure, their tone and register, the way in which characters are drawn and plots resolved. Jack Lule has written a book about 'the mythological role of journalism' which approaches news as 'eternal stories' with deep anthropological meanings for a society (2001). From this perspective journalism is just another form of story-telling, a form which happens to be 'true' where novels and other literary forms are imagined or invented. Journalism is narrative, presenting the 'facts' of a situation in a structure which has beginning, middle and end.

Conversely, much that is presented as literary invention is based on actual events, or inspired by incidents drawn from a writer's experience. 'Write what you know' is standard advice for a creative writing student, reflecting the core truth that all art, including the literary variety, must be based on experience. The purpose of literature, or one of its purposes, is to tell the truth about human experience in an original and insightful way. Great literature is no more, perhaps, than the application of an outstandingly creative and sensitive mind to the mysteries and complexities of the real, combined with the capacity to shine a light on the apparent banalities of the everyday in a way that makes them seem fresh and vital, and that reveals elements we had not perceived before. Literature and journalism, if this is accepted, are just different pathways to the same destination – that of understanding the real, recognising complexity, accepting the relativity of truth.

It can be argued that the marketing power of the concept of objectivity, which developed only in the late nineteenth century (borrowed from the world of natural science) and was applied to journalism in an environment where there were many news accounts competing for attention,[5] prevented this acceptance of the underlying similarities between good journalism in particular and good writing in general. The two types of text had different cultural functions, different uses and exchange values in the growing media marketplace, and thus different socio-economic statuses. That this was linked to a hierarchy of taste in which objective journalism was deemed inferior to subjective art can be read as part of liberal humanity's affection for all things judged to be somehow beyond the realm of bureaucratic and organisational rules, and thus in some sense 'free'.

This attitude changed in the twentieth century, for a number of reasons. First, one might argue, it was simply unsustainable in a world where writers of the stature of Dickens, Hemingway, Greene and Orwell wrote journalism, and where broader and broader swathes of the population were accessing writing of quality through popular news and periodical media (such as those run and contributed to by Dickens). The elitism of the view that there was something called 'literature', easily separable from popular modes of writing such as journalism, began to creak as the twentieth century got under way, and as new mass media such as cinema, radio and then TV emerged to challenge the 'high culture' platforms of the past. Graham Greene, one of the century's greatest novelists, wrote film reviews for the London *Times*, the *Spectator* and *Sight & Sound*,[6] as did many other acknowledged literary artists. In those circumstances it was probably inevitable that the largely arbitrary, socially constructed line between high and low culture would begin to be eroded.

THE EPISTEMOLOGICAL CHALLENGE TO OBJECTIVITY

If the connections and similarities between journalism and art were becoming more obvious in the early twentieth century, thus challenging the objectivity/ subjectivity binary, also of importance in the emergence of a more self-consciously literary journalism was the epistemological revolution in scientific method, and the erosion of the concept of objectivity as commonly understood. Developments in natural science, such as the discovery of relativity in physics, of the uncertainty principle and quantum mechanics, problematised the hitherto dominant view of detached observation, and reportage of that observation as the only scientific method available to the objective observer. It was not that reportage was declared redundant (just as laboratory experimentation remained central to natural science, reportage and the standards associated with it were and remain at the core of journalism of quality), but that ideas about the nature of reality, and of how to retrieve reliable accounts of reality from inherently subjective observers, had to adapt to a world in which the concept of relativity had been accepted, and the role of observer viewpoint had acquired enhanced significance.

The impact of these advances was felt also in philosophy, and in the growth of analogous concepts such as that of cultural relativism: the idea that the meaning of human behaviour can only be understood in the context within which it occurs. In journalistic terms this meant that there was, in principle, more than one objective or true account of events available for extraction by a reporter; that how things looked depended on one's viewing position, which could change, and which was shaped in part by individual history and context. This idea could not form and spread until it had been accepted in the realms of science and philosophy which had traditionally provided journalism with its epistemological models. Journalism had long looked to science for legitimation of its truth claims. Objectivity functioned as the seal of approval on journalistic endeavour from the point at which it become necessary to market news as a commodity. As science abandoned simple notions of objectivity, so over time did journalists. The notion of Absolute Truth, of a pure knowledge which could be extracted from the coarse ore of reality, gave way to acceptance of truth as something which could legitimately and in good faith be contested, debated, argued over, between sides which might both believe that they were telling the truth, because this was how events and issues looked to them.

THE RISE OF PUBLIC RELATIONS

Another factor driving the decline of a certain notion of objectivity around this time was the rise of a parallel profession, or craft, or trade known variously as public relations, public affairs or press counselling.

While public relations, defined as the practice of managing communication, and its meanings as understood by various publics has a long history, it begins to be recognised as a professional communication practice only in the first decades of the twentieth century.[7] Only then, as mass democracy became a political reality and mass media correspondingly expanded their reach and influence, did the importance of managing meaning and thus influencing public opinion become apparent, and a profession emerge to carry out the work of what Walter Lippman called without apology 'manufacturing consent'.[8] For Lippmann and others, the complexity of twentieth-century life would require not merely competent, objective journalism to help the newly enfranchised citizenry make sense of it, but another kind of communicator able to make sense of things for the journalist.

Facts may be 'spun', to use contemporary vernacular, at the same time as they are given the necessary shape and structure for use by journalists. Truth may be manipulated, constructed, bent and twisted. And thus we have another reason to be suspicious of those claiming to be the purveyors of pure objectivity, or uninterested truth. Not only are meanings the product of particular viewpoints on the 'facts'; they are moulded to suit particular interests. And with that understanding already clear to journalists nearly a century ago, the line from objectivity to subjectivity in reportage, from professional detachment to passionate propaganda, was not difficult to cross.

TWO BOOKS THAT SHOOK THE WORLD

In the early twentieth century American journalist John Reed published what was undoubtedly intended as a work of, if not propaganda then eulogy, and which can be read now as one of the pioneering works of self-consciously produced 'literary journalism': *Ten Days That Shook the World*, his eye-witness account of the Bolshevik Revolution of October 1917. Reed was a foreign correspondent, a reporter, and also a revolutionary socialist who believed in the power of journalism to change things. Presented with the opportunity of a real live socialist revolution in Russia, he travelled there and put together a book-length account of how Lenin and the Bolsheviks took power. In his preface he observes that while 'my sympathies were not neutral ... in telling the story of those great days I have tried to see events with the eye of a conscientious reporter, interested in setting down the truth' (2007: 13). In his introduction to the Penguin edition, historian A. J. P. Taylor acknowledged the book as a political classic, and warned that Reed's account was not a detached or objective account of the revolution, but one in which the drama was heightened, and 'imaginative detail' added. 'Much of Reed's book is fiction', he observes. The book became the source of a subsequent mythology of the events it describes, including a Soviet government-sponsored film directed by Sergei Eisenstein in 1927.

John Reed's short life became the subject of *Reds*, directed by Warren Beatty (who also played the lead role) and released to huge critical acclaim in 1981 (it won three Oscars, for Best Director, Best Supporting Actress, and Cinematography). Described by Peter Biskind as 'one of the most audacious and politically literate movies ever to come out of Hollywood',[9] *Reds* told the story of Reed's relationship with fellow-socialist and journalist Louise Bryant, and his epic project to both report on and participate in the experience of the Russian Revolution. As is typical for mainstream movies, *Reds* played fast and loose with the facts of the Reed-Bryant story, emphasising its tragic-romantic elements, but as Biskind's *Vanity Fair* article notes, for a movie made by a top Hollywood studio at the onset of the Ronald Reagan presidency and what would soon come to be known as the 'New Cold War' it is a remarkable achievement, reclaiming a period of American left history that had been ignored and forgotten by mainstream cultural producers.

Figure 19 *Reds* (Warren Beatty, 1981). Source: BFI

In its 195-minute running length the aesthetic dimension of Reed's journalism, and his qualities as a writer, are rarely the primary focus of the film, but throughout there is substantial engagement with the question of the journalist's responsibility to the facts of a situation when he is politically committed. Should he be an enthusiastic participant in the events being reported and, if so, does he risk becoming a propagandist? And if so, can this ever be justified? In the scenes at the end of the film, when he is trapped in Russia and under pressure to work in the service of the Communist party, Reed begins to assert his liberal credentials as an independent figure. While the senior party figure Georgy Zinoviev presents the Leninist approach to journalism – that there is no such thing as 'freedom' of the press, no such thing as objectivity, which is a bourgeois ideological myth[10] – Reed sticks to his guns, becoming increasingly disillusioned. He dies a broken man in Moscow in 1920, Bryant by his side (which really *did* happen).

Reds has the distinction of being the only big-budget Hollywood movie ever made which dares to make a sex symbol of an American Communist. It also rescues from the margins of history a key work of twentieth-century journalism, and one that pioneered the long-form literary style of later decades. *Ten Days* ... can be read by unreconstructed Marxist-Leninists as an inspirational, rabble-rousing account of their movement's greatest revolutionary triumph, and by historians as a documentary source for the October events. It is also, for we journalism students, a pioneering experiment in the interplay of detachment and participation, of objectivity and subjectivity, which acknowledges the capacity of the reporter's emotional involvement to generate a kind of truth that mere reportage on its own cannot. The structure of the film, in which Jack Nicholson plays a key supporting role as playwright Eugene O'Neill, places journalism alongside literature and invites us to consider them aesthetic equals in their capacity to evoke and comment on the real.

Of particular importance in Reed's book is its stress on the epistemological value of authorial participation, of emotional engagement with the material about which one is, as a journalist, striving to be accurate and honest. This principle had always been accepted in fiction, but had not really been considered as relevant to journalism, except perhaps in the context of the research undertaken to prepare a story. *Ten Days* ... is an acknowledgement of the inevitable partiality of the journalistic observer, and a plea for the value of the reportage which such partiality permits. *Reds* takes us beyond Reed's book, to the point where partiality becomes mere propaganda and, in Beatty's account of Reed's final months, something to be resisted.

IN COLD BLOOD

The seeds of what Tom Wolfe called 'New Journalism' were already being sown, then, in the early twentieth century, if not before (was there ever a time, indeed, when the techniques and tricks of the creative writer were not being applied by journalists, and vice versa, whether either group admitted to it or not?). It was not until the 1960s, however, and the emergence of a distinct group of journalists who, like Wolfe, rejected the inferiority complex which had surrounded their profession and proclaimed the literary qualities of good journalism that its status as Art began to be widely accepted. Before this, recalls Wolfe, 'no-one was used to thinking of reporting as having an aesthetic dimension', and certainly not in the context of popular journalism.

> There was no such thing as a *literary* journalist [his emphasis] working for popular magazines or newspapers. If a journalist aspired to literary status – then he had better have the sense and the courage to quit the popular press and try to get into the big league.(1975: 21)

Thirty-five years later Wolfe's essay remains essential reading for all students of a journalism that, if no longer 'new', does have an aesthetic dimension in so far as it aspires to the qualities of art, while remaining in the service of reportage; and who are prepared to believe that the application of 'artistic' tools are the path to a deeper, higher truth than mere objectivity alone can enable.[11]

Truman Capote was a key figure in the New Journalism movement described by Wolfe, mainly because of his long-form 'non-fiction novel'. *In Cold Blood* was published first in the *New Yorker* magazine and then as a book (Capote 1966). Unlike John Reed's *Ten Days ...*, *In Cold Blood* (subtitled 'A true account of a murder and its consequences') is not a political book, nor a work of propaganda for anything other than the author's own interpretation of events, but it is closer to Reed's reportorial approach than to anything we might view as 'objective journalism'. At nearly 100,000 words in length, it is novelistic in form, divided into four chapters (the four *New Yorker* pieces) with sections of dialogue, description and authorial intervention. It is a murder mystery – who killed the Clutters, and why? – but one constructed from personal research and observation, as well as official documents and other sources of information familiar to journalists. Capote writes in his acknowledgements that 'all the material in this book not derived from my own observation is either taken from official records or is the result of interviews with the persons directly concerned'. *In Cold Blood* is a 'true crime' story, as the genre is popularly known, but written with all the skill of a recognised literary genius who employs his powers to create a work which quickly became a classic not just of late twentieth-century journalism, but late twentieth-century literature. In doing so, Capote highlighted the problematic nature of the distinction between the two.

CAPOTE AND INFAMOUS

We wait for nearly a century of cinema history for a film which explores in depth the subject of journalism-as-art, and then two come along at once. Not only that, but both films are about the same journalist, Truman Capote. Even more remarkably, both are about the same piece of journalism, a series of feature articles published by *New Yorker* magazine in 1965 about a hitherto obscure murder case in Kansas, and a subsequent work of non-fiction entitled *In Cold Blood*. Would you credit it?[12]

Both *Capote* and *Infamous* take as their subject the potential unreliability of the journalistic narrator, and the validity of using literary techniques (Capote was already an established novelist, short story and screenplay writer when he embarked on the project which became *In Cold Blood*) to convey a more intense truth than conventional reportage alone could achieve. We are shown, for example, how Capote never uses tape recorders when interviewing the killers of

Figure 20 *Capote* (Bennett Miller, 2005). Source: BFI

Figure 21 *Infamous* (Douglas McGrath, 2006). Source: BFI

the Clutter family, or others involved with the case, but reconstructs conversations from memory. He has, he claims, a photographic memory. But he would say that, wouldn't he, and how from this distance would we be able to prove otherwise? Journalists embellish things, after all. Maybe he made up some, if not all of the intimate details that make *In Cold Blood* so gripping. In *Capote* we see the author confess to fictionalising his written description of a visit to the mortuary where the bodies of the murdered family are laid out. His point, though, is that the details do not matter as much as the essence of the scene, which he insists he has captured accurately. In going along with this argument, we accept that truth is indeed a largely subjective matter, constructed not just from facts and figures but moods and feelings, from impressions as much as observations.

Both of the Capote films are remarkable for their interest – given the popular medium in which they work – in the complex matter of where the boundaries exist between Journalism and Art, if indeed they exist at all.[13] Both films dare to make the radical suggestion that the gap between fiction and fact is narrow, even as both narrativise and inevitably fictionalise the 'true'story of how Capote came to write *In Cold Blood*. *Infamous* goes rather too far, in my view, when it has Capote kiss an imprisoned, muscle-bound, guitar-strumming Perry played by Daniel Craig – an incident for which there is precisely no evidential basis. *Capote*, on the other hand, and Philip Seymour Hoffman's Oscar-winning performance, gives the author a more commanding physicality than he is reliably reported to have had. No matter. The relative nature of truth, its constructedness, is embedded in both films, and we must accept them on those terms or not at all. Neither account is absolutely 'true', nor do we expect it to be. Both tell different untruths, eroding our faith in their narrators, just as the narrator who is their subject comes to be seen as unreliable. Unreliable narration is, indeed, their subject. Why apologise for artistic licence in films about a journalist-artist who crossed the line between the two practices with such bravado? There is no single Truth, only the account of what happened, inflected by the creative imagination of the author, and which may recreate a deeper, more authentic truth than that contained in the police documents and court files.

Capote's *In Cold Blood* – what he deliberately called his 'non-fiction novel' – was one of the first examples of a journalism which consciously, and without apology, blurred the traditional dividing lines between fact and fiction. *In Cold Blood* was itself made into a film in the 1960s,[14] and both Capote bio-pics explore the process of researching and writing it, inviting their audiences to reflect on the balance it strikes between reportorial objectivity and personal subjectivity. Both ask the question: is *In Cold Blood* a work of journalistic reportage, or novelistic imagination? Which is the pathway to the greater truth – objective accuracy in reportage, or sensitivity and subjectivity – creativity, in short – in rendering the facts as feelings and emotions to which we can relate and empathise as fellow human beings? Are the two qualities reconcilable within a single text?

Asking these questions in the mainstream movie multiplex in 2005–6, as Miller and McGrath were able to, was the culmination of a long process encompassing almost the entire twentieth century in which liberal capitalist societies gradually came to accept that there was more to journalism than the detachment of the reporter; that 'truth' was a quality not reducible to factual accuracy; that there was a valuable dimension of truth to be gleaned from the application of novelistic techniques to reportage; that the boundaries between fact and fiction were indeed breaking down. Such boundaries were always porous, and scholars have been critiquing the 'myth' of journalistic objectivity for decades,[15] but such was the legitimising power of the concept for journalism as a profession that it could not be fully acknowledged until the end of the century, when the awareness of something loosely called 'postmodernism' or 'cultural relativism' had emerged into public discourse, problematising the notion of Absolute Truth as an entity extractable from reality by the application of appropriate reportorial techniques. By then, capitalist societies had acquired both the vocabulary and the philosophical tools to grasp that the truth of 'what really happened' in a given situation is much more complex and difficult to ascertain than the confident application of something called 'objectivity' might suggest. The dedication of such a quantity of film-making resources to telling the story of a dead American writer and his book about a tragic 1950s murder case reflects the impact of that awareness.

FEAR AND LOATHING

Operating in the same zone of epistemological relativity and generic ambiguity as Truman Capote, but with a very different style and aim, was the inventor of what came to be known as 'gonzo' journalism, Hunter S. Thompson. When Capote published the first instalment of *In Cold Blood* in September 1965, Thompson was a rising twenty-eight-year-old features writer for the *National Observer*. There is nothing in his letters of the time to suggest that Thompson, who was a notoriously macho writer, found anything to like about the effeminate, homosexual Capote, but in their attempts to cross the fact/fiction boundary with a journalism saturated in literary technique they undoubtedly have much in common.

Thompson was a typically frustrated fiction writer of the kind written about by Wolfe in 'The New Journalism'. He regarded his 1962 novel *The Rum Diary*, based on his experiences as a reporter in Puerto Rico, as inferior and hardly worthy of publication, and he was probably right (the novel was eventually published in 1998, by which time anything written by Thompson had acquired a market value). The first volume of his letters, *The Proud Highway* (1997), makes it clear that from an early age his ambitions were novelistic rather than journalistic, and that his model, or hero, was Ernest Hemingway, another journalist who saw fiction as the more worthy form. Where Hemingway successfully made the leap from reporter to novelist, however, Thompson by his own account stumbled on another path to literary greatness, defining his own journalistic sub-genre – gonzo.

Reported by one source to have its roots in Boston bar culture, and referring to the last man standing after a heavy drinking session, the adjective 'gonzo' describes a form of journalism which took the literary elements of the New Journalism identified by Wolfe and embodied in Thompson's 1966 book *Hell's Angels*, and then added something else – not merely authorial presence at the scene of the events being reported; not only active participation in those events (as dramatised by Warren Beatty playing John Reed in *Reds*); but provocation by the reporter of those being observed and reported on. The consequences of this participation-provocation would then be described in prose heavily influenced by alcohol and other drugs, undermining the reliability of the narrator but heightening the descriptive power of the prose and the force of its author's message. Thompson was clearly an angry man in the 1960s and 1970s, as well as a man more or less permanently stoned. His journalism reflected this unapologetic hedonism, as well as the ethos and lifestyle of the youth sub-culture going on around him. His style was transgressive and anti-authority, yet controlled and efficient, spawning countless imitators. To this day, Thompson's florid phrasing and stream of consciousness narration inspires journalism students to attempt emulation, if rarely with the success of the original.

Hanging over Thompson's work is the question: is it journalism, or art? Fact or fiction? Where Wolfe welcomed the emergence of a journalism which used literary devices, and Capote talked about the non-fiction novel as a valid literary form whose time had come, Thompson invited the reader not to worry about such distinctions. There was no such thing as objectivity, in his view, but neither did it matter if his most famous book, *Fear and Loathing in Las Vegas*, was an objective, true account of a weekend spent covering a motorcycle race in the southern desert city, or a series of drug-fuelled impressions recording the end of the American Dream and the onset of the Nixonian nightmare (as Thompson characterised it). Thompson happily drew attention to his own unreliability as a narrator, while insisting that there was some kind of essential truth in his account of events. One *had* to be stoned to understand America and see it for what it was, was his point, or at least to be able to live in it with any dignity. But was the product of this approach journalism, and why would Thompson be so concerned to label it as such?

Figure 22 *Fear and Loathing in Las Vagas* (Terry Gilliam, 1998). Source: BFI

In his foreword to *The Proud Highway* William J. Kennedy describes Thompson as 'a journalistic fictionist' (Thompson, 1997: xvii). The first genuinely 'gonzo' piece, 'The Kentucky Derby is Decadent and Depraved', was where he discovered, as Kennedy puts it, 'that confounding sums of money could be had by writing what seemed to be journalism, while actually you were developing your fictional ouvre'. Thompson created himself as a character in his own writing, and it was never entirely clear if this character was real or imagined. In claiming to be a journalist, however, Thompson also laid claim to the privileged cultural status of factuality.

Terry Gilliam's 1998 film of *Fear and Loathing in Las Vegas* seeks to capture this heightened reality, or sur-reality, by means of special effects and close adherence to Thompson's written text. Johnny Depp and Benicio Del Toro play Thompson (or Raoul Duke) and his 'lawyer' with their usual skill (Depp truly looks the part, and became a genuine friend of Thompson as a result of the production). But something is lost (or so it seems to this writer) in the translation from page to screen, as if by faithfully playing out Thompson's scenes to a late 1990s audience, including the most misogynistic and cruel episodes, the script misses out on the late 1960s/early 1970s context of the original material. Separated from their original time and place by three decades, the satirical force of the transgressions of Duke and his lawyer is blunted.

Fear and Loathing ... is a flawed adaptation of a great book, but stands as a late twentieth-century recognition of the power of Thompson's journalism, and clear evidence of our fascination as a culture with those journalists who boldly stray across the fact-fiction boundary.[16] The success of first the book, and then the film of the book, followed by the ever-expanding industry devoted to excavating Thompson's career which followed his suicide in 2005 signal our readiness to see the world not through the eyes of the objective reporter alone (and gonzo has never replaced conventional journalism, merely challenged its self-proclaimed monopoly on truth) but also through the eyes of the artist in journalist's clothing. Through the unique perspective of the aesthetically gifted, sensitive individual, we approach a truth which the best and most diligent of BBC News or CNN reporters may miss.

By 1975, as Alex Gilbey's documentary shows (*Gonzo*, 2008), Thompson's best work was done, and the rest of his life was spent mainly as a celebrity columnist and then, towards the end, on the effort to make money from his unpublished writings such as *The Rum Diary* and the letters (the latter are essential reading for their awe-inspiring picture of a hugely prolific young writer finding his voice). And why not? His ten years of greatness made him not merely a celebrity journalist, but a legend and icon. Most will agree that he was entitled to make something of that status while he remained alive and in a position to benefit from it. He died in 2005, at his own hands, with a shotgun, in the manner of his literary hero Ernest Hemingway and for broadly the same reasons – alcoholic burn-out, masculine melancholia, fear of growing old.[17]

CONCLUSION

The interest of contemporary film-makers in journalism-as-art (and of documentary-makers in cinema as a journalistic medium) does not signal the end or death of objectivity as a guiding principle of journalism. Far from it. Objectivity – what it means, why it is important, how to go about applying it in one's work – are essential starting points for the twenty-first century journalist. S/he, even more than the journalist of the late nineteenth and twentieth centuries, inhabits an almost infinitely complex media environment, where news is globalised, networked, decentralised; where the boundaries between professional journalist and amateur blogger, social networker or citizen journalist are porous and shifting. This is an environment of exponentially expanded and accelerated information flow, where the provenance of news and thus its reliability and veracity are not always clear. In such an environment quality standards become more important than ever, both as a branding tool for news organisations, and as a guarantee that user-generated content (UGC) and other forms of journalism provided by non-journalists can be relied upon to tell the truth (in so far as there is truth available to be told). In the past journalists sifted and sorted reality, ordering and structuring events in the form of news, making them intelligible to an audience. Today, allegiance to at least the *aspiration* to objectivity permits us all, whether producers or consumers of news and journalism, to sort and sift through the immense quantity of information which circulates on the internet. People may lie about their objectivity, or fake it, as some in the journalistic profession have always done, and it is necessary to maintain vigilance when using the expanded, globalised public sphere as a news source. But in adherence to the concept of objectivity we have at least one criterion by which to measure the quality of information.

What the cinema of journalism-as-art tells us, however, is that while striving after objectivity may be a necessary condition of 'good' journalism, it is not sufficient to guarantee *a* (or *the most*) truthful account of events. The telling of a journalistic, fact-based story, no less than that of a fiction, while founded on observation and accurate reportage of what is observed, may acquire greater truth value when subject to the interpretative, sense-making powers of the observer.

NOTES

1. Wise, Damon, 'Gonzo's back', *Guardian*, 6 December 2008.
2. Kevin Macdonald subsequently directed *State of Play* (2009), about a journalist investigating political corruption, released after this book was completed and thus not available for inclusion in the main narrative. The film, starring Russell Crowe, was adapted from a 2003 UK television production.
3. Hitchens, C., 'The Grub Street years', *Guardian*, 16 June 2007.
4. For an account of *The Printing Revolution in Early Modern Europe* and its impact on the commodification of culture, see Elisabeth Eisenstein's 1983 book. She shows how the development of a reading public in Europe created a demand for literary personality, a cult of the individual author which had not existed before
5. This is the account provided by historians such as Michael Schudson (1978) and Dan Schiller (1981) with specific reference to the United States, where the expansion of the telegraph and the proliferation of news agencies across a vast territory required the development of standards for judging the quality of news – one of these being 'objectivity'.
6. For an essay on a particular episode arising from one of these reviews, when Greene and his publisher were taken to court for alleged libel, see Keeble and Wheller (2008).
7. For a more detailed account of the history of public relations see my *Introduction To Political Communication*, 4th edition (McNair 2007).
8. From Lippmann's *Public Opinion*, pp. 314–15, first published in 1922 (1954).
9. Biskind, Peter, 'Thunder on the left', *Vanity Fair*, March 2006.
10. For a discussion of Marxist-Leninist press theory, and its evolution following the October revolution, see McNair 1991 and Anna Arutunyan's recent *The Media In Russia* (2009).
11. Wolfe argued not only that journalism could have an aesthetic dimension, and could at its best be literature of the highest quality, but that literary journalism had by the late twentieth century replaced the novel as the great 'social realist' form. For Wolfe, the journalistic writing of Breslin and others was doing in the 1960s what the novels of Dickens and others had done in the late nineteenth and early twentieth centuries – documenting and dramatising

the dysfunctional aspects of capitalist social relations, dissecting and commenting upon them in a form accessible to mass readerships, in a popular cultural context. This important function of literature (as Wolfe perceived it) had been abandoned by the self-obsessed navel-gazing of post-war, postmodern literary fiction, leaving the new journalists to carry on the work of writing about lived social reality in a creative but still authentic way. Dickens, Steinbeck, Zola, in Wolfe's view, wrote novels full of documentary detail, often based on personal observation, about subjects that mattered to people. What the new journalists did was not so different in method from great literature, even if it enjoyed nothing like the same status. Perhaps one day it would, Wolfe clearly hoped. Indeed, his own non-fiction books, such as *The Right Stuff* (1979), would contribute substantially to that effort, while his later novels (*The Bonfire of the Vanities* (1987), *A Man In Full* (1998), *I Am Charlotte Simmons* (2004)) were an attempt to reclaim the high ground of social realism from cinema, which had become, as he put it in *Hooking Up* (2000), 'the great naturalistic story-telling medium of the late twentieth century' (160).

    Hooking Up, and the essay 'My Three Stooges' in particular, provides a coda to *The New Journalism*, and brings Wolfe back full circle to the novel. Attacking Norman Mailer, John Updike and John Irving for their 'otherworldly preciousness', in 'My Three Stooges' Wolfe recalls that 'in 1973, while I was still exclusively a writer of non-fiction, fourteen years before I published my first novel, I wrote an essay on what was known then as the "New Journalism". In it, I said that the American novel was in bad shape, but that there was a tremendous future for a sort of novel that will be called the journalistic novel, or perhaps documentary novel, a novel of "intense social realism based upon the same painstaking reporting that goes into the New Journalism"' (2000: 147). Wolfe's three novels to date were written to this brief, and achieved varying degrees of critical and commercial success. A fourth novel, *Back to Blood*, was published in 2009.

12. The film industry is a business, and investors routinely hedge their bets. Production companies hear about this or that project underway at a rival studio, and decide they better have something like it in production, just in case it is a big hit. Just as TV channels engage in competitive scheduling, film production companies do not want to be made to look slow or old-fashioned by the competition. This is why films often come in cycles. The fact that these films were made is worthy of note, however, as the sign of a particular cultural moment, an indication of the extent to which by the early twenty-first century public interest had grown in the subject of journalism-as-art.

13. James, N., 'Capote', *Sight & Sound*, volume 24, number 3.

14. *In Cold Blood* (Richard Brooks, 1967).

15. This is a central theme of academic media and journalism studies from the 1970s, exemplified by the work of the Glasgow University Media Group (1976, 1978), Gaye Tuchman (1972) and Judith Lichtenberg (1991).

16. Thompson's life and work were the subject of an earlier, much less successful film directed by Art Linson and called *Where the Buffalo Roam* (1980). Starring a youthful Bill Murray as Thompson, this film has the ramshackle look and feel of a home movie made by his friends and admirers, all of whom appear to be as stoned as their subject.

17. For a critical take on *Gonzo*, see Cox, David, 'Gonzo and better forgotten', *Guardian*, 22 December 2008 (http://www.guardian.co.uk/film/filmblog/2008/dec/22/hunter-s-thompson-gonzo-and-better-forgotten).

Part III
Villains

CHAPTER 9

Rogues, reptiles and repentant sinners

Journalists are heroes, their watchdog duties inscribed in the founding mythology of liberal democracy. They are also villains, when they fail to perform these duties adequately, or if they disregard or neglect their normative functions as watchdogs and witnesses to become, instead, manipulators of the truth, fabricators of the facts, abusers of the monitoring power which has been bestowed upon them. In this guise journalists are represented in cinema as, at best, lovable rogues; at worst, loathsome reptiles for whom death itself is not too severe a punishment. The chapters in Part III explore examples of each.

At the outset, and as a generalisation, one can say that films in which journalists are represented as heroic tend to be those in which as investigators, watchdogs and witnesses they are seen to challenge power, or to have power challenge them, as they go about their democratically ordained functions of monitoring and surveillance, analysis, critical scrutiny and commentary. These films tend to be critical of power (or more precisely, its abuses), and celebratory of the role of the journalist in facing down that power, be it in the political, economic, or military spheres (or media power, for that matter – as we have seen, journalists such as Lowell Bergman and Ed Murrow have been represented as heroic in their struggle with their own managers and proprietors). Films about journalists as villains, on the other hand, tend to critique the media institutions themselves, and those who work in them, and in particular the popular, 'tabloid' media. In a similar fashion to much scholarly critique of journalism, film-makers tend to equate popular with degenerate, damaging, noteworthy.

At the same time as film-makers attack the news media, they may defend the actions of power elites, or at least attempt to present sympathetically those elites' perspectives on events, and to frame their consequent desire to constrain or control rogue journalists as having validity. Journalists may be accused of subverting legitimate (and very necessary) authority, or of undermining good government. They may be accused of inappropriate or unjustified interference in the private lives of those whom they write about. They may be blamed for damaging society itself, of degrading, dumbing down or otherwise corroding the cultural life in which they play so central a role by flooding it with sleaze and infotainment. Where journalists are represented as the villains of the piece, movies become the watchdogs of the watchdogs, a third tier of critical scrutiny overseeing both the fourth estate and those institutions and individuals which the fourth estate is charged with overseeing.

There is an important difference between the two modes of scrutiny, of course. In contrast to the practitioners of liberal journalism movie-makers are not bound by objectivity and the professional rules designed to ensure journalistic authority by mobilising consent around perceptions of reliability, accuracy, honesty and integrity. The media critiques constructed by film-makers appeal to their audiences by reference to other criteria – aesthetic and stylistic innovation, the application of personal judgement (legitimised because of the recognised creative status of the author responsible), and the mobilisation of story-telling techniques and resources which, when all are put together to make a finished film, might win over audiences and capture the *zeitgeist* in a way which gives them resonance beyond the cinema. Where journalism in its normative mode avoids emotion and polemic in favour of detachment and seriousness of tone (a style echoed in classics of heroic representation such as *All the President's Men* and *Good Night, and Good Luck*), the film-maker concerned to represent journalistic villainy is more likely to dramatise and exaggerate for effect, to play to the gallery with the crudest of stereotypes and caricatures.

Many such films (Sydney Lumet's *Network* comes to mind [1976]) are satirical in tone, and thus licensed to go over the top in pursuit of their point. This has led to some ripe portrayals down the years, and satires such as *Natural Born Killers* and *Rag Trade* have been harshly criticised for their lack of believability, which probably misses the point of satire. On the other hand, some of the very best movies ever made about journalism have been those which portray the most villainous characteristics of the profession in bold, primary colours. Nor should this be surprising. Heroes, if truth be told, can be dull and boring, and villains much more interesting both for actors to play and audiences to watch. The most appealing characters in movies, including movies about journalism, are often those which combine heroism and villainy –Walter Burns in *His Girl Friday*, for example. Nicole Kidman's performance in *To Die For* – the most irredeemably loathsome of all the characters she has ever played – is regularly cited as one of her best. Likewise, Kirk Douglas in *Ace in the Hole* and Burt Lancaster in *Sweet Smell of Success* are cast-against-type villains whose performances drive classic movies of the journalism genre. We love to hate them.

Movies, then, in their function as meta-media engaged in the construction of regulatory and legitimatory myth, are not merely celebratory of journalism at its idealised best, but interrogative and critical of the journalist's flaws and failings. This reflects the duality of journalists' oscillating social contribution as either heroes or villains.

HEROES OR VILLAINS? JOURNALISTS ON SCREEN, 1997–2008

In a 2008 piece for the *Guardian* Stephen Armstrong observed that 'recently, the screen seems to have fallen out of love with the [journalism] trade'.[1] I disputed this assertion in a letter to the same newspaper published a week later,[2] citing *A Mighty Heart* and *Good Night, and Good Luck* as recent examples of journalists being portrayed as heroes. Are they typical, however, of the journalism movies released in the period 1997–2008? As we saw in Chapter 4 the majority of those films portrayed the journalist as, in general terms, heroic. But there were villains aplenty, as there have been throughout cinema history. These representations can be grouped into three categories:

- The lovable rogue.

In this category the villainy is of the kind we can live with, may indeed be attracted to; the charming fellow (and such villains are usually men) who is, with the best will in the world, not to be trusted; the cad, or 'bad boy' whom women love, but would never dream of marrying. He is often played by the leading men of the time – Clark Gable, Cary Grant, Richard Gere, George Clooney.

- The reptile.

This is the figure with few, if any redeeming qualities, who embodies without apology or hesitation the very worst of what journalism can be in a market-driven media culture. He or she (and there are some memorable female reptiles in cinema) is wholly loathsome.

- The repentant sinner (or reformed rogue).

This is the category of celluloid hack who knows that he or she is violating the normative principles of liberal journalism, for whatever reason (usually professional advancement) and feels guilty about it. Such a representation will tend to involve a struggle between heroism and villainy, or between good and evil – between the conscience of the journalist and the pragmatic realities within which he or she works.

THE LOVABLE ROGUE – FROM *HIS GIRL FRIDAY* TO *RUNAWAY BRIDE*

There is a long and honourable tradition of films about journalism which have featured what I will characterise as the lovable rogue – the figure who displays many of the characteristics of journalism which we love to hate, such as lack of trustworthiness, but who is nevertheless a sympathetic, even sexy character. The lovable rogue is nearly always played by a leading actor of his time (and the sub-genre is very much a male-defined form). The lovable rogue is glamorous and sexy, his sexiness enhanced by a hint (or more than a hint) of naughtiness. In films about journalism the rogue tends to appear in romantic comedies, opposite a leading Hollywood lady, often one who has herself played a journalist such as Rosalind Russell, Michelle Pfeiffer or Julia Roberts.

Lovable rogues tend to play it for laughs, then, but with an element of sexual tension as the stars duel with each other, and a sometimes sophisticated engagement with the ethical issues raised by roguish behaviour. *His Girl Friday*, starring Cary Grant, is the paradigm case. Chapter 7 discussed Rosalind Russell's performance as Hildy Johnson in this film, noting the strength of her character and its significance in the history of films about female journalists. Cary Grant's Walter Burns is also an iconic portrayal, exemplifying a type

Figure 23 *His Girl Friday* (Howard Hawks, 1940). Source BFI

which is at the same time both admirable and despicable. We know we are supposed to disapprove of Walter's populist news values, and the ruthlessness with which he pursues his journalistic goals, but we cannot help but love the way he goes about it, wise-cracking, chain-smoking, undermining his rival for Hildy's heart (and her time – Walter, as her ex-husband, may want to sleep with Hildy, but he also wants to re-acquire her services on his newspaper). Walter engineers the fiancé's arrest on a false shop-lifting charge, and engages in merciless verbal humiliation of the hapless Bruce, who in the end must retreat to Albany without his bride-to-be.

On its re-release in 1997 Laura Mulvey noted that *His Girl Friday* was the Howard Hawks' film in which 'everything seems to work as it should',[3] fast-moving dialogue in perfect harmony with visuals, and 'in which the reporters provide a chorus to ongoing speech and action'. An exemplary scene is that in which Walter takes Hildy and Bruce to lunch, all innocence and profes-sionalism, only to make clear his contempt both for insurance salesman Bruce and Hildy's marriage plans, albeit in a manner which exudes charm and sexual energy. As the cigarettes are lit and the lunchtime martinis are ordered (this film, like so many movies about journalism in the monochrome era, looks today like pornography for nicotine addicts), we watch Walter work his roguish magic.

Walter: Well, well, well, so you two are gonna get married, huh? How does it feel, Bruce?

Bruce: It feels awful good, yes sir.

Walter: You're getting a great little girl for yourself.

Bruce: I realise that. Things have been different for me ever since I first met Hildy. Everybody else I've ever known, you could always tell ahead of time what they were gonna say or do. Hildy's not like that. You can't tell that about Hildy, and that's nice.

Walter: Well, you're getting something else too, Bruce. You're getting a great newspaperman, one of the best I ever knew. Sorry to see her go, darned sorry, Hildy.

Hildy: I'd like to believe you meant that.

Walter: I do mean it. Listen, If you ever want to come back to the newspaper business ...

Hildy: Which I won't. In spite of everything, if I ever do, there's only one man I'd work for.

Walter: You bet your life. I'd kill you if you ever worked for anyone else.

Hildy: Now you hear that Bruce? That's my diploma.

Bruce: It must be quite a business if ... Hildy, are you sure you want to quit?

Hildy: Now Bruce, what do you mean?

Bruce: Well I mean, if there's any doubt about it, if there's anything ...
No, this is your chance to have a home and to be, like you said, a human
being, and I'm going to make you take that chance.

Walter: Certainly. Why, I wouldn't let her stay. No, she deserves all this
happiness Bruce, all the things I couldn't give her. Yeah, all she ever
wanted was a home.

Bruce: Well I'll certainly try to give her one.

Walter: I know you will, Bruce. Where you gonna live?

Bruce: Albany.

Walter: Albany, huh? You get a family up there, then?

Bruce: Just my mother.

Walter: Oh, you're gonna live with your mother?

Bruce: Well, just for the first year.

Walter: That will be nice. A home with mother, in Albany too.

Throughout this exchange Walter's demeanour portrays his view that he can
think of no better definition of a living hell for his ex-wife than 'a home with
mother in Albany'. His roguish qualities are also reflected in his attitude to his
journalism. At one point Hildy says to Walter, 'You'd hang your own mother
for a scoop', and she isn't joking.

The moral ambivalence represented by the lovable rogue reflects public
attitudes, past and present, to the field of popular journalism from which they
are usually drawn. *His Girl Friday* was adapted from stage play *The Front Page*,
written by former journalists Ben Hecht and Charles MacArthur and first
produced in 1928 as a satirical take on the then-ascendant popular press and
its excesses. Nearly a century ago, when the 'tabloids' were still a relatively new
phenomenon, *The Front Page* interrogated their unethical news values, but
with a nod to the fact that such values were driven by an apparently insatiable
public taste for the lurid and the sensational. People were entertained by the
popular media, morbidly attracted to tales of scandal and excess even when
they knew that, really, they should not be. Thus, pleasure was tinged with guilt.
Walter Burns in *His Girl Friday* exemplifies this tension – he is a rogue, yes,
prepared to make the most appalling ethical compromises to maximise sales
of his newspaper in a market hungry for drama. But there is a bit of all of
us which cannot resist the kinds of stories popular newspapers deal in. And
without us, after all, the readers, such journalism would not exist.

The lovable rogue, then, is not a truly bad or evil figure. Rather, he represents the often absurd distortions of normative journalistic values generated by
a popular market place of readers who cannot get enough of the stuff. He has
redeeming features and a capacity for good which, as played by these leading
men of the movie business, tends to come through before the final credits roll.
George Clooney's columnist in *One Fine Day* (Michael Hoffmann, 1996),

Jack Taylor, presents a more recent example of the type, with his less than reliable performance of parental responsibilities and general self-centredness morphing by the end of the film into a more considerate, family-oriented figure.

Runaway Bride (Gary Marshall, 1999) stars Richard Gere in the lovable rogue role, opposite Julia Roberts as a woman, Maggie Carpenter, who repeatedly jilts her fiancés at the altar. Gere as columnist Ike Hoffmann specialises in provocative attacks on women – he admits to a penchant for writing 'inner diatribes at the opposite sex' – and writes a column labelling Maggie the 'runaway bride'. His writing is lazily inaccurate, however, and Maggie complains to his editor (and ex-wife), who dismisses him on ethical grounds. 'Journalism lesson number one', she tells him as he is canned, 'if you fabricate the facts, you get fired'. Ike then travels incognito to Maggie's town in order to prepare a devastating, fact-based exposé of her character that will redeem him in his editor's eyes. Instead, he begins to fall in love with her, and thus to question the ethics of a journalism which depends so much for its raw material on the violation of another's personal privacy.

As with other films in this sub-genre, the main marketing attraction of the film is the romantic interaction of its two A-list movie stars. Gere and Roberts had performed opposite each other in the huge 1990 hit, *Pretty Woman* (also directed by Gary Marshall) and *Runaway Bride* was a transparent attempt to repeat that success (and just about did so, making $309 million at the global box office). The plot device (reportedly based on an actual incident) of creating conditions where a journalist is brought into close contact with the victim of one of his dashed-off pieces is in the first instance precisely that – a device which exploits the licence of journalism to invade the lives of others, and allows us to criticise those who abuse that licence. In terms of our classification it is a secondary representation, and much less focused on the practice of journalism than, say, *His Girl Friday* (where journalism is primary – one of the reasons why it can be regarded as a classic of the journalism genre). However, and in keeping with many rom coms and other genres in which journalism has formed the backdrop or stage for the action but is not the narrative centre of the piece, the script of *Runaway Bride* does address in an insightful manner the ethical questions raised by Ike's polemical brand of journalism and invites its audience to reflect on them, if in a viewing context which is above all about entertainment and romance.

Our relationship to the lovable rogue is, then, like our relationship to the popular media in general: ambivalent. We are attracted to him, as to the racy headlines of the *Sun* or the *New York Post*, with the feelings of guilt associated with the consumption of any forbidden fruit. We know it is a little unseemly to read about the latest misadventures of Britney Spears or other celebrities, or to know the gory details of a grisly murder case or a motorway pile-up, but it is hard to resist when the stories are lying there on the news stand, headlines and photographs demanding our attention. The lovable rogue represents in human form that dimension of journalism which we both love and hate. He embodies that promise of naughtiness and transgression which is at the root of much human desire, and which so frequently gives him the mystique of a sex symbol.

THE REPTILE

The lovable rogue is entertaining, but perhaps the most fun, and mischief, which movie-makers have with journalism is when they enter the territory of the tabloid reptile: the repulsive, loathsome hack with few, if any redeeming features; the figure conjured up by Hunter Thompson in Chapter Two, and by Ralph Steadman in the scary sketches which illustrated Thompson's books and articles (lizards, literally, reproduced to some effect in Terry Gilliam's adaptation of *Fear and Loathing* ...). If the lovable rogue is the kind of cultural transgressor with whom we may feel some affinity, since deep down we all have a guilty fascination with the kinds of story he deals in (even if we may not admit it), and who can therefore be played by a handsome star such as Cary Grant or Richard Gere, the reptile is a true villain. His (and occasionally her) function is to embody the very worst that journalism can be in a commercialised media system, and to appall us with its excesses.

The representation of the journalist-as-reptile may be viewed both as a warning to the public in a democracy that their media are at worst akin to predators running wild, and that they – the public – bear some responsibility for putting them back in their cage; and also as a form of vengeance waged by one sector of the culture industry against another found wanting. In a few cases, such as *Paparazzi*, directed by Paul Abascal in 2004 (and given limited cinema release in the UK in January 2005), the vengeance may be more personal. Produced by Mel Gibson, who has the briefest of cameos in it, the film was reviewed on its release as a self-indulgent vanity project, allowing Gibson to articulate his wrath at the celebrity media who have dogged his career. According to one reviewer, observing the Diana-inspired plot in which a wronged celebrity wreaks vengeance on the journalistic scum responsible for his unhappiness, the film is 'sadistic in the extreme and lacking any moral compass. It's the kind of film only OJ Simpson would enjoy'.[4] Another noted that, while the actions of some celebrity photographers are surely worthy of condemnation, '*Paparazzi*'s vilification of the profession is so over-the-top you can't take any of its objections seriously ... Is executive producer Mel Gibson, who has famously had "issues" with the media's coverage of his private life ... using the film to work through his own anger about press intrusion?'.[5]

Quite possibly. Central character Bo Laramie becomes involved in a feud with a group of four paparazzi photographers, led by the evil Rex. The script is peppered with sarcastic digs at the tabloid media, such as the scene where Vince Vaughan (in another blink-and-you-missed-it cameo), playing an actor alongside Bo in one of his action movies, says with heavy irony:

> Says here [holding up the front page of a supermarket tabloid] – this came out in England so it must be true – 'Unnamed sources say Laramie took a private jet to Switzerland, where the young star reportedly went for a penile enhancement, surprising his wife on her birthday'.

The newspaper headline visible on screen reads: 'Laramie underwent penile enhancement'. Lead reptile Rex, defending his profession to a girl he meets in a bar, says:

> *Rex:* I'm a photojournalist.
> *Girl:* Your pictures hurt people.
> *Rex:* Do they? The irony is, everybody wants to have steak, but nobody wants to date the butcher. My job is to provide a window on reality for society. It's up to them whether they want to look through it or not? You never bought a tabloid?

We the public, he suggests, are as much responsible for the villainous excesses of the paparazzi as the journalists. This is a valid point, well made, but it is undermined in the rest of the film by reducing the celebrity-paparazzi battle to a Good versus Evil melodrama. So angry is the script with its journalistic subjects that Laramie is allowed to kill three paparazzi and get away with it. The satire is crude and clumsy, and nowhere near as effective as in the UK-made *Rag Tale* (see below).

PAPARAZZI, AND A NOTE ON CELEBRITY JOURNALISM

The term 'paparazzi' was coined by Federico Fellini in his 1958 film, *La Dolce Vita* (not released until 1960), now regarded as a classic of the journalism movie genre. His character, Joe Paparazzo, is a photojournalist who spends his days snapping the celebrities who hang around Roma's Via Veneto and other locations. Joe was based on an actual person, Tazio Secchiaroli. *La Dolce Vita* was not widely acclaimed on its release. It became a recognised classic, however, as the *Guardian* explained in an editorial to mark the fiftieth anniversary of the film (itself a rare accolade for a piece of cinema, no matter how exalted): 'Fifty years on, *La Dolce Vita*'s preoccupation with celebrity, sex and hedonism seems a presciently modern cultural turning point'.[6] As the popular media became more demanding, and the numbers of paparazzi grew to service them, late twentieth-century capitalist societies saw the growth in their midst of a 'celebrity culture' distinct from the way in which celebrity was constructed and reported in pre-Warhol, pre-Fellini times. There was always celebrity, of course, and one of the pleasures of Amanda Foreman's volume of popular history on *Georgiana, Duchess of Devonshire* (made into a film starring Keira Knightley in 2008) is its revelation that even in the late eighteenth century there was a form of celebrity journalist active in London, obsessively and often irreverently reporting the doings of aristocrats and other famous people. At this time coverage of the rich and famous, though satirical and often scurrilous, functioned as a form of politicised critical scrutiny, drawing the common people's attention to aristocratic excess and the elite abuse of early democratic processes. In England, and in France, as John Hartley has noted (1996), this journalism of sensation and scandal (which often crossed into the realm of the pornographic), by demystifying and exposing the human flaws and weaknesses of the landed gentry made an important contribution to the erosion of feudal class distinctions and the emergence of democratic societies.

It is safe to say that contemporary celebrity journalism is rarely motivated by such lofty goals, and is seen as a damaging rather than democratising force by most commentators, including most movie-makers. The argument, in simple terms, is that journalists construct celebrity as a commercial instrument for selling newspapers (or TV programmes and now websites), paying no regard to the attributes held by a person which might justify their elevation. Fame is an arbitrary quality, awarded to people for any number of reasons apart from the fact that they are talented in some field of human endeavour. Fame is a machine for generating stories in popular media, devoid of substance and authenticity.

In the 1990s and since, the artificiality and emptiness of celebrity has been accentuated by the rise of reality TV. With the explosion of docu-soaps and fly-on-the-wall documentary strands in the 1990s, then of competitive reality TV shows such as *Big Brother* and *Survivor* in the 2000s, the notion that anyone, literally, can become famous and rich has never been more prevalent. The celebration of ordinariness has become ubiquitous, and celebrity culture banal (where it used to be glamorous and exciting). Moreover, celebrity journalism is increasingly packed with coverage of reality TV stars falling drunk out of night clubs and showing their knickers. People with real talent have been squeezed out of celebrity culture by the media's fascination with ordinariness. This phenomenon reached its peak, the critics argue, with the media circus which surrounded the Big Brother-fuelled career and untimely death of Jade Goody in March 2009.

There is a counter-argument that these trends represent a democratisation

Figure 24 *La Dolce Vita* (Federico Fellini, 1960). Source: BFI

of capitalist culture appropriate to the times we live in; that by celebrating ordinariness, reality TV and the forms of journalism which feed off it, no doubt parasitically at times, subvert the once-powerful monopoly on what constitutes talent once exercised by the self-appointed taste dictators of the arts and entertainment industry. Celebrity was never much more than a media construction anyway, and has today become much more accessible to many more people than ever before. Those who believe that they have some special talent dispute the worth of these ordinary celebrities, of course, but from the cultural democratisation perspective Jade Goody and Katie Price (Jordan, mainly famous for the size of her breasts, and her willingness to display them in public) have just as much popular relevance as more obviously 'talented' individuals. Reality culture, and contemporary celebrity journalism, celebrate ordinariness in a manner which accentuates the value of everyday human experience. They reject the social deference of the past, which was routinely extended to the kind of bored, vacuous rich kids depicted in *La Dolce Vita*.

Among those films which explore celebrity culture Woody Allen's *Celebrity* (1998) is a little-seen meditation on its artificiality, and the complicity of the media in fuelling the seemingly endless succession of relatively talent-free individuals who become famous (and rich). *Celebrity* was a commercial and critical failure, and failed even to get a cinema release in many markets (like Allen's *Scoop*, made in 2005). *Celebrity* illustrates an interesting feature of movies about celebrity journalism – they are rarely very good, at least in the eyes of the majority of film critics. *Celebrity*'s failings were linked by some reviewers with Allen's own negative opinions of celebrity journalism (and the scandalous coverage he received of his affair with the adopted child of his then-partner Mia Farrow, Soon Yi, in particular), as if he had allowed personal prejudice to drive his take on the subject.

A similar critical fate befell Mary McGuckian's *Rag Tale* (2005), a satire about red-top journalism in the UK, which is heavily dependent on celebrity culture for its daily diet of coked-up starlets and dysfunctional footballers' wives. Dismissed on its release by one newspaper as 'an unbelievable tale of tabloid hell', full of clichés and unrealistic stereotypes such as the notion that 'journalists are often drunk and sometimes dishonest',[7] *Guardian* film reviewer Peter Bradshaw called it 'a boring mess' and 'intelligence-insulting nonsense'.[8] Critic Philip French saw 'a satirical farce presenting the staff of a British tabloid as drunken, lecherous, treacherous, foul-mouthed, unprincipled, vindictive, coke-snorting hacks'.[9] Gritty realism, then, if let down by hyper-active cinematography of the type briefly fashionable in the early to mid-2000s.

Like *Celebrity*, which boasted a cast list to make any Hollywood producer weep with envy, *Rag Tale* boasted a very distinguished cast of British and American actors (Jennifer Jason Leigh, Malcolm McDowell, John Sessions, David Hayman and others). I am less critical of the film than most reviewers, seeing both entertainment and education in its fast-moving script, its evocation of the paranoia of a news room in crisis, and the macho thuggishness of its editorial meetings. *Rag Tale* is merciless in dissecting the commercial logic of celebrity culture, and of tabloid newspaper culture more widely, the hypocrisy of many of those who condemn it, and the woefully ignorant state of the people who buy it. I am rather alone in this view, however, which may stand as an example of the fact not only that good films about tabloids and celebrity culture are indeed difficult to find, but even more difficult for newspaper film critics to swallow. Too often (though not, I suggest, in the case of *Rag Tale*) the satire is lazy and self-satisfied, crafted by individuals who take for granted the superiority of their own talent and cannot understand why that of others should be celebrated. Let me turn, then, to four films which are more highly regarded, and which exemplify the journalist-as-reptile sub-type: *Ace in the Hole*, directed by Billy Wilder in 1951 and known in the United States as *The Big Carnival*; *Mad City* (Costa-Gavras, 1998); *To Die For* (Gus Van Zant, 1995); and *Natural Born Killers*, Oliver Stone's 1994 study of the relationship between crime and the media in the United States. All are satires, with strong critical messages about how the media relate to public perception of crime and deviance. In all of them, reptilian journalists meet grisly ends.

ACE IN THE HOLE

The power of Billy Wilder's 1951 film, from this distance, lies not only in its piercing critique of popular journalism's propensity to manufacture problematic reality rather than report it, but in its resonance for and relevance to our own twenty-first century times. The film tells an appalling story of journalistic cynicism, but with hindsight it is one which could have been told in any decade, in just about any country in the years since it was made.

Figure 25 *Ace in the Hole* (Billy Wilder, 1951). Source: BFI

The film stars Kirk Douglas as Chuck Tatum, a down-on-his-luck journalist whose car has broken down and who is stranded in the desert town of Albuquerque, New Mexico as the story gets going. Tatum has been used to working on the big East Coast newspapers, and is dismissive of local journalism (a common trope of journalism movies). Out of necessity he talks himself into a job at the *Albuquerque Sun-Bulletin*, introducing himself to the editor in the following terms.

> I'm a $250 newspaperman. I can be had for fifty. I know newspapers backward, forward and sideways. I can write 'em, edit 'em, print 'em and sell 'em. I can do big news and little news, and if there's no news I'll go out and bite a dog.

After a year or so of covering boring local non-stories (as he views them), assisted by young photographer Herbie, he is desperate for 'something big' that will propel him back to the top of his profession. He stumbles on an accident in the desert. A man – Leo Minosa – is trapped down a cave, and Tatum begins the process of turning what should be an easily remedied inconvenience into a major news event. Seen from today's vantage point, the film is exhilerating in its echoing of contemporary debates (a feature it shares with *His Girl Friday*). Everything we thought we knew about the flaws of late twentieth/early twenty-first-century popular journalism (what used to be called 'tabloid' journalism, before most newspapers adopted the tabloid print format) is exposed here. As Tatum and Herbie head in their open-top automobile for a story about rattle-snakes being smoked out from the desert underbrush, Tatum articulates the cynicism which drives his end of the journalism business.

> *Herbie:* You know, this could be quite a big story, Chuck. Don't sell it short.
> *Tatum:* Big deal. A thousand rattlers in the underbrush. Give me just fifty of them loose in Albuquerque … a whole town in panic, deserted streets, barricaded houses, they're evacuating the children. Every man is armed. Fifty killers on the prowl. Fifty! One by one they start hunting them down. They get ten, twenty, it's building. Forty, forty five, they get forty-nine. Where's the last rattler? In the kindergarten, in the church, in a crowded elevator? Where?
> *Herbie:* I give up. Where?
> *Tatum:* In my desk drawer, fan, stashed away only nobody knows it, see? The story's good for anther three days and then when I'm good and ready we come out with a big extra. *Sun-Bulletin* snags number fifty.
> *Herbie:* Where do you get those ideas?

This approach to journalism – the readiness to manipulate reality in pursuit of the bad news story – will now be applied to the rescue of the trapped Leo. We quickly learn that he could be rescued quickly and easily. Tatum, however, senses a story in Leo's predicament, possibly a Pulitzer prize, and proceeds to turn the incident into a media circus involving the corrupt local sheriff, Leo's equally corrupt wife (with whom Tatum has a fling), the East Coast media and then the great American public who begin to treat the incident like a carnival (hence the US title of the film – *The Big Carnival*). A theme tune is written, souvenir stalls are set up, train and car loads of tourists arrive, lots of money is made. To achieve this degree of newsworthiness, however, Tatum allows Leo to remain trapped underground for a week, even after he is warned of the risks. When it becomes clear that Leo is dying, the journalist has a brief moment of conscience, but it is too late. Leo dies, and the media circus evaporates. In the final act Leo's wife shoots Tatum and he falls dead in the offices of the *Albuquerque Sun-Bulletin*. Moral order is restored as the journalist who has sacrificed a life to his greed loses his own.

The film is successful both as satire and as tense, noir-ish drama, and embedded in the script are frequent monologues by Tatum on the nature of news. At one point, he explains to Herbie the nature and appeal of human interest.

> One man's better than eighty four. Didn't they teach you that [at journalism school, the idea of which Chuck despises]? Human interest. You pick up the paper and read about eighty-four men, or 284, or a million men like in a Chinese famine. You read it but it doesn't stay with you. One man's different. You wanna read all about it. That's human interest. Somebody all by himself like Lindbergh crossing the Atlantic ...

Wilder's script is merciless in portraying the very worst of liberal journalism, and is hardly more forgiving of the public who make such excesses possible and profitable. In one of the most memorable sequences we see a train pulling in to a railway stop near the cave. The doors open, and a wave of excited humanity exits the train and runs towards the crowd. Leo's theme tune is playing, the burgers and candy floss are selling like hot cakes, and we are left in no doubt of Wilder's view that the reptilian journalist is our creation (the public's) as much as that of a media so commercialised that it has lost all moral sense. In the decades since this fictional episode there have been many similar real-life incidents, in which tragedy has become entertainment for newspapers and their readers. There have also been other movies presenting similar scenarios, such as *Mad City* (Costa-Gavras, 1998).

Costa-Gavras' film, though a minor work of cinema, presents an interesting contrast with *Ace in the Hole*. Both films suggest that the demands of the news media for a good story (meaning one that will attract and build an audience in a competitive media market place) take precedence over the innocent victims who have been caught up in a tragically newsworthy situation. In *Ace in the Hole*, as we saw, Chuck Tatum's greed for a story leads directly to Leo's death deep in the cave. Chuck is little better than a murderer, and pays for his crime with his own death. In *Mad City* Dustin Hoffman plays a TV news reporter who by coincidence becomes involved in a hostage situation inside a public library. The hostage-taker, played by John Travolta, is mentally ill rather than evil, and as the story unfolds there are opportunities for him to be talked out of the building and the crisis defused. Already inside, however, Hoffmann's character spots the opportunity for a scoop, and gets his producers involved. From this point on the situation is driven by the needs of the media rather than the hostages. He gets his story, played out on live TV news across the nation, but Travolta's character pays for it with his life.

Unlike Wilder's film, Hoffmann comes to see the error of his ways and tries to redeem himself by saving the hostage-taker from being shot down – he is a repentant sinner (see below). Where Wilder is unforgiving in the punishment he metes out to the reptilian Tatum, Costa-Gavras gives us a more conventional Hollywood resolution, and one which does not require the death of the journalist in question. In contrast to Chuck Tatum in *Ace in the Hole* Hoffman's character is much more aware of the ethical transgression in which he is taking part, and ambivalent about the use made of the story both by himself and his employers at the news station. Forty years after Wilder's film the journalist, like his public, is much more troubled by the realisation of how news works, of what news is.

NATURAL BORN KILLERS

Closer to Wilder's bleak vision, if very different in plot and tone, is Oliver Stone's *Natural Born Killers* (1994), a film which was widely condemned on its release for its portrayal of violence but can now be recognised as a perceptive and principled satire about celebrity culture and the corrupt relationship between crime and the media in the United States (the film has an American focus but its themes are highly relevant to comparable countries like the UK).

In a manner which recalls Terence Mallick's *Badlands* (1973), *Natural Born Killers* has two young outcasts from superficially stable families go on a killing rampage through America, growing steadily more notorious as they go. Stone enlists our sympathy for Mickey and Mallory (Woody Harrelson, Juliette Lewis) by alluding to her history of sexual abuse (in early scenes shot to look like a TV sit com we see Mallory being groped lasciviously by her father, and we can imagine the rest), and Mickey's rejection by the same father, prompting the first of the many murders which drive the narrative. In this way we are shown that, senseless and cruel as most of the subsequent killings will be, there is context and causality behind them.

Stone's romantic treatment of the killers provoked huge controversy on the film's release, and *Natural Born Killers* became a key piece of evidence for the prosecution in the case against violence in mainstream cinema. Stone's aim, however, is to make the media complicit in the morbid fascination with which the killers come to be held by the US public. First, there is the frequent reference to news coverage of their nihilistic road trip across America, an exaggerated if highly plausible recreation of how many actual cases have been reported. Disapproval and moral panic blends with the media's need to highlight the grim and gory details as the killers become media celebrities.

Then they are caught, and the satire grows even more savage. The presenter of a TV true crime show, Wayne Gale (played by Robert Downey Jr in the period before his re-emergence as one of America's most highly-regarded actors – see his role as a less villainous journalist in David Fincher's *Zodiac*), enters the high security prison where Mickey and Mallory are being held, and persuades the authorities to grant him a live interview with Mickey. The episode expertly pastiches the fascination of contemporary TV audiences with liveness, and the way in which producers manipulate their viewers' sympathies. Murderous Mickey, by now beyond reason or redemption, is constructed on the show as a hero, and the TV audience encouraged to root for him as a victim of the system rather than a cold-blooded killer of innocent people. Downey Jr's character is a cartoonish figure, utterly lacking in positive qualities, and prepared to unleash chaos in pursuit of his ratings. When, during the interview and thus live on TV, Mickey breaks free and sparks off a bloody prison riot, Downey Jr and his crew follow and film the escaping convicts as they kill and wound their guards, delighting in the televisual spectacle they have managed to create.

Natural Born Killers shares with *Ace in the Hole* an appalled interest in the fact – as true in the 1990s as it was in the 1950s – that there are journalists who do not merely report events. They will influence them, manipulate them, sometimes even manufacture them in pursuit of the story and without regard for the human cost. Chuck Tatum causes the death of Leo Minosa. Gale, by his recklessness and irresponsibility in setting up a live interview with a psychopathic killer, and then encouraging him in his anger and self-victimhood, causes a riot and many deaths, all of it available to his audience in real time. This is what his form of tabloid TV journalism demands, and what his audience are entranced by. Unlike Chuck Tatum, however, there is to the end no hint of remorse by this hack, and it is left to the film-maker to dispense justice to someone who is a truly sinister, amoral individual. In the final scenes Mickey and Mallory are re-united and preparing to head off down the road together.

Downey Jr's journalist pleads with them to let him accompany them, so that he can record the next act in their drama and continue to make folk heroes of them. Instead, Mickey coldly and without hesitation executes the journalist, with whom we are encouraged to feel no sympathy. His death is wholly deserved. His journalistic crimes are even more reprehensible than those of the killers whom he has helped elevate to celebrity status. They, indeed, drive off into the sunset and a life of implied domestic bliss, to the sound of Leonard Cohen's 'The Future'.[10]

HACKESSES

Screen journalists of such undiluted villainy as Tatum and Wayne Gale are nearly always men. Indeed, I can think of only one female who comes close to those excesses in her pursuit of professional success – Suzanne Stone (Nicole Kidman) in Gus Van Sant's *To Die For*. The paucity of female baddies reflects the gender balance of good and evil in other movie genres, and probably too in the journalistic profession. As we saw earlier, women have historically been under-represented in the profession. They have, as a consequence, fewer opportunities for badness.

This fact – that women in journalism have not been regarded as the equals of men by their male counterparts, and have been pushed into 'women's issues' and required to use their preferably beautiful bodies as much as their journalistic talents to advance their careers – is the main justification presented by Van Sant for Suzanne Stone's numerous transgressions as she seeks to make her way in TV. The world she wishes to succeed in is very much a man's world, and we do not blame her for using her feminine charms as an aid to making her way in it. She goes too far, however, engineering the murder of her own husband (because she believes that he is a hindrance to her career) and manipulating a group of vulnerable young people into assisting her ruthless rise to the top. In the end, since her husband's family are Italian Americans with connections, she is assassinated by the mafia.

Suzanne, like Downey Jr's character in *Natural Born Killers*, is a caricature, a cartoon character in a satire with no pretensions to realism. Her dramatic function is to suggest that the evil she represents is the product of the media environment we today inhabit, an environment in which everyone is encouraged to believe that they too can be famous, they too can be on TV. Suzanne's methods are extreme, but her ambitions are routine.

THE REPENTANT SINNER

There is a category of movie which deals with the critical self-reflection of the journalist who one day discovers that he or she can no longer live with him or herself. This is the theme of Stephen Frear's *Accidental Hero* (1992), starring Geena Davis as TV news reporter Gayle Gayley, who comes to question the news values she works by, and who then recants and reforms, thereby re-asserting the normative principles which every journalism student is taught to revere.

At the centre of the film is the metaphor of the news story as an onion, comprising multiple layers which are peeled back to reveal ... what? The artificiality and constructedness of news, and of celebrity culture in particular, are treated here with a sophistication not seen since *Ace in the Hole*. Although the plots of both films are very different, the target of their satire is the same – the readiness of market-driven news media to manufacture and narrativise the problematic realities which they will then present to their audiences as objective news. In *Ace in the Hole* Chuck Tatum manufactures a prolonged and tense rescue situation, heightening the drama in order to maximise the newsworthiness and saleability of his story. In *Accidental Hero* Gayle and her employers manufacture dramatic coverage of a rescue from a crashed airplane, endowing the wrong person with heroic qualities which then become the basis of a false and corrupt media celebrity. Both films expose the ethical flaws of such journalism, and invite the media to reflect on their complicity in such manipulation.

Gayley is returning from an awards ceremony where she has been honoured for her reportorial work – in particular, her live on-the-scene coverage of a man's suicide after being exposed in the media – and her flight comes down in the city. Immediately before this scene we hear her deliver an acceptance speech in which she dissects with rare economy the manufactured nature of the modern news story.

This is an onion [holds up an onion, and begins peeling it, eyes watering as she proceeds]. It's a metaphor for a news story. Only a few hours ago I was sitting on a ledge, sixteen stories above the street, interviewing a man who subsequently jumped to his death. $40 million in the bank, happily married, good health, great story.

But there's gotta be more. I mean, we're pros, right? Extramarital hanky panky, maybe? [continues peeling] another great story. Maybe the guy's been accused of child molesting? Terrific story.

What? Turns out the accusations were false? Wonderful, more story. Maybe the alleged mistress was lying, setting the guy up, huh? Sensational story.

So we keep going, keep digging, expose the guy's family, his whole life. Why? Because we're pros. Because we're looking for the truth. What if it turns out, for all our digging, for all our painstaking investigation, what if it turns out there wasn't any truth? Just stories. One story after another, layer after layer, until there's nothing left, and if it's like that, do we have any obligation to stop at any point? Or do we just keep going, digging, digging, peeling, peeling, until we've destroyed what we were investigating in the first place?[11]

The speech allows us to see her character's unease with the job she does, based on her recognition that much of what counts as 'news' is in fact mere artifice. News is indeed a form of story-telling, positioned in the cultural universe somewhere between fact and fiction, and with no necessary or inevitable relationship to the truth of what happened.

This idea is then developed in the subsequent plot, which sees Davis' character rescued from the burning aircraft wreckage by a mysterious figure who then disappears. This is Dustin Hoffman, a small-time crook trying to go straight, and who has accidentally (and reluctantly) found himself in a position where he demonstrates heroism, saving not only the journalist but the lives of many others on the plane. Sensing a story in the episode, and with her own personal involvement ratchetting up the human interest value, Gayle goes in

Figure 26 *Accidental Hero* (Stephen Frears, 1992). Source: BFI

search of the 'Angel of Flight 104'. By way of various plot machinations she comes to believe that the accidental hero is John Bubber (Andy Garcia), and proceeds to turn him into a media celebrity. Director Frears now embarks on a satire about the manufacture of reality and celebrity in TV news, showing how the actual details of the rescue are transformed into an uplifting, quasi-religious tale. The rescue is reconstructed for the cameras, moving testimonials are broadcast for the 'Angel' (who is, of course, an imposter, and himself becomes increasingly uncomfortable with the media circus he is colluding with). We see how mediated reality diverges from the actuality, which in this case is itself sufficiently remarkable not to require this kind of mythologising. Finally, Garcia retreats from his unearned fame, allowing Hoffman's accidental hero to take his due credit. With the corrupt nature of the mediation process thus exposed for all to see, Davis finally sees the error of her ways, and repents.

CONCLUSION

Journalistic villains have not become more visible over time, or more villainous than they were in the monochrome days of *His Girl Friday* and *Ace in the Hole*. The roguish and reptilian stereotypes of those movies continue to be replayed in contemporary cinema. Now, as then, journalistic villains are associated with the popular media – the tabloid or (in the UK, red top) sectors of print and TV, and celebrity journalism in particular. Women are rarely represented as villains, and in the 1997–2008 period there was no character nearly as reprehensible as Suzanne Stone in *To Die For*. The bad girl trio depicted in *Rag Tale* (see appendix, p. 229) were as bad as it got in that decade and these women, one might argue in their defence, were only doing what they had to do to get by in a working environment of brutish male hacks. Neither was there any recognition (though it must surely come) of the villainous potential of online journalism, with its accelerated, globally networked rumour-mongering and gossiping.

There is another category of journalistic villain, however, who received some attention from film-makers in the 1997–2008 period, and it is to those that we now turn.

NOTES

1. Armstrong, Stephen, 'From hero to zero', *Guardian*, 12 May 2008 (*http://www.guardian. co.uk/media/2008/may/12/itv?gusrc=rss&feed=media*).
2. I must disagree with Armstrong's view that while the great majority of such portrayals have showed hacks as 'hardworking forces for good', the recent trend is towards images of sleaze and venality (as evidenced by James Nesbitt's character in *Midnight Man*). In fact, there have been both positive and negative images of journalists in film ever since the medium first took an interest in the subject. Stephen mentions *Ace in the Hole*, surely the most savage

portrayal ever made of how news manufactures reality, and nearly sixty years old. MacKendrick's *Sweet Smell of Success*, made half a century ago, has Burt Lancaster as the sinister king-maker J. J. Hunsecker, surely a model for rottweiller journalists down the years.

On the positive side, Michael Winterbottom recently made a poignant film about Daniel Pearl, while George Clooney portrayed Ed Murrow as near saintly in *Good Night, and Good Luck*.

As an academic currently working on a book about journalism in the movies, I find that there are plenty of lazy stereotypes to be found on our screens, past and present. The best movies about journalists, the ones that have survived the test of time, are those, like Oliver Stone's *Salvador* or Winterbottom's *A Mighty Heart*, which avoid stereotypes and engage with the complexity of the profession in an increasingly uncertain world.

3. Review by Laura Mulvey, *Sight & Sound*, volume seven, number three, 1997.
4. For a review of *Paparazzi*, see Neil Smith at http://www.bbc.co.uk/films/2005/01/13/paparazzi_2005_review.shtml.
5. Lawrenson, Edward, *Sight & Sound*, volume 15, number 3, 2005.
6. *Guardian*, 26 November 2008. A few years after *La Dolce Vita* modern celebrity culture reached maturity and became mainstream in Andy Warhol's New York, symbolised by the artist's aphorism that in the future, everyone would be famous for fifteen minutes (a film of that name about tabloid television journalism was made in 2001). What precisely he meant by the phrase is less important than what it has come to mean in the public imagination – that we inhabit a culture in which anyone (if not, actually, everyone) can achieve the kind of media celebrity which in the past was restricted to people who were truly talented in some way – actors, writers, musicians, sports men and women. Modern media, Warhol understood, had the capacity to elevate the ordinary to the heights of public visibility and acclaim, even if it was only for a short time. The ever-expanding media's appetite for new faces, new trends and fashions provided those with little to offer except their newness unprecedented scope for attracting media attention.
7. O'Brien, J., *Guardian*, 12 September 2005.
8. Review, *Guardian*, 7 October 2005.
9. Review, *Observer*, 9 October 2005
10. John Herzfeld's *15 Minutes* (2001) stars Kelsey Grammar as a similarly cynical tabloid TV presenter, who works with celebrity cop Robert De Niro to get the most sensational exclusives. Although Grammar's character is reptilian, it is De Niro's media-obsessed detective who pays with his life for his celebrity.
11. I first quoted this extract in my essay 'What is journalism?', in Hugo De Burgh's edited collection *Making Journalists* (2005).

CHAPTER 10

Fabricators, fakers, fraudsters

If there is one thing deemed worse by journalism's many critics than the cynical manipulation of reality in pursuit of the saleable news story it is, surely, the deliberate fabrication of the facts themselves – the invention of stories and sources, the presentation of lies as truth. Chuck Tatum in *Ace in the Hole* may have 'manufactured' problematic reality in a manner which is indefensible to any but the most cynically commercial of news editors but his story was at least founded on an actual event, in the reportage of which he then expended considerable newsgathering and reporting energy (albeit without concern for the victim of his manipulation). Lies were told in the process of turning his predicament into a news story, but Leo Minosa *did* exist, and he *was* stuck in a cave. Richard Gere's Ike in *Runaway Bride* got himself into trouble because of 'journalism lesson number one. If you fabricate your facts you get fired'. But he was guilty principally of laziness in fact-checking the lead supplied by a source encountered in a bar (and the runaway bride was, in fact, a serial jilter of fiancés at the altar). The true journalistic fabricator avoids even this outlay of effort and simply makes things up, gambling that he or she will not be found out.

If the greatest ethical sin of scholarship is plagiarism, journalism's greatest ethical sin is to invent stories which are not true; to lie, and then to use the privileged cultural status of journalism to have those lies believed. To be published in an established newspaper or online publication or to have a story broadcast on a TV news bulletin or current affairs magazine, in most countries, carries with it some guarantee of authenticity (how strong that guarantee is depends, of course, on the publication's reputation). Whether the outlet in question is elite, mid-market or popular, if it comes to the marketplace bearing the imprint of an established news brand the expectation of the audience is of authorial integrity. It is a cliché, but true, that we tend to believe what we read in the newspapers, or see on the TV. More than that, we *must* have a degree of trust that what we are reading or seeing or listening to is what it says it is. Without it there is no basis on which to expend one's time and money on the consumption of news. Journalism *has* to be believable, if it is to have value as a cultural form.

It is generally understood that mistakes will be made by journalists and editors from time to time, and that there may be inaccuracies in reportage of a story arising from any number of causes, but these are not assumed to include deliberate fabrication on the part of the author. A publication's reputation for, if not objectivity, at least honesty, and thus its position in a competitive information marketplace, excludes tolerance for journalistic invention, be it in the pages of the *Sun* or *Mirror* in the UK, the *New York Times* in the US, or on CNN and the BBC. The more competitive and global the information marketplace becomes, moreover, the more important is the maintenance of this reputation.

By 'invention' I do not mean the imaginative embellishment of reality seen in almost all the elements which make up a media outlet's information package, from the graphic packaging of a weather report to the deliberately florid language of the controversialist rant, or to the blurring of fact and fiction which occurs in the writing of Truman Capote and Hunter Thompson. As argued in Chapter 8, the latter device is by now understood and accepted in the context of late twentieth-century cultural relativism, and the associated idea that objectivity and truth are, while entirely legitimate aspirations for journalism (and necessary for competitive reasons, to repeat), less absolute than was once believed to be the case. Having lost much of the epistemological naivete of the past, modern audiences are more receptive to the idea that journalism is the creation of human beings, and bears their subjective characteristics. The growing popularity of first-person journalism in the late twentieth century suggests indeed a demand for accounts of the world which depart from sterile objectivity and incorporate creativity, even to the point where the line between fact and fiction is unclear.[1]

The unacceptable breach of the contract between journalist and public, the crime which puts its perpetrators firmly in the category of villain, occurs when a story which has been invented, wholly or in part, is presented to the reader as true, in a context where the audience is entitled and likely to believe the truth claim. It is a deception not only of the audience for the fabricated piece, and thus a violation of public trust in journalism as a cultural form, but of the editors of the publication or outlet in which it appears, who are rarely complicit in the fabrication (except in so far as their editorial procedures have failed to spot it). I therefore exclude here the 'journalists' and editors of publications such as the *National Enquirer* in the United States and the *Daily Sport* in the UK, which regularly invent sensational stories about celebrities, both dead and alive, and present them as true. Do readers believe it when they read that Elvis

Presley has been spotted in a supermarket in Delaware, or that – as in the fictional publication featured in *Paparazzi* (see previous chapter) – fictional movie star Bo Laramie has had a penile implant when he has not? Some may, just as there are some who believe that men never walked on the moon, and that 9/11 was not a jihadi attack but a zionist-neocon conspiracy. There are some very gullible people in the world, and our sympathies go out to them, but for the great majority of the public these publications are peripheral to journalism, parodic mutations of the form positioned in the media market more as comic books than news outlets. Most people (if not all) understand their function as fantasy-based entertainment rather than fact-based news. Fabrication, to be a violation of journalistic ethics, must occur in a context where the trust between public and journalist is consciously and deliberately betrayed for the sake of a journalist's personal advancement.

A HISTORY OF JOURNALISTIC HOAXES

There have always been professional liars in journalism. Some of the best-known examples from recent times include Janet Cook, whose heart-wrenching account of a young heroin addict called Jimmy was published in the *Washington Post* in September 1980, and won her a Pulitzer prize in 1981.[2] She had in fact made the story up.

In the 1990s Channel 4 television in the UK received substantial fines for broadcasting documentaries in which evidence and sources had been fabricated. In one example, from the *Cutting Edge* current affairs strand broadcast in 1996, ostensibly about the cocaine smuggling trade between Columbia and Britain, the *Guardian* newspaper discovered that supposed Columbian gang members were actually actors.[3] The production company, Carlton TV, was fined £2 million. In another case, again on Channel 4, the maker of a documentary on child prostitution in Glasgow used members of the production team to impersonate 'johns' on camera. On this occasion a fine of £150,000 was imposed. In 1999 the *Vanessa* daytime talk show on the prestigious BBC1 was revealed to be employing actors to impersonate 'real' people in its Springer-lite tales of family dysfunction and sexual deviation, sparking a wave of moral panic around the incidence of 'faking' in British public service broadcasting, and the BBC in particular.

These examples show that, despite the tenor of media coverage (and scholarly commentary) which frequently accompanies these cases when they are exposed, journalistic fabrication is not a new problem. Public concern about the issue tends to be cyclical, usually sparked by one high profile case which puts it on the news agenda from where, in the manner familiar to students of agenda-setting, editorial sensitivities are raised, other cases of varying seriousness identified, then fed into a narrative of worsening journalistic unreliability. Each new cycle tends to be forgetful of an ignoble tradition, and to present evidence of fabrication as if such things have never happened before. A rhetoric of decline kicks in, suggesting that standards are getting worse, or that they have never been so bad as now.

That is in the story-telling, narrativising nature of news, and if it leads to an exaggerated picture of how commonplace journalistic liars are, we should nevertheless welcome the fact that news media are often the first to expose their own, and then become their severest critics. This confirms the continuing importance to journalism's survival of trust in journalistic integrity (we would *really* be in trouble if journalistic lying no longer attracted opprobrium from news media). In the late 1990s and into the 2000s, however, anxiety about the level of journalistic fabrication in the media, and associated declines in recorded levels of public trust in journalism as a whole coincided with the trauma of technology-driven transition from the great journalistic carrier media of the twentieth century – print and analogue broadcasting – to the internet and multi-channel digital TV (and radio). This parallel structural trend threw up new challenges to the notions of journalistic truth, objectivity and reliability. The result was a transnational, even global collapse of trust in journalism, as examples of fabrication and sloppy editing became the subject of an expanding online sector eager to assert its rights vis à vis the 'old' media.

THE CRISIS OF JOURNALISTIC TRUST

In April 2003 *New York Times* reporter Jayson Blair was discovered plagiarising an article which had originally appeared in the *San-Antonio Express News*. In what the *New York Times* apologetically described as 'a low point in the 152-year history of the newspaper',[4] it was subsequently revealed that Blair had fabricated and plagiarised dozens of articles. More damaging than this was the fact that his lying had fooled his editors, confident and self-satisfied as they had hitherto been in their status as a 'quality' news organisation, and *the* newspaper of record in the US. The *NYT* was embarassed, humiliated, compromised, at the very time when the rise of online journalism was beginning to seriously challenge the traditional dominance of print and analogue broadcast news media.

The *NYT* was not alone, however, in harbouring journalistic fraudsters. In early 2004 *USA Today* conceded that one of its staff reporters, Jack Kelley, had fabricated parts of at least eight stories, 'offering readers a lengthy apology in an attempt to avoid the damage to its reputation endured by the *New York Times* last year'.[5] In the United Kingdom in May of that year, photographs said to be of British troops abusing prisoners in Iraq were published on the front page of the *Daily Mirror*. In the aftermath of the Abu Ghraib story the photographs – which included scenes of soldiers urinating on prisoners – had credibility and the story 'legs'. Less than one year after the Andrew Gilligan affair, and the related suicide of a government scientist, there was a hunger amongst anti-war organisations such as the *Mirror* for stories which would show British forces in Iraq, and thus the UK government which put them there, in a negative light. However, the British Ministry of Defence alleged that the images had been faked, citing the fact that items of equipment seen in the frames were not used by British forces in Iraq. After initial denials from defiant editor Piers Morgan the fraud was conceded and he was forced to resign for being taken in by what the *Mirror*'s owners called a 'calculated and malicious hoax'.[6]

At the BBC, meanwhile, perhaps the most trusted news organisation on the planet, the effects of the Gilligan affair and its aftermath had been extremely damaging.[7] This was not a fabrication scandal, but a case of a journalist allegedly misrepresenting the views of a source in order to present a misleading story about the government, and to characterise the prime minister as a liar. The details of the case are available on the website of the Hutton inquiry set up by the UK government to investigate the affair.[8] Suffice to say here that the British government of Tony Blair was accused in May 2003 of 'sexing up' a dossier on Saddam Hussein's possession of weapons of mass destruction, in order to encourage parliamentary support and pro-war public opinion in advance of the March 2003 invasion of Iraq. The journalist concerned, Andrew Gilligan, speaking on the BBC's flagship radio *Today* programme cited an official source, later named as David Kelly, but in a way which was (the government and its supporters argued) dishonest and misleading. The government was furious, and in a tragic turn of events David Kelly subsequently committed suicide, leading to a major investigation by Lord Hutton. In August 2003 the Hutton inquiry reported its findings, which were highly critical of the BBC's editorial procedures.

The findings of the Hutton inquiry were contested by many observers, who accused it of being a whitewash of governmental duplicity. Others, such as journalist John Lloyd, urged the BBC to accept that on this occasion its editorial practices had been found wanting.[9] The director general and chairman of the corporation both resigned, and the lingering impact on the BBC was to undermine public confidence in its editorial standards and in the accuracy of its reporting.

On 10 October 2005 one of Britain's most trusted and successful newspapers, the *Guardian*, published on its front page the story of a Chinese dissident who had been brutally beaten and was now missing, possibly dead. The story was accompanied by pictures and a graphic eye-witness account by the reporter. It later emerged that much of the story had been invented. On 17 October, the *Guardian* apologised for the story's 'gross errors and exaggerations'.

By the mid-2000s, therefore, on both sides of the Atlantic, the issues of journalistic fabrication and invention, of fakes and hoaxes, were high on the news and public agendas. For the BBC the issue was not fabrication but editorial standards, but it too was swept up in the wave of negative stories about journalistic integrity. In a trend fuelled not least by the networking potential of online technology the established news media of print and terrestrial broadcast TV and radio were going through a generalised crisis of public trust in their output, caused by the perception, fair or not, that their content was vulnerable to inappropriate editorial manipulation, slack and sloppy production, and downright fabrication and lying.

THE CRISIS OF TRUST AND THE DIGITAL DIVIDE

Chapter 5 referred to the downbeat state of investigative journalism in the twenty-first century as the editorial resources devoted to this key journalistic specialism were cut back in the wake of competitive pressures. Other kinds of journalism were also under unprecedented scrutiny, not least from the rise of online news-makers, also known as 'citizen journalists', content-generating users, bloggers and social networkers who as the 2000s progressed spent a great deal of their time checking up on, and then spreading the news about, errors of judgement or fact, not to mention deliberate deception on the part of the 'old media'. If the established news media had acted as a fourth estate watching over political power, emerging online media acted as scrutineers of print and broadcast journalism, harrying them and deflating their presumptions of superiority with repeated examples of fabrication and plagiarism.

The principal victims of this 'crisis' of trust – and for once, crisis is an appropriate term – have, as noted above, been the *New York Times, USA Today*, and CBS in the United States; the *Mirror* and the BBC in the United Kingdom. These familiar, once trusted institutions now faced the emergence of an online, twenty-four-hour, globalised news culture in which ordinary people – amateurs in journalistic terms – had unprecedented capacity to follow stories back to their source, and to communicate their own take on these stories to a global audience, at great speed and with relatively few opportunities for censorship or control.

This trend has been welcomed by many, including this writer, as amounting to a decentralisation and democratisation of journalism, liberating it from the stultifying effect of the old, top-down, capital-intensive media organisations, as well as the authoritarian control of governments.[10] There is a downside to technological change, however, in that many of the elements of traditional print and broadcast journalism which we have good cause to value are also at risk from the internet.

Journalism on the internet, it is argued by some observers, suffers because of the dissolution of the boundary which has traditionally existed between the professional and the amateur. There are concerns that in the era of the blogger and the 'citizen journalist', where user-generated content is often king, the professional standards of journalism such as reliability and accuracy of sourcing are eroded. The consumers of news find it more difficult to distinguish truth from falsehood, and reasonable speculation from gossip and rumour. There is a lot more information out there in the globalised public sphere, yes, more than any human being has ever had access to before, but much of it is flawed because of its doubtful provenance. Who has originated it? What checks have they carried out on the reliability of their sources? Can we trust it, in the way that we have traditionally trusted, say, the BBC? A number of observers have acknowledged the important democratising effects of the new media, while balancing these against the degenerative effects of so much information that is untested and potentially untrue. Oliver Kamm in a 2006 article for the *Guardian* observed that the blogosphere (that sector of the internet where so much of this information circulates) is a 'democratic medium, allowing anyone to participate in political debate without an intermediary, at little or no cost. But it is a direct and not deliberative form of democracy. You need no competence to join in'. However:

> Blogs are providers not of news but of comment. This would be a good thing if blogs extended the range of available opinion in the public sphere. But they do not; paradoxically, they narrow it. This happens because blogs typically do not add to the available stock of commentary; they are purely parasitic on the stories and opinions that traditional media provide. In its paucity of coverage and predictability of conclusion, the blogosphere provides a parody of democratic deliberation.[11]

While online journalism *is* often flawed (is often not 'journalism' at all), for all the reasons cited in the above works and elsewhere, it should also be acknowledged that it has no special relationship to error in news-gathering and presentation, nor to the fabrication of facts. Nor indeed to commentary, despite Kamm's condemnation of the blogger. 'Old' print media are full of opinion, polemic, punditry – far too much, many have argued. The online commentariat, though much more numerous and independent of organisational affiliations, does not qualitatively differ in its output from the old media punditocracy. There have been online journalistic hoaxes, of course, but as we have seen this deviation from the normative standards of liberal journalism has a long history which predates the internet. On the plus side, online journalists have broken important stories which print and broadcast media were simply unable or unwilling to (such as the Clinton-Lewinky scandal first reported by the *Drudge Report*). Online journalists have played a valuable role in exposing a number of old media fabrications and hoaxes, including the Jayson Blair scandal at the *New York Times*. In doing so, they have challenged long-established presumptions of where in the media environment journalistic and ethical superiority reside.

SHATTERED GLASS AND THE CRISIS OF JOURNALISTIC TRUST

Online journalism is a recent phenomenon and thus not one which had been extensively addressed by film-makers as this book went to press. The world awaits a movie about blogging and its cultural impact. But there has been one important film in recent years which deals with precisely these issues as they impact on the 'old' media. With fortuitious timing given the wave of faking scandals which broke in the preceding months, including the Jayson Blair case, Billy Ray's 2003 film (released in the UK on 14 May 2004, by coincidence the same day as Piers Morgan resigned as editor of the *Mirror* over the hoax Iraqi prisoner abuse story) returned to a 1998 case, that of Stephen Glass and the extended hoax he played on the *New Republic*. Adapted from a *Vanity Fair* article by Buzz Bissinger,[12] *Shattered Glass* marks the moment when authority and influence in the public sphere began to shift from print to the internet.

Figure 27 *Shattered Glass* (Billy Ray, 2005). Source: BFI

For one reviewer, 'the film plays like a cautionary tale about rotten practices in the fourth estate'.[13] The film focuses in on the *New Republic*'s meticulous editorial process, with a sequence portraying the checking and revising stages through which every article passes. Not only is the sequence an interesting lesson in one dimension of 'objectivity' – the importance of checking sources, and verifying claims – it raises the question: if such a rigorous process is in place, how on earth could a young novice such as Glass so abuse his employers' trust and get away with it?

It is ironic that the fabrications and lies of Stephen Glass, which fooled editors at one of the world's most respected and editorially sound publications, should have been uncovered by what was then, in 1998, the very new medium of online journalism, in the form of *Forbes Digital Tool*. As *Shattered Glass* shows, it was this online publication's editor, Adam Penenberg, after conducting his own research on a Glass story ('Hack Heaven') he had found to be suspicious, who finally blew the whistle. In a piece for *Forbes Digital* published on 5 November 1998 Penenberg gave an account of the steps he and his colleagues took to establish the truth or otherwise of the Glass story.[14] The internet was a key tool in doing so, as search engines failed to show up any reference to the company, Jukt Electronics, referred to by Glass in 'Hack Heaven', or to enable confirmation of any of the other details in the story. An online publication, using internet search methods, had proven the unreliability of one of the great US media of record. For Penenberg:

> It is ironic that online journalists have received bad press from the print media for shoddy reporting. But the truth is, bad journalism can be found anywhere. It is not the medium; it is the writer.[15]

In another piece written by Perenberg's colleague Kambiz Foroohar, he wondered if he (or *Forbes*) should have blown the whistle sooner, and with more forcefulness since, in his words, 'we had enough information to run a story casting serious doubts on [Glass' piece]'.[16] Rather than going public with their doubts about Glass, they gave him the benefit of the doubt, and Charles Lane several days to establish the truth and avoid embarrassment for the *New Republic*. In the end, Glass had to concede that his story was faked, and he was fired that weekend. Justifying *Forbes*' decision not to publish immediately suspicions were raised, Foroohar wrote:

> We were convinced that the story was a fake but we thought that no sane person would create such a ridiculous fiction. We called the Mountainview, Calif. number but only got a suspicious-sounding voice mail. Investigating further, we discovered that the supposed corporate phone number was for a cell phone. It was very odd.

On Friday, May 8, there followed a series of conference calls between senior editors at *Forbes Digital Tool* and the *New Republic*'s Lane and Glass. I assumed that a clever hoax had been set up to embarrass a journalist whose reporting left a lot to be desired. Although *Forbes Digital* had enough information to run a story on how the *New Republic* had been fooled, we held back. We decided to delay publishing our story for a few more days to find the hackers who had perpetrated the hoax. On Sunday, the *New Republic*'s editor issued a press release announcing that he had fired Glass. According to Lane, Glass had fabricated the whole article. Should we have published our story on Friday? It is a cliché, but hindsight is always 20/20. We erred on the side of caution. In today's climate of trigger-happy journalism it is better to lose the scoop than have egg on our faces.

Unlike many films which have been critical of journalistic ethics, *Shattered Glass* received generally positive reviews. Howard Good observes that Sydney Pollack's *Absence of Malice* (1981), starring Sally Field as a reporter who flouts her own ethical conventions in order to get the story her editor requires, was 'an antagonistic portrayal of the press' (1989: 2), and that journalists were duly antagonised. Billy Ray's account of an even more despicable journalist was not received as anything but a realistic, understated, even sympathetic account of the predicament of an editor when he discovers that his star reporter is a fake. By 2003/4, perhaps, the crisis of journalistic trust was so advanced that for journalists to attack its cinematic treatment would merely have made matters worse. And indeed, *Shattered Glass* is not a film which accuses US journalism of anything more than naivete and gentile arrogance. Peter Sarsgaard plays Chuck Lane as a kindly, supportive boss who is cruelly misled, and who deserves our understanding. He stands, we might also say, for the better instincts of the US media as they confront the uncertain and dangerous environment of the twenty-first century.

Positive reviews aside, the remarkable fact is that *Shattered Glass* was initially released in only eight cinemas in the US, and made less than $3 million at the worldwide box office (approximately one hundredth of the revenues taken by *Borat*). The reason for this is not clear, although it is consistent with the pattern of many other movies about journalism which are now recognised as classics. Both *Ace in the Hole* and *The Sweet Smell of Success* were commercial flops, and are now revered by critics and scholars of the journalism genre.

SHATTERED GLASS, SHATTERED DREAMS –
THE COMING DEATH OF PRINT JOURNALISM?

Following the release of *Shattered Glass*, though not necessarily because of it, the crisis of journalistic trust continued to build, and to coincide with other perceived transgressions. CBS coverage of the 2004 presidential election campaign was found to have been taken in by forged documents and accused of liberal bias. At CNN in 2005 chief news executive Eason Jordan was forced to resign after alleging in public that the US military was targeting journalists in Iraq. In 2007 the BBC experienced another wave of faking scandals (not journalistic this time, but inevitably incorporated within the same narrative framework as the Blair and Glass examples) when it was revealed that programme makers had invented the names of competition winners on children's TV, and that voting on phone-in shows was perhaps less rigorously managed than it should have been (a criticism made too of the commercial broadcaster ITV). Back on the terrain of journalism, a reality TV-style documentary on the Queen was condemned for misleading editing. In one scene the Queen appeared to have grumpily walked out on a photo session with celebrity photographer Anne Liebowitz. She had done no such thing, it turned out, but the producers of the show felt the appearance of drama would increase its appeal.

The overall impression given by these incidents was of a media under unprecedented scrutiny for practices which had probably always been present in news and other categories of output, but to which opponents and rivals had become hyper-sensitive. Even the long-standing trick of using 'noddies' in TV interviews (that is where, after the completion of an interview, the camera films the interviewer from behind, 'nodding' in agreement with the interviewee, thereby giving the impression of continuity) was condemned as fakery, and banished from its programmes henceforth by Channel Five News. In this respect, reportage of the crisis of trust at the BBC and elsewhere had many of the structural features of a moral panic, fuelled not least by the anti-BBC motivations of big commercial media such as News Corp and Associated Newspapers. Undermining the BBC and the UK's system of public service broadcasting in general had been a favoured past time of these organisations since the Thatcherite 1980s, and the various lapses and failures which came to light when the press started to look for them provided useful ammunition for those such as News Corp who wished to break up the BBC monopoly. That said, the lapses, and the crisis of public trust in the BBC, and in journalism generally which they fuelled, were real.

In a lengthy article for the *New Yorker* magazine published in March 2008 Eric Alterman considered these issues of trust against the background of a newspaper industry in 'life or death' mode. As he observed, the American newspaper (and the argument applies also to those newspapers of comparable societies such as the UK) is 'designed to appeal to a broad audience, with competing values and opinions, by virtue of its commitment to the goal of objectivity'.[17] Alterman noted that this model was being replaced by online news aggregation sites, such as the *Huffington Post* and the *Drudge Report*, which do not originate stories but bring them together under one banner, where they become the subject of online debate. 'Surrounding the news articles are the highly opinionated posts of an endless army of both celebrity and non-celebrity bloggers'. This is good for democratic discourse, Alterman concedes, but at what cost in terms of our capacity to trust what we read in the news?

> It is impossible not to wonder what will become of not just news but democracy itself, in a world in which we can no longer depend on newspapers to invest their unmatched resources and professional pride in helping the rest of us to learn, however imperfectly, what we need to know.
>
> We are about to enter a fractured, chaotic world of news, characterised by superior community conversation but a decidedly diminished level of first-rate journalists. The transformation of newspapers from enterprises devoted to objective reporting to a cluster of communities, each engaged in its own kind of 'news' – and each with its own set of 'truths' upon which to base debate and discussion – will mean the loss of a single national narrative and agreed-upon set of 'facts' by which to conduct our politics.

It is no bad thing, many will think, that the journalism of the future is likely to be premised on the broad acceptance of interpretative plurality, the idea that there is indeed no 'single national narrative and agreed-upon set of facts' to which we must all defer, but a multiplicity of perspectives on events and issues. And yet, we still need to know who is trustworthy and who is not, given that we cannot experience directly all the events which make the news, or have direct access to the 'facts' behind every issue. Journalists in the twenty-first century, to a greater extent than ever before, are needed as sense-makers and sifters not just of ever-more complex reality, but of the many and diverse ways in which reality will be reported in the digital future. Whether these sense-makers operate on paper, TV, radio or online, they have to be trusted, which requires their acceptance of certain standards of quality control. A trusted voice need not be a paid staffer of an organisation like the BBC for us to trust him or her, but we still need assurances of some kind, do we not, to separate the journalistic wheat from the chaotic chaff?

The capacity of the internet to spread the news, to disseminate by online word-of-mouth who in the blogosphere is to be trusted and who is not, whose views are perceptive and insightful, and whose are not, will be key here. As is already the case online, where of the millions of active blogs in existence only a few are read by anyone other than their creators, quality journalism will rise to the top, in an evolutionary process which weeds out the malicious rumour-mongers, the deliberate liars, the lazy thinkers, and elevates those worth reading and listening to to the top of the internet ratings. This will happen without central direction (which is just as well, since there is none on the internet) but through the more informal processes of sharing and networking which online media permit.

It does not happen without toxic material leaking down and through the internet's myriad pathways but since, as *Shattered Glass* shows, this has always happened even with the most respected of old media outlets, it is unlikely to bring democracy crashing down. It should be our aim, perhaps, if the strengthening of mediated democracy is the goal, especially at the global level, to preserve the strengths of the old media, harness the opportunities presented by the new, and develop our critical faculties and reading skills in telling the difference between quality and rubbish in the online journalism environment. The dynamism and lack of deference for establishments of all kinds (including media establishments) shown by the online producers of news and journalism are qualities to be welcomed and encouraged. So too is the importance to all stakeholders, not least the online producers, of standards of quality control which enable material accessed online to be trusted and used. In the end a happy medium, an historic compromise will be found which enables these two, increasingly blurred groups of writers to co-exist.

CONCLUSION

The lesson of *Shattered Glass* is not that the established media of record are fatally flawed, and that online journalism is in some sense superior; merely that the mantra of old media good, new media bad is simplistic. For all that there are legitimate concerns around the impact of the internet on the gathering, production and dissemination of news and journalism, it is the case that lies, mistakes and gossip have been part of the journalistic media for centuries, firmly embedded even in the most highly regarded of media outlets. The capacity of the new media to act as watchdogs and whistleblowers over the old is one of the most welcome features of the internet.

At the end of 2008, just as the crisis of trust which dominated much debate about journalism in the early 2000s was melting away (until the next iteration of the cycle), concern began to grow that the long foreseen death of print as a journalistic medium was finally upon us. The tension between print and online journalism dramatised in *Shattered Glass* had, it was argued, become a life-and-death struggle for survival in a recession-hit world of declining circulations and advertising revenues. Newspaper is a carrier medium for journalistic content, and may indeed be in terminal decline, as circulations fall by 3 per cent a year and rising.[18] The news brand continues to be central to the functioning of journalism, both as a political force and a commercial product. The BBC and the *Guardian* provide examples of two 'old' media brands which have successfully made the transition to the internet, at no perceptible cost to public views of their journalistic quality. Journalism of quality can and will thrive on the internet, just as it survived the transition from print to radio and then TV. Methods will change, there will be formal evolution. The presentation and packaging of journalism will adapt to the online environment and the interactive, participatory ways in which people use it. The lines which have separated professional and amateur journalists for centuries will dissolve further, and may even disappear entirely (although I doubt it). But journalism will survive, for at least as long as liberal democracy. It is just that it will look different. *Shattered Glass* will come to be seen as a key movie by future audiences, because it marks the moment at which that transition from old to new really began to be felt for the first time.

NOTES

1. Fans of Hunter Thompson derive much of their pleasure in reading his work from deciding whether this or that episode of drug-fuelled mayhem could possibly have happened, or if it is the creation of the author's imagination. What's more, they don't really care which it is, because these episodes feed into a broader vision of the world that is uniquely the journalist-artist's own, and transcends the question of what actually happened that weekend in Las Vegas.

2. For details of this and other journalistic fabrications see the Museum of Hoaxes website (http://www.museumofhoaxes.com/).

3. For a discussion of this period in British current affairs and documentary-making, see Winston, B., 'The primrose path: faking UK television documentary, 'docuglitz' and docusoap' (http://www.latrobe.edu.au/screeningthepast/firstrelease/fr1199/bwfr8b.htm).

4. Barry, D., et al, 'Times reporter who resigned leaves long trail of deception', *New York Times*, 11 May 2003 (http://www.nytimes.com/2003/05/11/national/11PAPE.html?ex=1367985600&en=d6f511319c259463&ei=5007&partner=USERLAND).

5. Lawrenson, E., 'It didn't happen here', *Sight & Sound*, volume 4, number 6, 2004.

6. Reported on the BBC's news website on Friday 14 May 2004.

7. See my *News & Journalism In the UK*, 5th edition, for an account of the affair and its aftermath (McNair 2009).

8. www.the-hutton-inquiry.org.uk/.

9. See Lloyd's book on *What the Media are Doing To Our Politics* (2004), and the debate hosted by the *Guardian* newspaper in December 2004.

10. See, for example, my essay in Chadwick and Howard's *Routledge Handbook of Internet Politics*, 'The internet and the changing global media environment'. This edited volume contains a large resource of essays addressing in detail the democratic implications of the internet, including the journalistic dimension.

11. Kamm, O., 'A parody of democracy', *Guardian*, 9 April 2007. Andrew Keen's *Cult of the Amateur* (2008) argues with even greater force that the democratisation thesis as applied to news online is a utopian illusion. Clay Shirky's 2008 book, *Here Comes Everybody* makes a similar case, if less emphatically. For a scholarly history of online news media, see Allan 2006.

12. Bissinger, B., 'Shattered Glass', *Vanity Fair*, September 1998, (*www.vanityfair.com/ magazine/archive/1998/09/bissinger199809*

13. Lawrenson, E., 'It didn't happen here', *Sight & Sound*, volume 4, number 6, 2004.

14. Penenberg, A., 'Lies, damn lies and fiction', *Forbes Digital Tool*, 5 November 1998 (www. forbes.com/1998/05/11/otw3.html).

15. Idem.

16. Foroohar, K., 'Tracking lies', *Forbes Digital*, 5 November 1998 (www.forbes.com/1998/ 05/11/otw2.html).

17. Alterman, Eric, '"Out of print": the death and life of the American newspaper', *New Yorker*, 31 March 2008.

18. For a recent overview of the state of print journalism in the UK, see my *News and Journalism in the UK*, 5th edition (McNair 2009).

CHAPTER 11

King-makers

News media are important cultural institutions, not least because it is perceived that they have the capacity to influence public opinion and political processes. Exactly how they do so, and with what consequences or effects, has always been a matter of debate,[1] but there is no doubt that the power of perception in itself means that the people and corporations who own news media and thus have final say on editorial policy, then the editors and journalists responsible for content and then, too, the communications specialists who aim to shape and manage that content for various purposes and ends, are to a greater or lesser degree political actors. Political journalism (and political communication) may win or lose elections (as was claimed of the Murdoch-owned *Sun* in the UK in the 1980s), make or break careers, elevate or lower individuals in the public imagination. They have influence on and through the public sphere, on public opinion, and thence on those institutions and individuals who feel as if they need to take into account the state of public opinion in decision and policy-making. This in turn gives rise to the parallel profession of public relations. Since the very existence of public relations is premised on the existence of journalism as an agent of public opinion and a factor in political decision-making, I include films about public relations in this chapter. PR professionals such as Max Clifford in the UK are powerful figures, with a potentially huge impact on how their clients – be they politicians, pop stars, or members of the public who find themselves at the epicentre of media feeding frenzies – are represented by journalists.[2]

To the extent that they are perceived to have influence news media – defined both as institutions and the individuals who own or staff them – can be viewed as king-makers. They have the power to build up the power of others, as vested in reputation, social status and wealth. They also have the power to attack those assets, and erode the power founded on them. In this final chapter we explore the ways in which cinema has represented these journalistic king-makers, and also the changing nature of media power in the age of the internet.

'HE'S TOLD PRESIDENTS WHERE TO GO AND WHAT TO DO' – THE PUNDITOCRACY AND *SWEET SMELL OF SUCCESS*

Journalists are required, first and foremost, to report events, then to make sense of complex reality, to bear witness to injustice and suffering, and to scrutinise power in the name of the people. In carrying out these roles and functions on behalf of the public in a democracy they themselves become, some of them, public figures of consequence, wielding significant power in their spheres of competence, be these the worlds of politics, sport or entertainment. A film reviewer can make an immense difference to the success or failure of a new movie. A leading sports columnist can use his space in a popular newspaper to make a struggling football coach's position much more fragile than it might otherwise have been. The very last film of the 1997–2008 period reviewed for this book – *Frost/Nixon* (Ron Howard, 2008) – focuses on one such journalist, David Frost, best known for his deceptively 'soft' interviewing technique as deployed on shows such as the BBC's *Frost on Sunday* and *Breakfast with Frost*. His 1977 interviews with Richard Nixon were possible in large part because of his power and influence as a journalist more famous than most of those whom he interviewed. The Nixon interviews, and the contest between two iconic public figures which they presented (Howard's film portrays it like a boxing match in which the protagonists slug it out for superiority, round by round) came to be seen as a key moment in America's (and Nixon's) coming to terms with the meaning of Watergate.

Other journalists have had different kinds of impact. In a career spanning more than forty years Australian investigative reporter John Pilger has frequently placed issues on the public agenda in the UK and elsewhere which might have been ignored had he not addressed them in documentaries such as *Cambodia – Year Zero*.[3] Michael Moore has had a comparable influence in the United States, and celebrated foreign correspondent Christiane Amanpour at the height of her fame needed only to turn up at an event for it to become news. Her presence endowed news value on events.

Media power of this kind is generated not by the journalist alone, but is also a function of the reputation of the news brand – the BBC, for example, or the *Wall Street Journal* – channelled through the personality of a particular journalist. In 2008 the BBC's business correspondent, Robert Peston, acquired huge influence as an astute reporter of, and commentator on, the credit crunch which first emerged in all its severity that year. The shocks of the fabrications perpetrated on the *New Republic* and the *New York Times* by Stephen Glass and Jayson Blair respectively were amplified by the power exercised by those publications in US political life. What they wrote – what anyone writes in the *New Republic* or the *NYT* – has greater influence and hence indirect power to make things happen than something written by an anonymous hack for, say, the *National Enquirer*.

Newspapers, TV, radio and online news outlets acquire through the performance of their normative democratic role a form of power which is autonomous and self-contained, and which is distinct from the power accruing to elected politicians, or appointed officials, or self-made millionaire businessmen and women. This power is a consequence of the normal functioning of news media when they are doing their job properly, and a necessary condition for journalism to perform the most important of its allotted roles in a democracy, since there can be no effective scrutiny without a degree of authority. Who cares what a journalist says about corruption if he or she has no influence with decision-making elites, no independent authority in the eyes of the public? Many cinematic representations of journalists, as we have seen, are driven by the watchdog's struggle to be heard in the face of the resistance of the powerful.[4]

But power, once acquired, can be used for more than just the public good. Media power in particular, with its potential impact on mass publics and thus on political processes, is a much sought-after resource for those with their own private interests to promote, but an obligation to be seen to operate within democratic standards, and to be responsive to public opinion. News media are usually constituted as private enterprises. This is their default mode in capitalist societies, where private ownership of media is reconciled with normatively approved levels of freedom and pluralism through the maintenance by regulation of editorial and ideological diversity. With that qualification, and with the exception of public-service broadcasters and a handful of niche publications operated on a not-for-profit basis by the memberships of political and other organisations, the preferred model for journalistic organisation in liberal democratic societies is that of the capitalist business, selling the news commodity to a market of readers, and those readers to advertisers.

But news is a *cultural* commodity, imbued with ideological power over and above its basic use value (that is, informing us about what is happening in the world). The commentary and analytic forms of journalism, and those who produce them – the sense-makers of complex reality – have a particular power in this respect. They are the *punditocracy*, the *commentariat*, the secular priesthood in whom we place our trust. They are the interpretative elite of the journalistic sphere, licensed to analyse complexity as experts, to define its essential meanings, to recommend and advise on individual and collective responses to events. The pundits are the most directly influential of journalists, because their voices are highlighted and often aggressively marketed as incentives to buy a particular newspaper or watch a TV news bulletin. Buy this newspaper and acquire access to his or her opinions, is the deal.

The phenomenon of the media pundit is not new, as is demonstrated by the recent reprinting of a 1945 book called *Molders of Opinion*.[5] As often happens with books written about journalism in decades past, one is struck by the relevance of the contents to present-day debates in journalism studies. Editor David Bulman, for example, observes from this vantage point (long before transnational TV and the internet accelerated the media trends he observed nearly seven decades ago), 'tremendous changes in the manner of gathering and interpreting news' (2008: v).[6] In particular, the velocity and quantity of journalistic information has increased hugely. In such an environment the public, 'confused by the abundance and complexity of the news' needs the pundit more than ever. 'Columnists and commentators are the Delphic Oracles of today' (ibid.: vii). They have 'more influence than any other factor in molding the opinions of adult Americans'. Bulman's book then presents a series of short essays about the well-known columnists of the time, such as Walter Lippmann (praised)[7] and Walter Winchell (condemned as an unethical, sleazy gossip columnist).

Neal Gabler's biography of Walter Winchell is rare in arguing that, far from being a reprehensible sleaze-monger, his rise was one manifestation of a democratising wave in American culture. Winchell, he argues, 'helped effect and then came to symbolise a cultural revolution in which control of the American agenda shifted from the mandarins of high culture to the new masters of mass culture' (1994: 645). Where Walter Lippman was a 'sage political columnist', and a 'sceptic of the rationality of the popular will', Winchell was 'the voice of the disenchanted and disenfranchised and the champion of democracy, the embodiment of the ascendant American masses' (ibid.: xiii). He was also, not least by Gabler's own account, a nasty piece of work, who revelled in his accumulation of power and did not hesitate to use it for personal gain.

At the peak of his influence Winchell is estimated to have reached two-thirds of Americans in his newspaper columns and radio broadcasts. Gabler suggests that he invented the gossip column as a form,[8] reaching out to the US masses first through the *Graphic*, a tabloid dedicated to the sensationalisation and dramatisation of news. For Winchell, argues Gabler, 'gossip, far beyond its basic attraction as journalistic voyeurism, was a weapon of empowerment for the audience. Invading the lives of the famous and revealing their secrets brought them to heel. It humanised them, and in humanising them demonstrated that they were no better than we and in many cases worse' (ibid.). For his critics, on the other hand, as for the critics of gossip and celebrity journalism ever since, the ethical violations of intrusion on privacy and catering to people's more voyeuristic tendencies outweigh any notional democratisation inherent in the form.

This argument takes us into a wider discussion about the ethics of the gossip column, and the place of celebrity journalism in the public sphere.[9] In the 1920s, observes Gabler, as Winchell's iconoclastic style was being established, his readers were dismissed by respectable journalists, scholars and the type of people who preferred the other Walter, as semi-literate morons. This, as John Carey's *The Intellectuals and the Masses* (1992) reminds us, was also the case in Britain, where the rise of mass and tabloid culture provoked scorn and anxiety amongst those who saw high culture as the only culture worth having. For decades since many scholars in media studies have interpreted the rise of this kind of 'infotainment' as a corruption or 'dumbing down' of the normatively preferred values of journalism, which from the critical perspective should favour information about the economy, politics, foreign affairs and so on. There is another body of opinion, however, which sees the interest of popular journalism in the more private, more personalised sphere of issues as entirely legitimate and healthy.

The critical view, less forgiving of the gossip columnist, is reflected cinematically in Curtis Hanson's 1997 adaptation of the James Ellroy novel *LA Confidential*. Danny De Vito plays Sid Hudgens, editor of *Hush Hush* magazine. Sid narrates what one reviewer at the time called 'Ellroy's magnificant Walter Winchell-inspired tabloid speak'[10] as we follow his pursuit (and occasional setting up) of Hollywood movie stars. In Ellroy's books, and in this film, the gossip columnist/celebrity journalist is a low-life figure barely less despicable than the criminal sadists and psychopaths who populate the rest of his fictional universe. Sid is eventually despatched in a manner that invites no sympathy from the audience.

Walter Winchell's career did not have such a dramatic ending, of course, and by the 1950s he had established himself as America's foremost journalistic king-maker. In this capacity he was the model for the character of J. J. Hunsecker, played with chilling menace by Burt Lancaster in *Sweet Smell of Success* (Alexander MacKendrick, 1957). Hunsecker is a king-making columnist – 'He's told presidents where to go and what to do', says his crony, press agent Sydney Falco (Tony Curtis) – who uses his power corruptly, to fight his personal battles. At the core of the film's plot is Hunsecker's quasi-incestuous relationship with his sister, who is in love with a left-liberal jazz musician. Hunsecker disapproves of the relationship and uses his column to smear the musician and (he hopes) reclaim his sister. We see how he exploits his contacts in an equally corrupt NYPD, ruthlessly calls in favours, and seeds an unfounded smear story in the attempt to destroy the musician. In the end he is defeated by his own immorality, but not before huge damage is done to innocent people. Scott Kashner writes that 'Winchell's special brand of nastiness is the evil heart' of the film.[11]

The script of *Sweet Smell of Success*, by Clifford Odets and Ernest Lehman,

Figure 28 J. J. Hunsecker, *Sweet Smell of Success* (Alexander MacKendrick 1957)

echoes the real-life relationship between Walter Winchell and his sister,[12] and
the propensity of that real-life king-maker to wield his journalistic power as a
weapon. In a key scene Hunsecker is meeting with a senator, Harvey, and his
female 'friend' in his favourite New York club. The female is an aspiring singer
and has her agent, Manny, by her side. Hunsecker is joined by Sydney Falco,
and we receive an explanation of what a press agent and a columnist do, and
can do to those with whom they fall out.

J. J.: This man [Manny] is not for you, Harvey, and you shouldn't be seen in public with him, because that's another part of a press agent's life. They dig up scandal about prominent people and shovel it thin among columnists who give them space.

Harvey: There seems to be some allusion here that escapes me.

J. J.: We're friends, Harvey. We go as far back as when you were a fresh-kid congressman, don't we?

Harvey: Why is it everything you say sounds like a threat?

J. J.: Maybe it's a mannerism, because I don't threaten friends. But why furnish your enemies with ammunition? You're a family man, Harvey, and some day, God willing, you might want to be president, and here you are, out in the open, where any hep person knows that this one [Manny] is toting that one [the girl] around for you? Are we kids or what? [stands up, signalling that the meeting is over]

The next time you come up, you might join me on my TV show?

Harvey: Thanks J. J., for what I consider sound advice.

J. J.: Go thou, and sin no more.

Lancaster's sinister and reportedly authentic performance as Hunsecker's bullying columnist with the barely repressed hots for his sister was too disturbing for mainstream Hollywood, and *Sweet Smell of Success* was not a commercial hit on its release. In Kashner's view it was 'just far too cynical for the times – in 1957, America was in no mood to see a film about its dark side'.[13] Today it is revered as a powerful and prescient exploration of the rising power of the journalist in democratic societies, and a warning against the abuse of that power.

As noted, the phenomenon of what we today call a punditocracy was already the subject of books being written in the United States in the 1940s (and Walter Lippmann's 1922 book on *Public Opinion* also reflects extensively on the nature of expert or elite journalism). In the intervening period, as print and radio were joined by TV and now the internet, the quantity of opinion and commentary in journalism as a whole has expanded. At the end of the twentieth century there was an upsurge of concern about the punditocracy, and associated trends such as the 'hyperadversarialism' of political journalists discussed by James Fallows in his 1996 book, *Breaking the News*. Commentators noted the commercially-driven growth of gladiatorial, confrontational punditry, driven by an 'attack dog' mentality. Journalists were neglecting their responsibility to inform, and accentuating their watchdog function to the point at which politicians were increasingly finding it difficult to communicate their policies, and their positions. In the UK former deputy press secretary to Tony Blair, Tim Allan, referred to the hyper-adversarial style of Jeremy Paxman, John Humphrys and others as a 'punk political journalism' which 'puts the journalist centre stage. It judges itself by how many hits it can rack up against the subject. Any communication by the politician on his or her terms is regarded as a failure'.[14]

John Lloyd's *What the Media Are Doing To Our Politics* (2004) written in the wake of the Gilligan affair accused journalists of corrosive cynicism to the point at which democracy itself was undermined. These arguments were given urgency by then-current trends on declining public participation in democratic processes. Observing record low rates of voting in the US, the UK and some other countries, these critics blamed journalists, at least in part, for what was assumed to be a broad public disenchantment with politics. By treating politicians with sneering contempt, went the argument, the average citizen was less inclined to feel any allegiance to the democratic process, or any respect for its elected representatives.

There are many complex issues raised in this debate. Where, for example, is the balance to be drawn between legitimate (and necessary) adversarialism on the part of the journalist towards the politicians, and illegitimate or 'hyper' adversarialism? When does the normatively ordained critical scrutiny of power become 'corrosive cynicism'? Does an excess of the latter in the public sphere erode public trust in politics and thus undermine the democratic system? When these trends coincide with the celebrification of politics, and the personalisation or privatisation of political journalism, is the public sphere thereby degraded?

These are questions to which there are no definitive answers, only subjective judgements based on interpretations of trends and assumptions about the chain of cause and effect between, say, gladiatorial interviewing technique and public cynicism about politics. As a citizen, I value the aggressive interviewing styles of journalists such as Paxman and Humphrys in an era when political actors come to the table armed to the teeth with all the tricks of media management and public relations. At the same time, there is excess here and there, as journalistic egos are inflated and they come to see themselves and their often entertaining interrogations as the point, or end of the exchange, rather than the means to informing audiences.

The so-called 'crisis of public communication' of the 1990s fuelled much scholarly debate around political journalism,[15] but has now subsided as voting trends improved in the 2000s and critical attention moved elsewhere. In relation to punditry, the major concern is now with the impact of the internet on the quality of the information presented by commentators, online and offline. In particular, and assuming that we do indeed have a need for the analytical, sense-making, commentary work of the interpretative journalist, what relationship do we have with the proliferating numbers of online pundits now active? How do internet users, confronted with thousands, millions of bloggers and other categories of online journalist (or those who see themselves as journalists, which may not be the same thing), distinguish authority from its mere appearance, or credibility from confidence trickery? As the old top-down world of print recedes into history, what are the mechanisms of quality control which will enable us to sort and sift the huge informational mass of the internet for the pearls of wisdom?

As this book went to press, no feature film had as yet been made about the online commentariat or punditocracy, no contemporary equivalent of MacKendrick's classic film. *Shattered Glass* does, as the previous chapter noted, mark the moment when power began to shift from print to digital, but it is really a film about the former's vulnerability to fraudsters, rather than the online media's huge expansion and what it means for the future of journalism as a cultural form. Maybe there is a script in production about Matt Drudge and his exposure of the Clinton-Lewinsky scandal, or the adventures of the Baghdad Blogger in war-torn Iraq.[16] If not, perhaps someone should write one?

Meantime, early 2009 saw the global release of Ron Howard's *Frost/Nixon*, about the 1977 interviews of former president Richard Nixon by leading British journalist David Frost. Where *Sweet Smell of Success* with its menacing of a senator by J. J. Hunsecker represents the dark side of the journalist-as-king-maker, the usurpation of legitimate democratic power by the unelected, self-appointed watchdog who then becomes a bully, *Frost/Nixon* gives us a representation of the normative ideal – the political journalist as hero. In these four interviews, conducted in a private home in California, a disgraced leader who has evaded the admission of guilt that will set his people free is brought to account by a journalist. Frost's critical scrutiny of Nixon presents a lesson in the proper functioning of the fourth estate, which is to watch over power and hold it to account. Nixon had resigned rather than be impeached, and then been pardoned by incoming president Gerald Ford. There had been no holding to account of the conspiracy until Frost came along with his inspired idea. In *Frost/Nixon* the king-maker becomes the one who escorts the king from power, who lances the boil which has been infecting the realm, and guides the old man into as dignified an exile as can be expected in such circumstances.

The script lays stress on the fact that Frost was not an established member of the political press corps, nor a heavyweight pundit, but a figure known for his comedy and light entertainment shows as much as his political journalism. Could such a journalist outwit Richard Nixon, it asks? Will he just throw 'puff balls' to be batted aside by the wily old president? The film has researcher James Reston Jr (Sam Rockwell) in despair at one point as he rails at Frost's failure to divert Nixon from 'the sort of banal anecdotes you'd expect from a talk show host'. Frost maintains a dignified silence on that point, and in the end vindicates himself by extracting the admission of wrongdoing he seeks. The episode dramatises a wider debate around the effectiveness of various interviewing styles which Fallows and others raised in the 1990s. Which style of interview is likely to produce the most information from a political subject, especially one with something to hide? The bulldog terrier approach of such as Jeremy Paxman in the UK, or David Frost's deceptively soft, friendly style, which here and in many subsequent interviews caught interviewees off guard? Both styles have their place, and so does every style in between. But no political interviewer was ever more successful in getting his or her man (or woman) than David Frost in 1977. Behind the smile there was steel, and Nixon did not see it coming.

SPIN DOCTORS

Nixon went on TV for the money, as Howard's film shows, and also because he knew that it was a way of speaking to the American people directly, of securing whatever legacy might remain to him. As the former president recalls at one point, TV images are crucial to a politician's reputation. He cites the case of his 1960 televised debate with John F. Kennedy, when it is widely believed that the sight of his perspiration, pale complexion and bushy eyebrows lost him the advantage (radio listeners favoured Nixon over the telegenic Kennedy). This case has become axiomatic in the study of political communication, and shorthand for the power of the media, and of television in particular. The perception of that power, and that it is open to abuse, has had another consequence: the rise of a parallel communication-oriented profession, known today as public relations.

Public relations is the management of communication between an actor in any sphere of public life and his or her publics. It is, in part, the attempt to shape, influence or manage how the media represents one's client, and thus how he is perceived by the public. In *Frost/Nixon* we see the former president acutely conscious of how he will look on TV, and surrounded by advisers dedicated to helping him in that task.

In common vernacular the public relations professional is better known as the spin doctor, the media advisor, the communications guru. Although not a new practice in itself, the profession of public relations dates back only to the start of the twentieth century, when the expansion of mass print media coincided with the extension of voting rights to the great majority of the people in democratic societies (women, for example, who had hitherto been denied the vote). The rise of PR in the century since then reflects the growing recognition amongst social actors of all kinds (and not only elite groups – many of the most effective deployers of PR techniques are single-issue pressure and campaigning groups unconnected with power elites) that because media are potentially powerful, or potentially influential on those who wield power, there is something to be gained by trying to influence what the media say about oneself, one's organisation, one's favoured political cause. Influencing journalism – media relations, or media management – has become a profession in itself, part of the broader field of public relations. There are indeed estimated to be more PR professionals in the US and the UK than journalists.

Such facts alarm many observers, and have contributed to a vast and still growing 'demonology' of spin which presents the rise of PR as synonymous with the decline of journalism (or of certain standards in journalism). The scholarly critique of public relations is extensive, and occupies a substantial sub-sector of media and journalism studies which views it as practically the same as propaganda.[17] Journalists are critical too, blaming PR for what is perceived as growing journalistic dependence on public relations as sources for news. In 2008 journalist Nick Davies made this case forcefully. When news organisations are under ever-increasing financial pressures, and journalists are required to meet tighter deadlines with fewer editorial resources, the temptation to use PR 'puffery' is understandable. The quantity of news 'supplied' by PR professionals, rather than gathered and independently sourced by journalists, has increased over time, which cannot be a good thing for the reputation and integrity of the fourth estate. The fifth estate of public relations practitioners has its place in a complex and fast-moving world, but it is, or should be, always a subordinate one.

Which brings us to the case *for* PR. Not only is it an organisational convenience, indeed necessity, for news-makers to have access to a regular supply of stories, but there is democratic value in individuals and organisations having the capacity and opportunity to communicate their considered positions on given topics to the public at large. This would be so even if the journalists always got it right, which of course they do not. In any conceivable circumstance, communication between, say, a government and its citizenry is essential, or between a party and those whom it wishes to enlist as voters, but in the media environment we today inhabit there can be no guarantes of communicative clarity or consistency. Government ministers disagree with each other or with their executive and may leak information, confusing the message a government may wish to present. A media frantic for story, and highly competitive, may easily misread the government's message, which should ideally be as clear and unambiguous as possible. In a word of chaotic communication any ambivalence or confusion in a message quickly gets blown up into a story of 'split' or division, which may come to overwhelm the substantive issues underpinning that apparent division. This is in the nature of contemporary political journalism, and a communicative reality for all political actors. For this reason, as Alistair Campbell and others argued when they were required to defend the New Labour spin operation in the 1990s, communicative co-ordination and clarity are essential.[18]

Most people, even the critics of PR, will accept this when pressed. Some of the best media communicators are figures such as Michael Moore, Noam

Chomsky and a myriad 'anti-establishment' public figures who use the techniques of persuasive communication with great skill. To communicate effectively, in a volatile media environment fraught with risk is unquestionably a good thing in itself, and an entirely reasonable aspiration for any political actor. Journalists sift and sort complex reality for their audiences. PR experts (professional and amateur) help journalists to achieve that sifting. They may also succeed in placing issues on the public agenda through the use of media-friendly demonstrations (or spectaculars), sound bites and other 'pseudo-events' designed purely to grab the media's attention. All this is fair and reasonable. Not good, from the democratic perspective, is the use of public relations techniques in ways which are dishonest or otherwise unethical. Just as journalists have ethical codes, so the practitioners of public relations – who also claim the status of profession – are rightly expected to behave within certain commonly agreed standards. When these are violated, which they frequently are, criticism and condemnation are entirely justified.

Another defence of PR is, of course, directly related to the previous section on the power of the journalist – when pundits and commentators threaten to drown out the opinions and policies of politicians with hyperadversarialism and corrosive cynicism (and not just politicians in the narrow sense, but all political actors), the latter require access to managed communication, designed and executed with the aim of effectively conveying their messages. How can citizens in a democracy make meaningful choices, if they are not permitted to hear the policy proposals of their aspiring and actual representatives from the horse's mouth rather than refracted though the journalistic prism?

In previous work I have argued that the rise of hyperadversarial journalism in the late twentieth century was an evolutionary response to the rise of public relations and spin.[19] Conversely, the need of political actors to be heard in a hyperadversarial journalistic culture justifies investment in the methods and tools of effective communication. Whether the logic of this communicative arms race is accepted or not, public relations is here to stay as an element of the media environment; one, moreover, which is growing in importance, as reflected in popular culture in a variety of ways. On TV there have been *Spin City* (US) and *The Thick of It* (UK), comic satires inspired by the communication practices of the Clinton and Blair administrations respectively.[20] The BBC also produced *Absolute Power* (radio and TV versions were made), starring Stephen Fry as a cynical, amoral public relations consultant.

PR's rise in the twentieth century parallels the rise of the cinema, and has been the subject of a number of movies, if not nearly as many as journalism. This reflects the relative newness and cultural marginality of public relations. It also confirms the particular esteem – ambivalent and contradictory though it often is – in which journalism is held. There is a popular fascination with

Figure 29 Tony Curtis as Sydney Fako, *Sweet Smell of Success* (Alexander MacKendrick, 1957). Source: BFI

journalism which is absent from the world of public relations, even though practitioners of the latter are more numerous, better paid on average, and live lifestyles which are probably just as glamorous. It is as if public relations is the unwelcome guest in the modern public sphere, a necessary but unloved element of the communication process. How else to explain the relative lack of interest in the profession (and I will call it that) amongst film-makers?

There have been *some* films made about PR, however, and more over time, with the status of the PR man (rarely a woman) gradually changing. Morris and Goldsworthy 2008 identify *Waikiki Wedding* (Frank Tuttle, 1937) starring Bing Crosby and *Four's A Crowd* (Michael Curtiz, 1938) starring Errol Flynn as early examples of the sub-genre. Some films about PR also qualify as films about journalism (*Sweet Smell of Success*, for example – see above), in so far as they represent the PR professional working alongside the journalist. Others barely address journalism, and focus entirely on the world of public relations.

As in films about journalism, cinematic representations of public relations professionals often combine grime with glamour, and positive with negative images. As Morris and Goldsworthy note, 'popular representations of PR exude glamour' (2008: 6), but it is glamour of an anti-heroic kind, set within critical studies of how unethical and manipulative public relations can be. The men and women of the PR industry are rarely portrayed as heroes, even when they are played by the leading screen stars of their day. In the period 1997–2008 key movies about PR included *Wag the Dog* (Barry Levinson, 1998) and *Thank You for Smoking* (Jason Reitman, 2006). In *Wag the Dog* a communications guru (Robert De Niro) enlists the help of a Hollywood producer (Dustin Hoffman, reportedly modelled on Robert Evans) after the US president asks him to manufacture a fake media war and thus distract the public's attention from a potential sex scandal. The film appeared in the wake of the Clinton-Lewinsky scandal, and President Clinton's authorisation of a missile attack on suspected jihadi sites in Afghanistan and Sudan. These were seen by many at the time as diversionary strikes with little military value. *Wag the Dog* took this notion to an absurdist level, suggesting that the American public could be fooled by an entirely fictional war played out on TV news (as with many satires about public relations, the film-makers often assume a gullible and stupid public easily taken in by the crudest PR stunts).[21]

In *Thank You for Smoking* Aaron Eckhart plays a top lobbyist for Big Tobacco, whose best friends and drinking buddies include lobbyists for firearms and alcohol. In what can be read as another take on the scenario depicted from the journalistic perspective in *The Insider*, Reitman's film explores the tools and techniques used by tobacco companies to manage public opinion in their favour. Both of these films reflect an era of heightened knowingness about public relations, an environment in which phrases such as 'on message' are part of the common parlance and the average citizen is quite likely to have a view on spin. They play as satire and invite the audience's contempt for a profession almost always portrayed as fundamentally untrustworthy, albeit one whose practitioners are glamorous and sexy as well as powerful. They are, in this sense, propaganda for the anti-PR lobby, who fear the growing influence of persuasive communication on the public sphere.

Contrast them with the figure of Sydney Falco (Tony Curtis) in *Sweet Smell of Success*, portrayed as a reluctant gofer for J. J. Hunsecker's king-maker columnist. Sydney represents the PR man as a sad, desperate figure, waiting for crumbs to fall from the more powerful man's table, prepared to do anything to curry favour. In a key scene which makes clear the low status of public relations in the 1950s Hunsecker explains Sydney's role to his companions in a night club.

> *J. J.:* Mr Falco is a hungry press agent, and fully up to all the tricks of his very slimy trade. Match me, Sydney!
> *Sydney:* Not quite this minute, J. J.
> *Senator:* May I ask you a naïve question, Mr Falco? Exactly how does a press agent work?
> *Sydney:* You just saw a good example of it, Senator. A press agent eats a columnist's dirt and is expected to call it manna [as in 'manna from heaven'].
> *Senator:* But don't you help columnists by furnishing them with items?
> *Sydney:* Sure, the columnists can't do without us, except our good and great friend. J. J. forgets to mention that. You see, we furnish him with items.
> *J. J.:* What, some cheap, gruesome gags?
> *Sydney:* You print them don'tcha?
> *J. J.:* Yes, with your clients' names attached. That's the only reason the poor slobs pay you, to see their names in my column all over the world. Now you make out you're doing me a favour?
> *Sydney:* I didn't say …
> *J. J.:* The day I can't get along without a press agent's handouts I'll close up shop and move to Alaska, lock stock and barrel.

Falco is the undervalued servant, sometimes the slave of the journalist whom he feeds with juicy titbits of celebrity gossip. In one scene, as Sydney encounters a dissatisfied client, the latter complains about what he pays his money to Falco for. 'It's a dirty job, but I pay good money for it, don't I?' Sydney is roundly despised and mocked wherever he goes. At the end of the film he is beaten and dragged away to an uncertain future by the same corrupt cops who have helped Hunsecker frame the musician who is in love with his sister.

By the time, thirty years later, we get to *Power* (Sydney Lumet, 1987) the public relations professional has acquired much greater, well, power. Richard Gere plays Pete St John, a media advisor for political parties and other clients employed to help them win elections. Gere's character educates his clients, and we the audience, as to the techniques of political PR in a media age. Crucially, he is the boss, sophisticated and in control, while his clients are the suppliants, desperate for his services and prepared to corrupt themselves at his bidding. There is cynicism in the script, but also a weary pragmatism, founded on the knowledge that this is how things are in the late twentieth century, and political actors better get used to it. In the opening scene we find Pete at the scene of an election rally in an unnamed Latin American country, risking death and articulating the principles of political success in a mediated democracy. Later in the film we see him flying in his private jet, playing the drums for relaxation, being glamorous and cool, as in the scene where he puts straight an aspiring state governor with principles by telling him how it is in the modern media world. Having lectured the politician on what colour of clothes to wear, how to speak in public and what kind of exercise machine to use (and for how long per week), the politician observes with exasperation:

Wallace: I am paying you. You work for me. You're trying to run my life here.

Pete (wearily): Wallace, Wallace, Wallace. You are paying me to make you a new life. Politics. And in order for me to do that I've got to be in charge of all the elements that go into it. It's the only way I work. That means framing the overall strategy as well as deciding all the specifics. The look of the campaign, the look of the billboards, the bumper stickers, what colours they're going to be. It means the polling, it means the ads, radio, TV, newspapers, it means co-ordinating every piece of information out of this office to make sure that it fits with what the polls are telling us the people out there are worrying about, and what they're feeling good about.

Wallace (fumbling for a sheet of paper): But aside from the campaign themes I want to address some of my long-term plans.

Pete: I'm sure they're great, but they're not important. My job is to get you in. Once you're there, you do whatever your conscience tells you to do.

Gere's performance in *Power* is about as heroic and glamorous as PR practitioners get in the movies. In more recent films such as *Thank You for Smoking* the projection of communicative power co-exists with encouraging audience revulsion at the amoral excesses of the profession, and its offshoots such as those who populate the world of party political campaigning. *The Contender* (Rod Lurie, 2000), a rarely seen story of dirty tricks in the US White House centred on efforts by a morally conservative congressman (Gary Oldman) to smear and destroy a vice-presidential nominee who is also a pro-choice feminist (Joan Allen), and *Primary Colours* (Mike Nichols, 1998) place public relations – and its more unsavoury elements in particular – at the heart of government and political campaigning, engaged in dirty tricks and other unethical practices in pursuit of so-called democracy. The latter, like *Wag the Dog*, was inspired by, if not absolutely faithful to, the actual history of the Clinton White House, as recounted in Joe Klein's source novel. There, and in these films, the media and the danger to political reputation they represent fuel the activities of the professional communicators, although they are rarely allowed to excuse their excesses.

BARONS

The perception, right or wrong, that journalism has influence is, of course, one of the main reasons why businessmen down the years have wished to acquire ownership of news media outlets, and to become media barons in charge of media empires. Lord Northcliffe, who launched the *Daily Mail* in Britain in 1896, is described by Michael Wolff as the founder of the 'world's first great populist media empire'.[22] Media empires, if this is true, are thus a feature of twentieth-century capitalism, and of the rise of popular journalism (formerly known as 'tabloid') which accompanied mass literacy and democracy. After the Northcliffe empire came Rothermere (Northcliffe's brother), Pearson, Hearst in the US, Maxwell, Springer in Germany, and others, all of them eclipsed by the towering figure of Rupert Murdoch, unquestionably the most powerful media baron of all time (and possibly the last).

Media companies are a vehicle for making profit and some owners treat them in precisely this way, as business opportunities, maintaining a 'hands-off' approach to editorial policy. Given the priority attached in democratic societies to media pluralism, such detachment is sometimes a condition laid down by government regulators for the purchase of this or that newspaper or TV channel, as in the 1980s in Britain when Rupert Murdoch's News Corp bought the *Times* and *Sunday Times*, having undertaken to preserve the independence of its editorial policy. Similar undertakings were given to the Bancroft family by Murdoch when he purchased the *Wall Street Journal* in 2007 (in both cases, separated by a quarter of a century, Murdoch side-stepped his undertakings and took control of editorial policy at the earliest possible opportunity following conclusion of the deals).

In 2008 News Corp's desire to take control of the UK ITV network was blocked by competition rules. Aware that news media companies are different in key ways from other companies, many governments, including those in the greatest champion of free markets, the USA, operate quite strict limits on the quantity and type of media which individuals and corporations may own. These rules are intended to limit ownership and prevent media power from being concentrated in too few hands, and thus preserve political pluralism and diversity. They express the recognition that media ownership is by definition media power, and that those who wield such power must be constrained. For the final category of journalistic screen villain explored in this book, and perhaps the most powerful of all the categories of communicative king-maker, we consider the representation of the media baron.

FROM *CITIZEN KANE* TO *CITIZEN MURDOCH*

Picture the scene, if you will. Oxford University, 1952, an overseas student surveys the gentle surroundings from his well-appointed rooms; the paths criss-crossing the quadrangle lead one way into the great hall where every night he and his peers take their meals and drink their claret in the shadow of the dons. In the other direction, the lecture theatres and the library where the actual learning is done. The student is a quick learner, who loses patience easily. He is also a rebel. Behind him on his desk there is a bust of Lenin. Vladimir Ilyich Lenin, who killed the Tsar and casually ordered the slaughter of thousands of bourgeois in the name of socialist humanity. His hero.

The student's name is Rupert Murdoch, and he is fed up to the teeth with the antiquated English elitism of this place, the rigid class system, the snobbery that makes him an outsider although he is as rich, if not richer than most of his fellows. He is an outsider because he is not English, but Australian, of the Melbourne Murdochs, the son of a journalist and now wealthy newspaper proprietor Keith, one of Australia's most powerful men, who is himself regarded with suspicion by the wealthier set in that city. Why? Because he has been a journalist, and journalism is not a respected profession in the Australia of those days. That makes Rupert angry, as he moves among these cloisters.

And then, one day, when he least expects it, he receives a letter. His father is dead. He is needed back home, to run the family newspaper business. Rupert is sad, but also relieved, elated even. Now he can give up the pretence of trying to become an English gentleman and start his real life's work, selling newspapers to the masses. He will take over the Australian media, then the world's, with popular, down-to-earth journalism the man in the street can understand. This will be his destiny, and his revenge on those who see journalism as a profession not fit for a gentleman.

At this point the man in the Orange advert[23] will crack a very cool joke about how to incorporate mobile telephones into this pre-mobile scenario, and the illusion will break down. But there is no pitch, pastiche or otherwise, as far as this writer is aware, for a film about Rupert Murdoch, the world's greatest media baron; at least not one that's been successful. And yet Murdoch's story is every bit as dramatic as the fictional Charles Foster Kane, whose life as a media baron (loosely based on that of William Randolph Hearst, the great pioneer of US popular newspapers) was the subject of what is in many people's estimation the greatest film ever made.

There is no Citizen Murdoch (although there is a biography of that name), despite the inherent drama of the story – the early inheritance of a troubled family business; the building of an empire, first in Australia, then in Britain, assisted there by a right-wing government which gave him carte blanche to smash the powerful print unions; and then in America, and thus the world, growing to contain within it hundreds of newspapers, satellite TV stations, social networking and online publications – the greatest media empire the world has ever seen, and as of this writing, growing still with the purchase of the *Wall Street Journal* in 2007 for a cool $5.6 billion. There is no narrative film of this story of media power, which is interesting in itself, and my starting point for this final section.

Rupert Murdoch, let us note, is not just a media baron, but a man who feels at ease with the business of journalism in all its facets, and whose impact on journalism as a form has made many others feel distinctly ill at ease. According to his most recent biographer he 'perhaps knows as much about the various aspects of putting out a newspaper – paper, printing, distribution, advertising, reporting, editing, headline writing, promotion – as anyone in the world' (Wolff 2008: 17). This may well be the case, but Murdoch's impact on journalism has been, or until recently had been perceived as, almost entirely negative. He it was who introduced the institution of the Page 3 girl to British tabloids in the 1970s, sparking the race downmarket to ever more sexually explicit content. It was his newspaper, the *Sun*, which attracted universal opprobrium for accusing Liverpool fans at the Hillsborough stadium disaster of looting and urinating on the bodies of the dead. It was his company which in 1986 smashed the Fleet Street print unions and ushered in a much more profitable, if largely de-unionised era for the British newspaper industry.

It was his newspapers' cheerleading which, many argued, kept the Thatcher government in power for more than a decade during which it presided over de-industrialisation, mass unemployment and inner city riots. It was Murdoch who successfully wrested ownership and control of the prestigious *Wall Street Journal* from the Bancroft family in 2007, amidst fears that he would corrupt this citadel of objective financial journalism. And it was Murdoch who, in his seventies, left his wife and married a woman nearly forty years younger.

His has been an eventful life by any standards, and he has become a global household name, even guesting on *The Simpsons*. He has been portrayed by Barry Humphries in the 1991 mini-series *Selling Hitler* (about a famous hoax involving the attempted sale of Hitler's diaries), and by Ben Mendehlson in the 2002 film *Black and White* (Craig Lahiff), where a young, anti-establishment Murdoch is seen putting his Adelaide newspaper to the aid of a campaign against a perceived miscarriage of justice involving an aboriginal man. No-one, however, has ever tried to make a feature film with Murdoch at its centre (there have been documentaries),[24] which immediately begs a question. Why, if *Citizen Kane* was such a great movie, and its subject matter so timeless, as is often and correctly suggested, has no comparable study of a contemporary, and much more powerful media baron, been made?

The answer, critics of Murdoch will reply, is right there. Apart from the fact that Rupert Murdoch is very much alive and can be assumed to enjoy access to the best lawyers money can buy, media power on the scale which he possesses, extending through News Corp's ownership of Fox Entertainment Group to the film-making business, acts to silence or deter the kind of independent artistic or critical voice who could craft a Murdoch bio-pic worth watching. Michael Wolff's 2008 biography, written with an unprecedented degree of co-operation from the man himself, signalled that Murdoch had entered a period when his legacy was becoming increasingly important. 'He is becoming a liberal, sort of', concluded Woolf on the basis of extensive interviews, although 'he remains a militant free-marketeer'.[25] As he neared his eighties, it seemed that he was mellowing and softening as a person, and more concerned to ensure that his enduring image was not that of a ruthless media baron only. And indeed, as the brutalities of Wapping in 1986, or the excesses of the *Sun* at its most intrusive and insensitive faded into history, his singular contribution to transforming the news media was coming to be seen as more positive than had been allowed in the past. A reputational make-over was under way, and had been for some time as this book went to press. But still no bio-pic, and none on the horizon.

Murdoch is not the only significant absence in cinema's representation of media barons. There have been very few films made about them, despite the potential richness of the material. Robert Maxwell's corrupt and bullying career, ending with his mysterious death by drowning off the Canary Islands in 1991, has never been dramatised in the cinema, although the BBC made a TV drama about his final days in 2007. Canadian baron Conrad Black, sent to prison in the US for corporate corruption, has escaped the attention of film writers. Apart from the risks to a producer or writer of approaching such figures as subjects for film (at least while they remain alive), perhaps it is thought that one of the greatest films ever made, a film about a fictional media baron but based on the life of William Randolph Hearst, has said all there is to be said on the subject.

The daddy of all movies about media barons is, of course, Orson Welles' *Citizen Kane* (1941). Not only is it the greatest movie about a media baron ever made (and there have not been that many, as noted), it is in many critics' view the greatest *movie* ever made, due mainly to the innovative and highly influential cinematography of Gregg Toland.[26] *Citizen Kane*, described by Laura Mulvey as 'a pseudo-biographical portrait of a major newspaper tycoon' (1996: 97) has been written about extensively within academic film studies, lauded as a ground-breaking work of cinematic art. The film adopts the structure of a journalistic investigation as a vehicle for propelling its story – the life of

Figure 30 *Citizen Kane* (Orson Welles, 1941). Source: BFI

Charles Foster Kane, from childhood to death, as represented in fake newsreel footage, the testimony of friends and colleagues, newspaper headlines and enacted scenes involving Kane. Mulvey notes as particularly innovative the way in which, by utilising this variety of sources, the script problematises truth and questions the extent to which any life can really be 'known'. 'The film's 'active spectator' is forced to look back at and re-examine events as though the film were suggesting that history itself should be constantly subject to re-examination and re-reading' (ibid.: 102).

The same narrative strategy is employed, in a deliberate homage to *Citizen Kane*, in Todd Haynes' fictionalised bio-pic of David Bowie and the glam rock era, *Velvet Goldmine* (1998). As in Welles' film a journalist (Christian Bale) sets out to trace what happened to 1970s glam rock star Brian Slade (David Bowie would not allow his own name, or that of Ziggy Stardust, to be used). In a series of interviews and flashbacks, including a key moment with a fictionalised Iggy Pop (called here Kurt Wild, and played by Ewan McGregor), the film comes close to, but ultimately fails to discover the core of Slade's personality, although it has a lot of fun trying. In an exhilarating queer homage to 1970s glam rock and its aesthetic roots the frequent references to *Citizen Kane* are just one of the film's many pleasures.

As a film about journalism *Citizen Kane* articulates both the normative liberal ideal, in Kane's youthful determination to represent the people before power, and the cynical reality, as an older, less principled Kane betrays his idealism in pursuit of personal power. The first half of the film evokes the spirit of a radical popular newspaper and the young men who make it happen while the latter half moves out of the news room and into the realm of media power and its abuse. In a key scene Kane's old friend and colleague, asked to do a review of the baron's girlfriend's dreadful operatic debut, writes the truth. Kane respects his right to criticise, and then sacks him for doing so.

Since the release of *Citizen Kane* there have been no movies in English which focus so centrally on the figure of the media baron, although they have appeared in various contexts here and there. In 2002 an episode from W. R. Hearst's life was portrayed in Peter Bogdanovich's *The Cat's Meow*. The film presented an account of a mysterious death which occurred aboard Hearst's yacht in 1924, during a weekend party attended by gossip columnist Louella Parsons (Jennifer Tilly), Charlie Chaplin (Eddie Izzard) and others. Although the facts of the death by gunshot wound of Thomas Ince have never been fully established, the film suggests that Hearst did it in a case of mistaken identity, while in a jealous rage, and that Louella Parsons' subsequent lengthy career as a gossip columnist for Hearst was the price she extracted from him for her silence on the matter.

In 1997 the James Bond film *Tomorrow Never Dies* (Roger Spottiswoode) featured as its chief villain a media baron named Elliot Carver (Jonathan Pryce), whom reviewers then and since have compared to both Rupert Murdoch and Robert Maxwell. Mary McGuckian's *Rag Tale* has a media baron in an important supporting role. Richard Morton (Malcolm McDowell), chairman of Global Media Incorporated, is a Murdochian figure, sitting isolated in his high-technology office surrounded by telephones and screens and electronic snooping devices, spying on his staff, his wife, his rivals. Two things distinguish him from the real Murdoch, however: one, Morton has no track record as an interfering proprietor, although it is his desire to interfere in the content of the *Rag* which generates the plot and the narrative tension. Second, he is easily outmanouevred by his staff on *The Rag*, who have secured his downfall by the end of the movie. Richard Morton is most emphatically not Rupert Murdoch, who has ruled his global media empire with unquestioned authority for half a century.

CITIZEN CITIZEN?

Rupert Murdoch may turn out to have been the last media baron. Not the last individual ever to hold or wield media power, but the last to be so in control of so much that he can be credibly compared to a feudal baron. The rise of the internet, and the decentralisation and fragmentation of media which it has produced, the emergence of citizen journalism, user-generated content, blogging and social networking, effectively ends the era of top-down control which began in the late nineteenth century with Lord Northcliffe and the *Daily Mail*. The established centres of media power and influence – proprietors, editors, senior journalists in print and analogue broadcast media – are under intensifying pressure from a 'new commentariat' or online punditocracy, operating on the internet through blogs and personal home pages, social networking sites and other network channels. Control of media is slipping away from the old power centres and towards a globalised, networked public sphere to which hundreds of millions, billions have unprecedented access, and not merely as consumers of journalism but as producers. After more than a century of mass media organisation based on centralised, top-down lines of one-to-many communication, the structures of media power are being radically transformed, with uncertain consequences for democratic and authoritarian societies alike.

NOTES

1. The scholarly literature on media effects, and political media effects in particular, is extensive. For an overview, see my *Introduction to Political Communication* (2007), and recent books by Sarah Oates (2008) and Karen Sanders (2008).
2. That said, this chapter discusses PR in the movies only in an introductory way, acknowledging that there is much more to be said on the subject than I have space for here. For a recent discussion of public relations' public image, see Morris and Goldsworthy's *PR: a persuasive industry?* (2008).
3. A box set of John Pilger's TV documentary work was released in 2008, accompanied by a book by Anthony Hayward on the journalist's career (2008).
4. As was the March 2009 Channel 4 adaptation of David Peace's *Red Riding* novels, in which

young investigative reporter William Dunford uncovers corruption in the West Yorkshire police, local government and building trade, forces which combine to overwhelm him.

5. Edited by David Bulman, and published by Bruce Publishing Company, 2007.

6. In contrast to the time of the Civil War (about the same span in time from 1945 as 1945 is from the present), he suggests: 'There are advantages – great advantages – in the speed with which news is now transmitted. But there are disadvantages too. In the old days the difficulty of communicating even news of importance automatically screened out the drivel that serves no higher purpose than a peep show. Furthermore, the reader had time for thought and discussion. He was not bombarded daily with problems of world-shaking importance, spiced with juicy bits of gossip. As a result of the speed and abundance of news, the modern is confused. His time and mental capacity are limited. He is painfully aware that an attempt to assimilate anything beyond the smallest fraction of the day's news would result in an acute attack of mental indigestion.

7. An essay by J. C. O'Brien argues that 'although he is called a columnist, about all that he has in common with most other practitioners of the trade is a comparable number of inches of space on the features page. Primarily he is a scholar and philosopher who has chosen the newspaper instead of the lecture platform as a forum. Unlike the commentary of most so-called interpretive columists, which is largely emotional reaction to events, Lippmann's is related to and grows out of long-pondered, basic philosophical conceptions' (2008: 47).

8. Gabler describes Winchell's innovative style as 'a high-velocity montage of snapshots, a fragmentary new journalistic form that mirrored the modernistic experiments in high literature then being conducted by Gertrude Stein, Hemingway, Celine and others' (1994: 80).

9. For recent scholarly discussion of this issue, see Michael Higgins' *Media and Their Publics* (2008).

10. John Wrathall, *Sight & Sound*, 1997.

11. Kashner, S., 'A movie marked danger', *Vanity Fair*, April 2000.

12. See Neal Gabler's biography of *Winchell* (1994).

13. Kashner, S., 'A movie marked danger', *Vanity Fair*, April 2000.

14. Allan, T., 'Puffed up punks', *Guardian*, 4 December 2004.

15. The phrase was the title of an influential academic book by Jay Blumler and Michael Gurevitch published in 1996.

16. For an update on the health and happiness of the Baghdad Blogger as of early 2009, see Plommer, L., 'He spared neither regime nor invader', *Guardian*, 15 January 2009 (www.guardian.co.uk/world/2009/jan/15/baghdad-blogger-iraq-media).

17. Recent book-length critiques of public relations include *Thinker, Faker, Spinner, Spy* by David Miller and Will Dinan (Pluto, 2007). Journalist Nick Davies's *Flat Earth News* (2008) is heavily critical of the corrosive effect of the news media's growing dependence on public relations.

18. For an account of this debate, see my *Journalism and Democracy* (2000).

19. See my 2001 essay on 'Public relations and broadcast news: an evolutionary approach', in Michael Bromley's edited volume *No News Is Bad News* (2001).

20. The writer of *The Thick of It*, Armando Ianucci, subsequently wrote and directed a feature film called *In The Loop*, released in 2009. *In The Loop* develops the framework of his BBC TV sitcom, and places its characters in the midst of the media management operation which accompanied the 2003 Gulf War.

21. Levinson also directed *Man of the Year* (2007), starring Robin Williams. As in *Wag the Dog*, Levinson aimed to critique the way in which American politics had become dominated by the machinations of media and image. The film was a commercial and critical flop, however.

22. See his biography of Rupert Murdoch, *The Man Who Owns the News* (2008). For a history of the British popular press, see Matthew Engel's *Tickle The Public* (1996).

23. At the time this book was being written, screenings of films in the Cineworld multiplex chain were prefaced by short comic advertisements featuring a team of Hollywood producers in meetings with real-life movie stars such as Dennis Hopper, Angelica Huston, John Cleese and Rob Lowe. Each short film revolved around a serious 'pitch' of a screenplay by the actor in question, which was then undermined by the producers' desperate efforts to find a role in the movie for Orange mobile phones.

24. *OutFoxed: Rupert Murdoch's War on Journalism*, directed by Robert Greenwald in 2004, is the most critical.

25. Woolf, M., 'Tuesdays with Rupert', *Vanity Fair*, October 2008.

26. 'An obvious reason for the astonishing audience response to this film is its look, the most remarkable aspect of which is the extraordinary sharpness of every element in every scene' (Turner, G., 'Sharp practice', *Sight & Sound*, volume 9, number 7, 1999.

CHAPTER 12

In closing

We have seen journalists portrayed in cinema as heroes and villains; as complex, richly drawn characters; and as crude stereotypes. We have seen lurid anti-tabloid revenge fantasies where journalists are exterminated like cockroaches; and poignant reconstructions of real-life tragedies in which the journalist is the victim, or the target. There are still stereotypes and caricatures of journalism on the screen, many of them crass and stupid. But there has been amongst film-makers a clear recognition of the importance and difficulty of the job journalists do in a modern democracy, particularly at a time of conflict. There were many heroic representations of journalism in the cinema over the period 1997–2008 – many more, indeed, than there were villains. Journalists, male and female, are represented in the cinema of this period as courageous investigators and witnesses, and as determined protectors of their sources and their freedoms.

There are some journalistic bad guys (and bad girls) still around in the movies, to be sure, as there are fakers, fraudsters, hacks and reptiles in real life, but for now at least, they are eclipsed by the more positive representations favoured by such directors as George Clooney and Michael Winterbottom. Public opinion may be ambivalent about journalists as a professional category, and trust continues to be an issue, but the success of films such as *Good Night, and Good Luck* demonstrates that we want our journalists to be heroic, and value their efforts to be so.

It is entirely coincidental, though fitting, that the final release of the 1997–2008 period was a film which portrays the scrutinising, adversarial, watchdog function of journalism at its best. One might think it relatively easy for a journalist to look good when placed opposite Richard Nixon, but the play did not have to be written, nor the film made by such a powerful Hollywood player as Ron Howard. If *All the President's Men* presented a positive image of journalism against the backdrop of the Watergate scandal, there is a pleasing circularity in Howard's returning to that subject for a new generation relatively unfamiliar with the magnitude of the scandal, and the role which determined journalists played in it.

We go out on a high note, then, but at a moment when the news media and those who work in them – in newspapers especially - were under unprecedented pressure from digital technologies and associated trends such as the rise of citizen journalists, content-generating users and bloggers. Future films about journalism will address these themes, no doubt, adding further chapters to the story begun by Billy Ray in *Shattered Glass*. The decline of print journalism, and its potentially adverse implications for democratic societies, inspired the making of *State of Play* (Kevin Macdonald, 2009). The film, released in the UK just after this book went to press, was intended to defend the value of 'grubby', old fashioned, adequately resourced investigative journalism in the era of 'sharp-suited bloggery and the internet'.[1] It will not be the last to do so.

NOTE

1. Appleyard, B., 'The genuine article', *Sunday Times*, 5 April 2009.

Films about journalism, 1997–2008

This appendix contains mini-essays on all the films classified in chapter four as being 'about journalism' made for the cinema and released in the United Kingdom between 1997 and 2008.

1997

Welcome To Sarajevo (Michael Winterbottom, 1997, 103 minutes)

This is the first of two films about war correspondents made by Michael Winterbottom in the period 1997–2008, both based on actual events. It is not generally regarded as Winterbottom's best film – for one critic, 'the second half falls flat: the film moves with the characters and the narrative, supporting them and offering no resistance … a stiff-upper-lipped tearjerker based on the true story of an ITN journalist who resolves to rescue and adopt a child from Sarajevo'.[1] *Welcome To Sarajevo* is flawed, but successfully conveys the surreal tragedy of the Bosnian-Serb siege of what had been a prosperous, sophisticated city at the heart of Europe. In particular, the director uses an innovative and chilling blend of enacted and actual news footage to convey the horror of the massacre of civilians, and the death by sniper of a mother on her way to her daughter's wedding.

The story is that of a disillusioned TV news reporter who, despite the professional requirement for objectivity and detachment in his coverage, becomes increasingly engaged with the tragedy of war and its impact on civilians. We begin with scenes in which the journalists comment with war-weary acceptance on the increasing commodification of their reportage, and the debased need for 'infotainment', meaning in this context suitably graphic images of people dying. In a key scene we see Michael, the reporter, instruct his cameraman (James Nesbitt) to make sure he gets a shot of a discarded loaf of bread after a grisly market bombing in which dead and mutilated civilians lie all around. The feelings and pain of the victims are less important to the war correspondent, this scene suggests, than getting the money shot which will lead the TV news that evening.

The film is flabby in its structure, as the above review suggests, with the poignancy of the human stories gradually pushing out the discussions of journalism which inform its first half. It is also, at first, smug in its dismissive references to news as entertainment. When asked by their producer why they have not got grisly footage of another atrocity which competing news organisations have obtained, Michael's cameraman Greg says 'It's all this news as entertainment bollocks, isn't it?' He implies that he and Michael are not driven by the crass values of news conceived as infotainment; that they are above such commercialism. Later in the film, however, Michael uses the most heart-wrenching footage he can obtain to mobilise international support for the plight of the orphans he finds trapped in Sarajevo (and one of whom he rescues, as did Michael Nicholson, on whose real-life experiences the film is based).

Woody Harrelson plays a stereotypically wild and crazy American reporter of the Hunter S. Thompson school, but with a degree of knowingness which convinces the viewer that such reckless behaviour is probably an asset for a war correspondent in a situation such as the siege of Sarajevo. The film also contains many genuinely poignant scenes, such as one where a local assistant for the news team carefully saves some eggs to take back to his Bosnian friends. In the heart of Europe, in the last decade of the twentieth century, as barbaric war rages, the image of an omelette shared amongst friends who hunger for a return to peace and normality is genuinely moving.

Box office: $334,000 (US only)[2]

LA Confidential (Curtis Hanson, 1997, 138 minutes)

James Ellroy's 'LA quartet' of novels are steeped in the tabloid and celebrity news culture of pre-war Hollywood, which continually overlaps with the parallel worlds of organised crime, corrupt politics and serial psychopathy. In this episode of the series, and by critical consensus the best film adaptation of an Ellroy novel, Danny De Vito plays Sid Hudgens, editor of *Hush Hush Magazine* (catch phrase – 'Off the record, on the QT, and very hush-hush'). Sid is a scandal-monger, a journalistic villain of the worst kind whose stock in trade is the exposé of Hollywood stars' substance abuse and sexual excesses. Working hand in hand with celebrity TV cop Jack Vincennes (Kevin Spacey) he sets people up for arrest and subsequent shock horror coverage in *Hush Hush*.

Although journalism is a secondary element of this complex crime thriller, the treatment is rich and evocative, drawing heavily on the real-life practices of Walter Lippmann, Louella Parsons and other gossip columnists of the era in which the story is set. In the end, Sid's moral corruption brings him too close to the real source of evil in Ellroy's novel, and he is violently eliminated. As with other tabloid villains portrayed in the 1997–2008 period, the script allows us to feel little sympathy for his demise, given the relish with which we have seen him plot and execute the downfalls of others.

Box office: $126,216,940

Tomorrow Never Dies (Roger Spottiswoode, 1997, 119 minutes)

In this Bond movie Jonathan Pryce plays Elliot Carver, a cartoonish media baron whose desire to break into the Chinese broadcasting market is the pretext for his engineering a war between China and the UK. The film is included here because it is a rare portrayal of a media baron, and a reflection of the fact that by the late twentieth century it was entirely credible that a megalomaniac Bond villain should be a character who, if not based on Rupert Murdoch, at least refers to him and his business activities (News Corp has been heavily involved in China).

Box office: $333,011,068

Midnight in the Garden of Good and Evil (Clint Eastwood, 1997, 155 minutes)

John Cusack plays a reporter assigned to write a 500-word piece on the high society of Savannah, Georgia, and in particular the legendary Christmas party of Jim Williams (Kevin Spacey). While undertaking his research for the piece, however, Williams is accused of murdering his male lover. Cusack's reporter senses a bigger story beneath the surface, and begins to research a book. There are echoes here of the real-life circumstances in which Truman Capote wrote *In Cold Blood*, as we see the journalist putting together his material, interviewing sources, overcoming the resistance of a closed society to the East Coast writer come to discover their secrets. The film fails, however, both as a drama and as a study of the journalistic process. Cusack's journalism functions merely as a plot device to give him (and the viewer) access to the information which drives the plot. Beyond making some early observations about the importance of a reporter's independence vis à vis his sources, the script has very little interest in how this kind of journalism works.

Box office: $25,105,255 (US only)

Mad City (Costa-Gavras, 1997, 115 minutes)

In a story with echoes of Billy Wilder's *Ace in the Hole* Dustin Hoffman plays disillusioned, dissatisfied local TV news reporter Max Brackett, who happens to be covering a routine story at the museum when a hostage situation develops. Sacked museum worker (John Travolta) has snapped after being made redundant, and taken a group of children hostage. Presented with a scoop, Max and his producers proceed to build the story into a national spectacle, further enraging the hostage-taker and endangering his hostages as they do so. As in Wilder's film the hunger for a saleable story leads to the manufacture of a crisis, and the amplification of the problematic reality which journalists are supposed merely to report. Max's bosses and rivals are portrayed as unsympathetic villains, ruthless in their exploitation of an unfolding human tragedy. Unlike Wilder's satire, however, the journalist on this occasion is a reluctant participant in the media circus. His motives are good, and in the end he rebels against the rampant commercialism of his managers. Fifty years after Chuck Tatum's unapologetic villainy, Max is a more knowing, reflective figure, unwilling to just play along with the demands of the news business, here portrayed as the enemy of truth and objectivity.

Box office: $10,541,523 (US only)

1998

Fear and Loathing in Las Vegas (Terry Gilliam, 1998, 113 minutes)

Terry Gilliam's adaptation of Hunter S. Thompson's best known book had a troubled production history (British director Alex Cox had been enlisted as director before Gilliam, for example, but was taken off the project reportedly after disagreements with Thompson). Starring Johnny Depp as Thompson and Benicio Del Toro as his Attorney, the script stays close to the language and structure of the book, describing a weekend of drug-fuelled deviance in Las Vegas, circa 1971. Ostensibly sent to cover the Mint 400 motorcycle race, Thompson's aim is to show, through the prism of his satirical, surrealistic prose (here translated into voiceover and dialogue), 'the American dream in action'. 'Our trip was to be a classic affirmation of everything right and true in the national character; a gross physical salute to the fantastic possibilities of life in this country, but only for those with true grit'. As readers of the book will know, everything Thompson writes is steeped in irony, and the only heroic thing about this journey into the 'savage heart' of the American dream is the level of consumption of illegal drugs achieved by the journalist and his attorney. That is his point, of course – only through the prism of hallucino-genics can the reality of the American dream be accessed.

From the viewpoint of 1971, and against the backdrop of Thompson's previous work, this was a radical journalistic strategy, making him one of the most celebrated journalists in the world. In 1998, deprived of that context, the film lacks the satirical edge of the book and proceeds as a series of transgressive episodes of drug-fuelled rebellion against all that Las Vegas represents (a supper show by Debbie Reynolds is disrupted by boorish drunkenness, for example, in the mistaken belief that this is some kind of 'statement'). There are moments of overt misogyny in the latter third of the film, and much of the humour of the book is drowned out by paranoia and threatened violence. By staying so close to the original source material, written nearly three decades before, the script lacks narrative drive.

The real Hunter Thompson makes a brief cameo in a scene where the Duke reminisces about San Francisco in 1965, signalling his close involvement in and endorsement of the film.

Box office: $10,680,275 (US only)

Almost Famous (Cameron Crowe, 1998, 118 minutes)

Cameron Crowe's loosely autobiographical film is a coming-of-age story about a young, would-be music journalist (Patrick Fugit) who finds himself at fifteen years old on tour with rising rock band Stillwater. Aided and advised by Lester Bangs (Philip Seymour Hoffmann), William learns how to become a journalist, and how to become a man as he negotiates life with the band and its groupies, or 'band-aids', led by Penny Lane (Kate Hudson). This is a gentle story, miles away from the more realistic portrayals of the rock and roll lifestyle depicted in *Velvet Goldmine* or *Twenty Four Hour Party People*. Compared to the reported antics of Led Zeppelin and other bands touring around the time when the film is set, 1972–3, the members of Stillwater are choir boys. They smoke a little pot, and have sex from time to time, but this is a sanitised picture of life on the road; a version fit for the US teenagers whom the film appears to be targeting with its focus on William's growing pains. This is a film you could take home to a mother as protective as William's is in the script.

Hoffmann's mentorly role is to advise William on how to be a good music journalist, and to represent authenticity in the face of the big industry sell-out. He warns William that despite the temptations he must never make friends with the rock stars, if he is to preserve independence and integrity as a journalist. 'You have to build your reputation on being honest, and unmerciful'. And in the piece William writes for *Rolling Stone* he tries to be honest, if hardly savage in his criticism. His honesty leads the band to disown him to his editor as a liar, but in the final sequence they apologise and repair the damage to his career.

Notable as a rare example of a film set in the world of music journalism, and with a generous approach to its characters (there are no bad guys – just a few inflated egos) this is a diverting, sweet account of its subject. At one point William's editor at *Rolling Stone* warns him that he is not travelling with Stillwater 'to party. We already have one Hunter Thompson'. A story further removed from the debauchery and excess of gonzo would be hard to imagine.

Box office: $47,383,689

Velvet Goldmine (Todd Haynes, 1998, 117 minutes)

Todd Haynes' affectionate study of 1970s glam rock pays homage to *Citizen Kane* in its journalist-seeks-answers-to-mystery investigative structure. Arthur Stuart (Christian Bale) is commissioned to find out what happened to Brian Slade, a Ziggy Stardust-like figure who disappeared from rock stardom in the 1970s. As in *Citizen Kane* the journalist proceeds through a series of interviews with those who knew and worked with Slade, gradually uncovering pieces of the jigsaw which will solve the mystery. As in Welles' film there are no easy answers or neat resolutions, but the journey is fascinating, especially for viewers, like this writer, who remember the glam rock era as teenagers. The practice of music journalism is a secondary concern of the film, which succeeds mainly as a multi-layered meditation on the nature of image and celebrity, and a celebration of glam. The film can be read as a fan's bio-pic of David Bowie in his Ziggy years, and also as a queer deconstruction of the glam aesthetic.

Box office: $1,053,788 (US only)

Deep Impact (Mimi Leder, 1998, 120 minutes)

Made just as end-of-millennium angst was peaking (Y2K, anyone?), *Deep Impact* tells the story of an MSNBC news reporter (Tea Leoni) covering the Washington political brief, who stumbles upon 'Ele', which she believes to refer to a sex scandal cover-up in government. An ambitious journalist eager to be promoted to anchor, she aggressively pursues the story until she arouses the wrath of the authorities. Ele, she then learns, is an acronym for Extinction Level Event – specifically, a comet speeding towards earth with the capability to wipe out all life. She is asked by the president himself (Morgan Freeman) not to break her story until the authorities are ready, in return for which co-operation she will be given the first question at the presidential news conference where Ele will be revealed to the public.

The first third of the film is the most interesting for journalism students. What we see is a late 1990s world in which the media are treated with deep cynicism by politicians, who are merely trying to do a difficult job. What at first looks like a sinister cover-up is quickly revealed to be a very necessary policy of controlling information to avoid panic. Should the journalist co-operate or not? Her ambition and her sense of ethics say not. The president, looking like an older version of Barack Obama, tells her, 'Congratulations [on getting to the story of Ele]. You now have the biggest story in history. I know you're just a reporter, but you used to be a person'. Is it appropriate for her to co-operate in keeping the secret for a little longer, he asks, if it is in the best interests of the nation? Is the Truth always in the best interests of the nation?

Leoni's character co-operates as requested. When the meaning of Ele is finally revealed to the world, the film becomes a sci-fi/action hero/ rescue mission drama, in which Leoni's character, and MSNBC News, are positioned as spectators, reporters, and then trusted guides through what is going to be a rough ride for humanity as the comet hits. Extended scenes of Leoni anchoring MSNBC's rolling news coverage of the US-Russian efforts to save the world act as a narrative device taking the audience through the technical details of how to land a space raft on a comet and blow it up with nuclear weapons. Amidst technological complexity, the journalist is positioned as our sense-maker and guide.

Box office: $349,464,664

Celebrity (Woody Allen, 1998, 109 minutes)

Kenneth Branagh stars as celebrity journalist Lee in a satire about modern media culture, and the shallowness of the people who inhabit it. Branagh imper- sonates Woody Allen's neurotic New Yorker, complete with physical and verbal tics, and the cast features cameos and supporting roles from a galaxy of stars, including Leonardo Di Caprio, Famke Janssen and Charlize Theron. Sven Nykvist's monochrome cinematography is reminiscent of *Manhattan*, and the ingredients are in place for a funny and sophisticated look at contemporary celebrity. The film is a wasted opportunity, however. Branagh's performance is brazenly contrived, and makes Allen's normally funny dialogue seem merely annoying. The plot lacks credibility, and the script and acting are wooden from beginning to end. Avoiding any serious engagement with the nature of mediated celebrity, or celebrity journalism (which Branagh's character openly detests and seeks to escape at the earliest opportunity), *Celebrity* fails on almost every level, and emerges as little more than an angry celebrity's (i.e., the director's) extended dig at the media which had hounded him ever since the revelation of his affair with his partner's adopted daughter. Allen's anger at Mia Farrow may also help explain the uncharacteristically sexist tone of a film in which almost every female character is a crude caricature of some patriarchal stereotype or other, from wacky blonde model to broken, bitter divorcee.

Box office: $5,078,660 (US only)

1999

True Crime (Clint Eastwood, 1999, 127 minutes)

In a story with some similarities to Alan Parker's *Life of David Gale*, Clint Eastwood plays maverick investigative reporter Steve Everett, who is assigned to do a 'human interest side bar' on the imminent execution of a convicted murderer. Everett becomes convinced that the convicted man is innocent, and embarks on a race to have his execution cancelled. The film uses journalism principally as a vehicle for access to a crime thriller narrative. The journalists and editors on Everett's *Oakland Tribune* are clichéd, and Eastwood's character lacks credibility. Entering his seventies, we are nonetheless asked to accept that he is a serial and highly successful pursuer of women young enough to be his grand-daughter, and that he has a five-year-old child. We are also given to understand that this is a journalist in mid-career, although no editor would employ someone so old as a staffer.

Notwithstanding some funny and insightful lines on the nature of popular journalism – James Woods' editor says to Everett at one point, 'Issues are shit that we make up so we can have good stories' – this is a film about journalism made by people who do not really understand how it works.

Box office: $16,649,768 (US only)

Runaway Bride (Garry Marshall, 1999, 112 minutes)

Richard Gere plays Ike Graham, a columnist for *USA Today* who specialises in 'inner diatribes at the opposite sex'. Over drinks in a New York bar, and eager for a story, he is told of Maggie Carpenter (Julie Roberts), a woman living in the small town of Hale who, he is unreliably informed, has jilted seven fiancés at the altar. He dubs her 'the runaway bride' and pens a cruel column about her man-eating tendencies. The article is inaccurate and Maggie complains. Ike is sacked by his editor, who also happens to be his ex-wife.

Ike sets out to vindicate himself by going to Hale and reporting Maggie's latest planned wedding. He is promised a cover story in *GQ* if she again jilts her fiancé, a kind sports coach named Bob. A warm-hearted, well-written romantic comedy ensues as Ike and Maggie at first clash, then gradually fall in love as both he and she come to see the error of their past ways, and to recognise that after a number of failed attempts to find love, they are right for each other.

In this film Gere plays the classic journalistic rogue, deeply attractive to women but not to be trusted. His journalistic ethics are questionable, and he is a cynic, but at core he is a good man. Maggie is the catalyst for exposing the best in him, and he in her. Designed as a vehicle for the director and stars who made the hugely successful *Pretty Woman*, and similarly light and upbeat in tone, *Runaway Bride* has quite a lot of value to say about journalistic ethics, and the work of Ike's brand of personalised column-writing in particular. Ike articulates the common view of journalism as somewhat less than worthy, when he tells Maggie that his father wanted him to be a novelist and notes that 'Journalism is literature in a hurry'.

Box office: $309,457,509

Three Kings (David O. Russell, 1999, 114 minutes)

A film in large part about 'the media war' of 1991 in Iraq, when US and other forces liberated Kuwait from Saddam Hussein's invasion and briefly entered Iraq. The film follows a group of soldiers who stumble on to a map describing hidden Iraqi gold, and seek to liberate it for themselves. Primarily a caper movie in its structure and pacing, though realistic and disturbing in its realism, and in the impression of early post-war chaos it delivers, *Three Kings* is also a penetrating study of the relationship of the media to conflict. The 1991 Gulf War was the first to involve twenty-four-hour real-time news media on the ground, here represented by the character of Adriana Cruz, an 'NBS' reporter modelled on CNN's Christiane Amanpour. Her character is presented as a sincere journalist, confused by what she sees as a senseless war. She embodies the celebrification of news, but is portrayed as a reluctant participant.

George Clooney plays her escort, charged with ensuring that she gets access to good news stories about the war. He is cynical about her presence, and the role of the US military in Iraq, asking at one point, 'what did we do here?' His first appearance in the film shows him having sex with another journalist, perhaps a reference to the film-maker's view that the military well and truly fucked the media in Iraq. 'What was this war about?' Adriana Cruz echoes Archie's earlier exasperation, and voices the corrupt, empty nature of news. 'This business is about sexual politics and style ...' In the end she redeems herself by helping Archie with the evacuation of civilians. By sacrificing their gold for the civilians, the soldiers are also redeemed.

Although Cruz's pursuit of her story is a secondary sub-plot, the presence of the media hangs over the narrative. *Three Kings* is not the first film to explore the relationship between journalism and war in the era of the always-on media, but its innovative cinematography and unsentimental treatment of conflict and its consequences makes it among the most effective. The US again went to war in Iraq twelve years later, with far more human casualties inflicted, making the carnage depicted in this film seem mild by comparison.

Box office: $107,752,036

Never Been Kissed (Raja Gosnell, 1999, 107 minutes)

Drew Barrymore (who also produced the film through her Flowers company) stars as Josie Celler, a dull but efficient copy editor on a Chicago newspaper given the opportunity to go undercover and write about teenagers at a local high school. Barrymore does not convince as a twenty-five-year-old impersonating a seventeen-year-old student, and the journalistic elements of the plot are clichéd and unrealistic. The script is lazy and lacks narrative credibility. Barrymore's character's status as a journalist gives her the licence to go undercover with the school kids, and thus drives the plot, but the film avoids the potentially interesting ethical or professional issues it raises (such as the pressure placed on Josie to entrap her teacher into a sexual relationship, and thus manufacture a big story for the newspaper).

Box office: $84,565,230

The Insider (Michael Mann, 1999, 151 minutes)

Michael Mann's contribution to the journalism genre takes as its subject the CBS *Sixty Minutes* investigation into the allegations of a former tobacco company researcher that Big Tobacco had been knowingly withholding information about the addictive properties of cigarettes. Jeffrey Wigand, the 'insider' of the film's title (played by Russell Crowe just before he became a global superstar with *Gladiator*), is sacked from his senior research post at the firm of Brown and Williamson (he is a vice-president) for challenging the firm's research ethics. By accident (he is preparing a story on the tobacco industry) CBS producer Lowell Bergman (Al Pacino) comes into contact with Wigand, whom he intends to employ as a consultant. Bergman, again by accident, although his razor-sharp journalistic intuition and nose for a story place him on permanently high alert, realises that Wigand is in possession of newsworthy information about his former employer, and begins the process of turning him into a whistle-blower. Bergman's goal as a senior producer at *Sixty Minutes* is to prepare an investigative report which will expose the self-serving propaganda of the US tobacco companies, who by then were already under growing pressure to meet at least some of the costs of compensating smokers who had fallen ill or died from tobacco consumption. Wigand is reluctant to be involved, having signed a confidentiality agreement guaranteeing his salary and health benefits. The plot is structured around Bergman's struggle to groom his whistle-blower, then to protect him (unsuccessfully) when the flak starts to fly.

By the late 1990s Mann was renowned as a style-defining director of the TV series *Miami Vice*, and thrillers such as *Manhunter* (1986) and *Heat* (also starring Al Pacino, and made in 1995). Mann's movies hitherto had been long, complex and wordy, shot in crisp, clean blues and whites, and imbued with philosophical weight. *The Insider* fits into all of these boxes, with a screen time of two and a half hours in which we move between grainy, washed-out images signifying Wigand's paranoia and ultimate nervous collapse to glossy interior shots of impeccably minimalist board rooms and sterile suburban homes. Pacino's journalist is given several lengthy monologues about the meaning of ojectivity, integrity, and the importance of standing by one's whistle-blower, or source, when the going gets tough, as it quickly does. As Wigand grows to trust Bergman, and begins to co-operate with the complex strategems which will enable a public, legal expose of Big Tobacco, Brown and Williamson unleash a campaign of harassment and intimidation, including bullets left in mail boxes, mysterious footprints in the garden, and death threats sent by email to Wigand and his family.

A central theme of the film is the impact on a family – any family – of whistle-blowing against a powerful corporate force. We see an ostensibly happy family (although there are hints of problem drinking and domestic violence) broken apart by the pressure on Wigand to stick to the terms of his confidentiality agreement. His wife leaves him, temporarily, and takes the children with her, one of whom is asthmatic and requires expensive health treatment. Wigand bears all of this, because he trusts Bergman's assurances that, having taken the risk of going public with his insider knowledge, his information will be aired and it will all be worthwhile. Unfortunately, Bergman has underestimated the forces aligned against him. A merger deal involving CBS and Philip Morris leads CBS Business to override CBS News, and Wigand's key interview is cut from the broadcast. Bergman retaliates against his employees, and by complicated manouevring manages to get the story out in its entirety. To do this he must betray his star presenter, Mike Wallace (Christopher Plummer).

The Insider is a 'true' story, but in traditional Hollywood manner a number of scenes are 'creatively imagined' in order to heighten the suspense of the viewer. The bullet placed in Wigand's mail box, for example, may or may not be real. As Wigand's suffering intensifies, melancholic soundtrack music of the type later used to great effect in *Gladiator* highlights his distress and appeals to our sympathies. Such details heighten the drama of the story, but are irrelevant next to the central myth relayed in the film – the courage of the key players, and the struggle to maintain the integrity, not just of the journalist as he balances truth against professional loyalty, but the former employee with some kind of debt to his employer. When is it right to violate an agreement of confidentiality, and when is it right to betray one's journalistic colleagues? Mann clearly goes with the whistle-blower and the principled producer, both of whom are established as individuals prepared to risk all, be it their lives, or their reputations for professional loyalty and collegiality, in the pursuit of exposing the abuse of power.

Box office: $60,289,912

Complicity (Gavin Millar, 1999, 100 minutes)

Johhny Lee Miller plays Cameron Colley, an investigative reporter for the Edinburgh-based *Caledonian* newspaper, in a thriller based on Iain Banks' novel. The film fails on almost every level, and was released straight-to-video in most markets (except Scotland, where it is set). Miller's clichéd reporter (he drinks whisky all the time, but is never drunk; he smokes cannabis and snorts cocaine on the job; enjoys rough sex) is too slight and boyish to be convincing. While attempting to portray a world-weary journalistic cynic, he looks and sounds (in an irritating voiceover) as if he is just out of journalism school, or maybe just school.

The plot contrives to have him framed for a series of gruesome murders, and entirely fails to suspend the viewer's disbelief. The script is laden with crudely reductive assertions about how journalism works, such as the moment when Cameron's editor spikes a mildly left-of-centre article he's written with the words, 'You're paid to toe the editorial line'. *Complicity* reinforces the conclusion that good movies about the more popular end of the journalism business are thin on the ground.

Box office: not applicable (released in cinemas in Scotland, but not in the wider UK or overseas).

2000

In the Mood for Love (Wong Kar Wai, 2000, 94 minutes)

Mr Chow (Tony Leung) is a journalist in 1962 Hong Kong. He and his wife move into a small flat, next door to Mrs Chan (Maggie Cheung) and her husband. Gradually we, and they, come to realise that the wife and husband respectively (whom we never see in full shot) are conducting an affair. Chow and Chan embark on their own relationship, taking comfort in each other's company but never sleeping together. 'We won't be like them', says Mrs Chan. As they fall more deeply in love, Chow moves first to Singapore, then to Cambodia, where the film ends, his love for Chan never consummated.

This is a film about love rather than journalism. Chow's status as a journalist allows him to be presented as a thoughtful, intellectual character, dissatisfied with journalism and an aspiring writer of martial arts novels. He and Chan spend their happiest times writing together. The film has nothing of significance to say on the nature of journalism, except that writing novels is better, and only glimpses of Chow's workplace are offered.

Box office: $12,854,953

2001

15 Minutes (John Herzfeld, 2001, 120 minutes)

Robert Hawkins (Kelsey Grammar) is a presenter for New York-based true crime TV show *Top Story* – 'the nation's newsreel'. Robert De Niro plays Eddie Fleming, an alcoholic cop who works with Hawkins to 'break the big news' by allowing him to turn up at the scene of dramatic arrests with a camera crew in tow. Comparable to Kevin Spacey's character in *LA Confidential*, Fleming is a cop aware of how the media operate, and how he can use them to professional advantage. Hawkins and his producers are, meanwhile, hungry for the 'bad news' stories to which he gives them access.

Into this scenario come two Eastern European criminal psychopaths, fascinated by the power of media celebrity to make them famous (hence the title of the film with its reference to Warhol's 'famous for 15 minutes' aphorism), and who embark on a campaign of murder and media manipulation. They, like Eddie, understand that 'it's all about image'.

Unlike *LA Confidential*, this thriller-satire on the relationship between crime and the media is crude and unconvincing. The violence is realistic, and the New York settings authentic, but the characters are clichéd and one-dimensional, and the tone uneven, veering from comedy to intense, sexualised violence in an instant. This mix, and the extensive use of hand-held video recalls *Natural Born Killers*, but the effect here is exploitative and irritating rather than mesmeric. Its treatment of TV crime journalism is shallow, posing again the question: why are good films about popular, tabloid journalism – films which avoid caricatures and cliché – so hard to find and, apparently, so hard to make?

Box office: $56,359,980

The Shipping News (Lasse Halstrom, 2001, 107 minutes)

Kevin Spacey plays Quoyle, an emotionally damaged single father who moves to Newfoundland after the death of his abusive partner. He takes a job writing the shipping news for the local newspaper, *The Gammy Bird*, and begins to rebuild his life. Adapted from the novel by E. Annie Proulx, the film presents a multi-layered narrative of family dysfunction, personal self-discovery and emerging love in which Quoyle's developing journalistic identity is secondary, but an important foundation for his broader personal recovery. As he is a novice to the business of writing, the film takes him, and the audience, through the essentials of local journalism. Car crashes, for example, of which there are many in this foggy, snow-bound part of the country, always make headlines. The cynical editor, played by Pete Postlethwaite, dishes out pearls of journalistic wisdom to the rookie, who is a quick learner and soon delivering copy which is more interesting than that of his more experienced colleagues. Through his journalism he discovers unknown depths in himself, and something at which he is naturally gifted – finding and writing up colourful local stories for *The Gammy Bird*.

The film suffers from trying to pack in too many narrative strands, but the treatment of local journalism in a rural backwater is funny, affectionate and genuinely educational.

Box office: $24,690,441

The Cat's Meow (Peter Bogdanovich, 2001, 112 minutes)

The film tells the (rumoured to be) true story of the mysterious and still unsolved death of Hollywood producer Thomas Ince while on board the yacht of media baron William Randolph Hearst in 1924. According to the script, Ince was shot dead by accident, mistaken by Hearst for Charlie Chaplin, who was having an affair with the baron's mistress, Marion Davies. The shooting is covered up, and the silence of rising celebrity columnist Louella Parsons (Kirsten Dunst) guaranteed by Hearst's promotion of her career thenceforth. It is notable as a rare cinematic depiction of Hearst, but more a meditation on the capacity of the powerful to preserve their secrets than a study of media power in particular.

Box office: $3,646,994

Kissing Jessica Stein (Charles Herman-Wurmfeld, 2001, 97 minutes

A gay-themed variation on the romantic comedy sub-genre of journalism movies, Jennifer Westfeld stars as a New York-based straight journalist who embarks on a fling with a bisexual woman she encounters through a lonely hearts advertisement. Jessica's status as a journalist, and her colleagues and friends at the newspaper where she works, are merely the backdrop to the story, and journalism is not the subject of the film.

Box office: $10,013,424

2002

No Man's Land (Danis Tanovich, 2002, 93 minutes)

The first full-length feature film by Bosnian director Danis Tanovich deals with the same subject matter as Michael Winterbottom's *Welcome To Sarajevo* – the fratricidal civil war which engulfed Bosnia-Herzegovina in the early 1990s. The perspective is that of a local man, however, and the form chosen that of satire, through which Danovich aims to penetrate the absurdity of a conflict in which people who once were neighbours are now killing each other. Like *Welcome To Sarajevo*, enacted sequences are punctuated with actual news footage of the horrors of the war, including bodies of civilians lying dead in the streets. Pitch black comedy is the film-maker's main tool here, but the violent reality of ethnic cleansing is never far from the surface, with shootings, stabbings and other acts gradually reducing the protagonists Ciki and Nino to bloodied wrecks. The film won the 2002 Oscar for Best Foreign Language Film.

The story concerns a relief group of Bosnian fighters who get lost on their way to the frontline somewhere outside Sarajevo. They come under fire from a Serbian unit, and only one man survives – Ciki (Branko Djuric) – who hides in a trench. Two Serbians come to check on the situation, and place a booby-trap mine under the body of one of the fighters. Ciki kills one of them and wounds the other. It then turns out that the booby-trapped body is still alive, but cannot be moved lest the mine explode. The rest of the film follows the playing out of this stalemate in 'no man's land', where the three men squabble and debate the issues, surrounded by fighters of the competing factions, as first the United Nations (UNProfor) and then the world's media become involved.

The film is clearly intended as an attack on the UN for its impotence in dealing with the abuses which characterised this war at the heart of Europe, and also on the global media, represented by the late Katrin Cartlidge's Jane Livingstone, a reporter for the fictional *Global News Channel*. Jane overhears UN and Serb communication about the stalemate, and descends on the scene with her camera crew, where she proceeds to turn it into a story of the type which would have been enjoyed by Kate Adie at her peak, or Christiane Amanpour. She is soon joined by other journalists, and the scene becomes a media circus.

The film engages with a popular criticism of the media's role in conflict and catastrophe – that they both amplify and trivialise tragedy, turning harrowing events into infotainment for the sake of audience ratings. But by comparison with Winterbottom's film on the same subject, the satire here is clumsy and crude. Jane Livingstone and her employers back at home base in London are portrayed as entirely shallow and self-serving in their efforts to get the story. Initially, the arrival of *Global News Channel* is welcome, and we see some exploration of the notion that the media can act as a journalistic conscience for the world – a crucial witness, indeed – in situations such as this, where bureaucracy and politics are preventing common-sense resolution of a resolvable situation. But the script leaves us in no doubt that the media, in their desperation for viewer-friendly visuals, their hunger for televisual drama, are equally culpable in the unfolding absurdist tragedy.

The journalistic characters are shallow caricatures rather than real human beings, evoking no sympathy from the viewer. The war correspondent in this film is not a hero but an opportunist, feeding parasitically on the misfortune of others, and adding nothing that is positive to the situation. In the end the stalemate degenerates into violence, the leading protagonists are killed, and the man under whose body the booby trap is placed is left to fend for himself. Jane and her colleagues get in their car and drive away, presumably to the scene of the next atrocity, where they will go about their work in precisely the same way.

Box office: $4,858,869

Spider-Man (Sam Raimi, 2002, 121 minutes)

Like *Superman*, the adventures of the comic hero, *Spider-Man* take place against the backdrop of news media, in this case the tabloid *Daily Bugle*. Mild-mannered Peter Parker, though not a full-time journalist, is a freelance photographer for the *Bugle*. Editor J. Jonah Jameson is portrayed as a ruthless, amoral hack, determined to portray Spider-Man as an evil force, and to uncover his true identity. The tensions between Parker's inherent goodness and Jameson's pursuit of an innocent hero have been a key structuring element in the *Spider-Man* stories ever since their appearance in comic form, and are prominent in the latest version, directed for the big screen by Sam Raimi. Jameson's character, and the representation of tabloid journalism in the form of the *Daily Bugle*, reflect the critical views of many towards what was known then as the 'yellow press', a sub-species of journalism not to be trusted. The film and its sequels were among the most commercially successful films of all time.

Box office: $821,708,551

Twenty Four Hour Party People (Michael Winterbottom, 2002, 111 minutes)

The lead character in Winterbottom's account of the Factory years is journalist and music industry mogul Tony Wilson (played by Steve Coogan), whom we first see filming an item for the TV current affairs programme on which he is a roving reporter with a brief to do wacky, human interest-oriented stuff like hang-gliding. Later we see him mess up a TV interview with the Conservative cabinet minister Keith Joseph. Wilson, of course, was destined to be not a great journalist, but a visionary manager of rock bands and founder of the Factory record label, which established Manchester and the North as the creative centre of the British music scene in the 1980s.

Box office: $2,781,211

Life or Something Like It (Stephen Herek, 2002, 103 minutes)

In this romantic comedy Angelina Jolie plays Lanie Kerrigan, a TV news reporter working for *KGMO News*, who is told by Prophet Jack, a 'street savant' whom she interviews for a human-interest item on his apparent ability to predict the future, that she has only seven days to live. The film unfolds as an exploration of the dilemma such a revelation would pose for a person, against the background of her awkward relationship with ex-boyfriend Pete the cameraman (Ed Burns). Jolie's character, who begins the film as a stereo-typically shallow media bimbo (Jolie wears blonde hair, high heels and tight sweaters throughout), is required to go on a journey of personal self-discovery, involving reconciliation with her own deep-rooted neuroses about family and childhood, and eventual union with Pete.

Like many other films in this sub-genre, and those starring Hollywood's leading ladies in particular, *Life or Something Like It* is not really about journalism, although it is set in that world. Jolie's status as a TV news reporter provides the plot device for her encounter with the savant, and the milieu within which the action unfolds, but the film does not engage in depth with the nature of TV news. Her shallowness and vapidity as a person and a professional are challenged, but these are not qualities the film associates with journalism in particular. This is a minor work in the canon of journalism movies, then, and also in the acting portfolio of Angelina Jolie, whose performance as Mariane Pearl in *A Mighty Heart* later confirmed how good an actor she is. Here, she is merely cruising.

Box office: $16,872,671

Black and White (Craig Lahiff, 2002, 99 minutes)

This true-life legal drama is notable for its depiction of a young Rupert Murdoch, proprietor of the Adelaide-based *News*, who puts his then-still fragile press power to the service of a legal campaign to save an aboriginal man from the death penalty. Supporting Robert Carlyle's persistent defence lawyer, Ben Mendehlson plays Murdoch as a hard-headed but passionate, anti-estab-lishment man of the people, delighted to set himself up against what he sees as the stuffy South Australian elite of the late 1950s. The script is pedestrian and the performances lacklustre, although Mendehlson's Murdoch at least holds the attention, probably because portrayals of him are so rare. The picture presented here of the future media baron is broadly sympathetic, if not heroic. The script allows us to see that his commitment to the aboriginal's defence is about selling newspapers and getting one over on the elitist snobs who hate his journalism, as much as upholding justice. Nevertheless, Mr Murdoch cannot have been displeased with this portrayal of him as an iconoclastic champion of the popular.

Box office: $5,541,431

Chicago (Rob Marshall, 2002, 113 minutes)

Based on the successful Broadway musical, *Chicago* explores the relationship between popular journalism, crime and celebrity in America of the 1920s. Notwithstanding its generic focus on music and dance, the script tells a quite sophisticated story of how tabloid celebrity is constructed, and deconstructed, and constructed again, often with the help of skilful public relations (Richard Gere plays lawyer and press agent Billy Flynn). There are no major journalistic characters in *Chicago*, but the press pack as a whole is a constant backdrop to, and catalyst for, the action.

Box office: $306,776,732

The Quiet American (Philip Noyce, 2002, 118 minutes)

Philip Noyce's adaptation of the Graham Greene novel was perfectly timed for the post-9/11 environment of contested US intervention in Iraq and Afghanistan. Michael Caine plays Fowler, a disillusioned foreign correspondent in 1950s Vietnam who becomes involved with Pyle, the 'quiet American' of the title. Pyle is a shadowy figure involved in covert US actions, and Fowler becomes increasingly angry with what he perceives to be his (and America's) ignorance and hubris. The portrayal of a US agent complicit in bombings of civilians and other nefarious actions in pursuit of a higher cause is prescient of what would come in Iraq and Afghanistan after 9/11. In this sense Greene's novel retains its relevance in the twenty-first century, and this is a watchable adaptation. Fowler is the classic journalistic witness, seeking to maintain his detachment from atrocity but compelled in the end to participate in the story.

Box office: $27,674,124

2003

Bruce Almighty (Tom Shadyac, 2003, 101 minutes)

Jim Carrey plays Bruce, a bored, cynical local TV news reporter, forever condemned (as he sees it) to the humiliating trivia of community-based journalism. Then he is endowed with God-like powers and embarks on a fantasy-allegory about what happens when a man can have whatever he wants.

In the end he comes to value the things he has, and his job as a local journalist. This is a phenomenally successful comedy, which nevertheless has a serious message about the importance of community, and the role of local news in binding it together.

Box office: $484,592,874

How To Lose a Guy in 10 Days **(Donald Petrie, 2003, 116 minutes)**

Much more successful at the box office than Angelina Jolie's attempt at journalistic rom com, this film stars Kate Hudson as style journalist, or 'how-to girl', Andie Anderson, commissioned to write a career-saving piece on how to lose a guy in ten days. Andie is a frustrated graduate of journalism from Columbia, who hungers for serious stories about politics, economics, foreign affairs. Her editor at *Composure* urges her to make her 'how to' column a must read, after which she can write what she likes. Until then, 'you write what we like'. A successful commission will give her more freedom, her editor promises, and so she sets out to win and lose her guy. From this point on, the film is essentially a battle of the sexes, in which gender stereotypes come into mildly comic conflict before love prevails. Andie delivers her piece, but is let down by her editor at the last moment and resigns from *Composure*.

As in other rom coms featuring female style journalists made in the 1997–2008 period, journalism is the setting for a flawed comic vehicle. The journalistic challenge of writing an article about relationships provides the plot, but apart from the contrast made throughout between 'serious' and 'not serious' content, and the portrayal of the all-female offices of *Composure*, there is little here to interest the student of journalism.

Box office: $177,371,441

Shattered Glass **(Billy Ray, 2003, 91 minutes).**

This is the story of journalist Stephen Glass, who in 1998 was discovered to have been 'cooking' feature articles for the distinguished US public affairs periodical, *New Republic* (that is, inventing sources and facts). Although it would be unfair to assert that Glass' successful fabrication of dozens of his *New Republic* pieces was or is representative of the editorial standards applied by the great majority of print media, the extreme nature of the case here comes to symbolise a wider theme – the gradual decline in the authority of even the most respectable and established of print publications, and the rise of the online upstarts such as *Forbes Digital*, the first daily online business news publication (launched in 1997).

The tension between print and online journalism is one strand of the narrative; the other is the gap between the normative ideals of liberal journalism, which Glass articulates with great eloquence and credibility throughout the film, and his own blatant violation of those ideals. Glass (Hayden Christensen) has a number of speeches in which he talks reverently about the nature of journalism, and its function in a democracy. Journalism of the sort he practises for *New Republic* is, he asserts to a classroom full of journalism students, both 'a privilege and a responsibility', because 'what you write can influence public policy'. Fully aware of this responsibility as he is, Glass' blatant flouting of the most elementary journalistic ethics is all the more breath-taking, and we cannot help but sympathise with his editor Chuck Lane (Peter Sarsgaard) as the scale of Glass' fraud becomes clear.

The script suggests that Glass succeeds in his fabrications (until he is caught out by *Forbes Digital Tool*) because he is, in essence, a nice guy. His problem, the roots of which are never explored in depth (although there are references to a dysfunctional family background), is simply that he is desperate to be liked so gives those around him, be they editors, colleagues or friends, what it is he thinks they want to hear, even if it is not true. His niceness quickly transmutes into creepiness, as the sociopathic aspect of his personality emerges. One can feel some sympathy for his character, but more for the studious, civilised Chuck Lane who, as editor, presides over what may justifiably be regarded as the greatest fraud ever perpetrated on a journalistic publication in the US.

The film was co-executive produced by Tom Cruise. It is, however, a much more powerful critique of the media's excesses than the Mel Gibson-produced *Paparazzi*. This is a sophisticated, nuanced tale of good, hardworking journalists being cruelly conned by one of their own, and thereby becoming among the first victims of the digital era. In the end, the film is a plea for journalistic integrity, and against any tendency to fabricate or embellish the truth. 'It's indefensible, don't you know that?', says Chuck to one of his staff who stands up for Glass. She does, and so do we.

Box office: $2,944,752

Veronica Guerin (Joel Schumacher, 2003, 94 minutes)

Cate Blanchett plays real-life Irish investigative reporter Veronica Guerin in Joel Schumacher's account of how tenacity in pursuing organised crime led to a violent and untimely death. The script is brutal and bleak, following Guerin as she encounters bureaucratic obstruction and criminal violence, including a vicious beating at the hands of the crime boss she is pursuing. Her family are threatened, and in the end she is assassinated.

Guerin is a classic journalistic hero(ine), but the script questions her motivation. Is she brave, or just reckless? Is she intent on justice, or just obsessed, to the point where nothing else matters but her story? Her performance as a wife and mother are questioned and found wanting. It is a heroic representation, then, and a cautionary tale for the aspiring investigative journalist, but also a rebuke to those journalists who sacrifice their families and friends for their calling.

Box office: $9,439,660

The Life of David Gale (Alan Parker, 2003, 130 minutes)

Kate Winslet plays Bitsey Bloom, a principled investigative reporter working for *News* magazine (her principles are signalled by lines such as 'I play by the rules, even if my colleagues don't like it. It's called objectivity'). Having just served a week in prison for protecting her sources, Bitsey is assigned to interview David Gale, a condemned murderer on death row (Kevin Spacey). At first she is sceptical of his innocence, but is gradually drawn into the attempt to save his life.

In the first half of the film Bitsey's journalistic status is the vehicle for David Gale to narrate his story. In the latter part, she becomes an investigator after the truth, and the film shifts into thriller mode. The film never convinces as an account of how investigative journalism works, and although there is a clever twist to the tale, the thriller element is also weak. Like Eastwood's *True Crime*, it is a film built on clichés and overacting.

Box office: $38,955,598

City of God (Fernando Meirelles, 2003, 131 minutes)

Set in the favelas of Rio de Janeiro, this is the story of slum kid Buscape, who grows into a photo-journalist and thereby finds a route out of the violence which claims most of his contemporaries. The script positions Buscape, and the newspaper in which he finds an outlet for his photographs of gang warfare and slum life, as a kind of conflict journalist, a necessarily detached witness. His perspective on the narrative allows the audience some distance from what are often harrowing events.

Box office: $28,758,747

2004

Spider-Man 2 (Sam Raimi, 2004, 127 minutes)

The first sequel to the successful *Spider-Man*, containing more of the same. *Spider-Man* is again being pursued by the *Daily Bugle* and its editor, J. Jonah Jameson.

Box office: $783,766,341

Anchorman: the legend of Ron Burgundy (Adam McKay, 2004, 90 minutes)

Anchorman, produced by Judd Apatow, belongs to the genre of retro-chic comedies made in the early 2000s which poked ironic fun at the pre-feminist, pre-gay rights, pre-political correctness of the 1970s. This is the story of super-sexy San Diego anchorman Ron Burgundy (as he sees himself), and of local TV in the days 'when women weren't allowed to read the news'. Ron gulps down a large whisky before going on air, everyone smokes in the studio, and institutional sexism is taken for granted. Into this macho milieu comes the beautiful and ambitious Veronica Corningstone (Christina Applegate), who proceeds first of all to be seduced by Burgundy then, by a sequence of tragi-comic events, to replace him.

Corningstone represents precisely the stereotype of blonde beauty so condemned by critics of TV news's alleged dumbing down in subsequent decades (the argument being that, for ratings reasons, beauty had gradually come to be preferred over journalistic ability in the presentation of news). Playing against type, however, she confronts the station boss from the outset and demands access to serious news stories, while giving as good as she gets in the battle of the sexes with Ron and his gang of overgrown school boys. She is a feminist from the future arrived in a pre-feminist world, armed with a post-Madonna understanding of the power of female sexuality.

As a parodic illustration of how institutionally sexist TV news journalism (and journalism in general) used to be, *Anchorman* is knowing and funny. Men and what look from this distance like their primitively patriarchal attitudes are its targets, and female journalism students in particular will, from the security of the post-feminist twenty-first century, enjoy this display of how things used to be in their chosen profession. The script loses its tightness in the final reel, but makes an ideal companion piece to James L. Brooks' more sombre take on sexual politics in the local TV news room, *Broadcast News* (1987).

Box office: $261,572,717

Paparazzi (Paul Abascal, 2004, 81 minutes)

Produced by Mel Gibson, who makes a brief appearance, *Paparazzi* was read on its release as an act of vengeance by the Hollywood star on the celebrity media, and in particular on the photojournalists who pursue movie stars and other celebrities as they go about their public and private lives. This is a film in which the paparazzi of the title are equated with evil, and savagely punished for their crimes by a protagonist who literally gets away with murder.

Bo Laramie is a rising Hollywood action star who falls foul of a group of paparazzi, led by Rex (Tom Sizemore). In a dangerous prank gone wrong, the journalists cause Bo's car to crash (in a manner unmistakably reminiscent of the death of Diana), injuring his wife and son. In a subsequent freak accident, Bo causes one of the paprazzi to run his motorbike off the road, and then deliberately allows him to die. Having got away with this transgression, Bo pursues the rest of his tormentors, while detective Dennis Farina (playing his character as a dead ringer for Columbo) becomes suspicious.

Bo Laramie is a decent fellow, family-oriented, willing to co-operate with the media in their work, but driven beyond endurance by a group of feral hacks who live for the stolen celebrity photograph. This is a potentially interesting idea, but here the heroes and villains are drawn as caricatures. Next to Bo's good old boy the paparazzi are portrayed as vicious, predatory, parasitic, relentless in their pursuit of the shot which will make the big money. In the car crash scene we see the journalists desperately photographing the blooded occupants, one even loosening Bo's wife's dress to allow a better view of her breast (another reference to how members of the media allegedly behaved at the scene of Diana's death in 1997).

The lead journalist, Rex, is given a few lines to justify what he does. 'The public wants raw and real', he tells a girl in a bar. 'That's what we give 'em'. The public gets what the public wants, in short, and don't blame us, the journalists. There is some truth in this argument, of course, but his defence is fatally undermined by the sheer monstrousness of Rex and his colleagues as they go about their business. 'Laramie', says Rex elsewhere, 'I'm going to destroy your life and eat your soul, and I'm going to enjoy doing it'. There is a defence of celebrity journalism, not least in the need to counter celebrity PR, but this appeal to public taste is lazy and tokenistic, and weights the argument wholly to one side, i.e., the celebrity's.

The film has the look and feel of a TV movie pilot, notwithstanding a big-screen budget, Farina's involvement and eye-catching cameos by Gibson and Vince Vaughn. Only eighty minutes long, it gives the impression of a good idea left undeveloped, a wasted opportunity to explore the impact of celebrity journalism on those who become celebrities. Fifty years after *La Dolce Vita* the world still waits for a credible study of the paparazzi phenomenon. Here, the journalists are simply too villainous to be believable, and the script too wooden to be anything other than distracting, as when one of the hacks says to the boss, 'Rex, what's your plan? You must have something up your sleeve?' As *Anchorman*-style comedy this might work. Here, it is delivered without irony.

Box office: $16,796,512

13 Going On 30 (Gary Winick, 2004, 97 minutes)

A romantic comedy in the same vein as *Life or Something Like It*, and in the sub-genre of movies which play with the idea of a child inhabiting an adult's body. Jennifer Garner plays thirty-year-old Jenna, an editor of fashion magazine *Poised* who wakes up one day to find that she is thirteen again, and that seventeen years of her life have been erased from her memory. As a successful thirty-year-old working in style journalism she is also an unscrupulous media bitch, shallow and materialistic. Suddenly viewing her glamorous surroundings with the naivete and delight of a child in a sweet shop, she comes to see how empty and worthless her lifestyle is, and to re-evaluate the role of friends and family in her life. She also rediscovers her childhood sweetheart, principled photographer Matt (Mark Ruffalo), and begins the task of winning his love after seventeen years. Like *Life or Something Like It* a supernatural occurrence forces Jenna to re-evaluate her relationships with her parents, and to rediscover her essential inner goodness, which has been submerged by the pressures of her fast-lane career.

Set in the world of the women's magazine, the film explores contemporary femininity and the style culture which supports it. In competition to find a new design for the relaunch of *Poised*, in which Jenna participates with a ruthless colleague, we see two models of women's journalism exposed to scrutiny. The first, developed by her rival, wishes to make *Poised* even more 'heroin chic' and sexually graphic than it already is. Jenna, on the other hand, wishes to target *Poised* at 'real women, who are smart and pretty and like being who they are'. This is, in post-feminist terms, a conservative pitch, which the script allows to triumph. In this respect the film is a critical commentary on that strand of women's journalism featured in *Sex and the City*, and an appeal for women to return to a less sexualised culture.

Box office: $96,455,697

Control Room (2004, Jehane Noujaim, 103 minutes)

This documentary follows staff at the headquarters of Arab-language twenty-four-hour news channel Al Jazeera as they cover the invasion of Iraq in March 2003. Shot on video, *Control Room* is an example of the rise of the low-budget documentary in global cinemas in the 2000s, and one of only two in the 1997–2008 period which took journalism as its subject (see Alex Gibney's *Gonzo*, below). Its subject is the pressures faced by Al Jazeera journalists and managers as they try to cover Operation Iraqi Freedom in the face of a hostile US administration.

Box office: $2,724,826

The Life Aquatic with Steve Vissou (Wes Anderson, 2004, 119 minutes)

Cate Blanchett plays features writer Jane Winslett-Richardson on an assignment to write about eccentric oceanographer Steve Vissou. Her role is a secondary one in the script, supporting a cast of endearing oddballs. Her journalistic character provides the audience with a point of access to the narrative, but is otherwise irrelevant to the story.

Box office: $34,808,403

2005

2046 (Wong Kar Wai, 2005, 123 minutes)

The sequel to *In the Mood for Love* follows Mr Chow to Hong Kong in 1966–7, where he is writing a sci-fi novel and trying to forget Mrs Chan. He earns a living as a columnist, and the film depicts the inconclusive, unsatisfactory relationships he has with the women who live around him, including the girl in room 2046 of the hotel where he stays. Like the earlier film, 2046 uses journalism merely as a device for establishing Chow's identity as a writer-intellectual; an 'artist', as the hotel owner calls him on discovering his profession.

Box office: $19,470,239

Good Night, and Good Luck (George Clooney, 2005, 90 minutes)

George Clooney's father was a news anchor who brought up his son to revere the iconic US TV journalist Ed Murrow. This 2005 production, as Clooney put it in one promotional interview, 'is a tip of my hat to what my old man has been fighting for all his life'.[3] It is unmistakably an homage to the heroism of a particular journalist and his co-workers as they strive to fulfil their role as watchdogs in a free society.

The plot concerns an episode in 1953–4 when Ed Murrow and the producers of the CBS current affairs show *See It Now* dared to challenge what is portrayed in the film as an intensifying anti-communist witch hunt in American society, led by the notorious senator Joe McCarthy. McCarthy's campaign against the perceived threat of communist influence on, and infiltration of, US institutions dominated the political environment in the country for a decade following the end of the Second World War. Through the hearings of his Committee on Un-American Activities, McCarthy and his allies targeted writers and film directors, government officials and business people, indeed anyone who was, or who might ever have been, connected to the communist movement. In an ironic parallel to the Stalinist show trials, targeted individuals were required to name others who might also be communist sympathisers, to make confessions of their own complicity, or to publicly deny their left-wing views. Those who did not were frequently blacklisted from working in their field.

In 1953 US navy pilot Milo Radulovich was discharged from duty on the grounds of an alleged association with the communist party (his ex-wife had been a member of a communist-supporting organisation in her youth). No evidence was presented by the military in Radulovich's case, and he was given no opportunity to defend himself. In *Good Night, and Good Luck* (Murrow's catch phrase, used as a sign-off at the end of his nightly appearances) the journalist spots the story in a newspaper. In a news room already tense with mounting signs of anti-communist paranoia (Robert Downey Jr's character is required, for example, to sign one of the 'I am not now and have never been a member of the Communist Party' declarations which came to symbolise the witch hunts) Murrow decides to investigate the Radulovich case. His producer Fred Friendly, played by Clooney, supports him, though not without reservations.

Taking on the story puts *See It Now* in conflict with the US military, and also with parent company CBS, which includes amongst its key advertising clients the Alcoa aluminium company. Since Alcoa sponsors *See It Now*, and also has lucrative contracts with the US military, the Radulovich story creates tension between Murrow, Friendly and station boss William Paley (Frank Langella). Reluctantly, Paley allows *See It Now* to cover the story but warns Murrow and Friendly that they are playing for high stakes and better have their facts right. He also warns the journalists of the dangers of trial by media, and requires *See It Now* to give McCarthy a right of reply (which he takes).

As the narrative proceeds, the Radulovich story is reported and a favourable outcome achieved. He is re-instated, and the episode is seen to contribute to the end of McCarthy's toxic influence over American political and cultural life. The heroic watchdog is victorious, though not without cost. One CBS news anchor, Don Hollenbeck (Ray Wise), commits suicide following a campaign of harassment by pro-McCarthy columnist Jack O'Brien, and Hollenbeck's on-air defence of Murrow. As for Murrow and *See It Now*, the programme is eventually moved to a lower-profile place in the schedule, signalling defeat at the hands of corporate decision-makers. The film is topped and tailed by speeches delivered by Murrow warning of the dangers of a media system – a system of television journalism in particular – which does not take politics with sufficient seriousness. These and other scenes connect the narrative to debates going on in the USA when the film was released, in particular the policies of the Bush administration in its post-9/11 attempts to deal with islamic terrorism.

The film is shot in monochrome, recreating the 1950s TV news room in shades of black, white and grey. Cigarette smoke features prominently in the frame, and a mellow jazz soundtrack combined with numerous nightclub scenes reminds one of MacKendrick's *Sweet Smell of Success*. J. J. Hunsecker can be regarded as a fictionalised version of the real-life 'king-makers' Jack O'Brien and William Buckley, referenced in Clooney's film. Punctuating the scripted scenes with actors, the film contains several scenes of actual newsreel footage, although its description in some quarters as 'docu-drama' does not do justice to the warmth and energy of the piece.

Good Night, and Good Luck is a relatively short, concise film, telling its story without much in the way of character development. A sub-plot involving Robert Downey Jr and Patricia Clarkson's secretly married couple (CBS policy of the time does not allow employees to be married) allows for a small measure of human drama, as does the descent into suicidal despair of news anchor Don Hollenbeck. But Murrow himself and Friendly are given no back story. Their emotional responses to the unfolding narrative, and the dilemmas they are faced with as they take on the network bosses, the military and McCarthy, are hinted at here and there, but they have little to say that does not directly drive the heroic watchdog plot forward. This emotional minimalism is clearly intentional on Clooney's part, perhaps because the drama of the journalistic story was considered sufficient to fuel the narrative. There is a parallel here to *All The President's Men*, which is similarly uninterested in the private lives and emotions of its protagonists. In adopting this style Clooney, like Pakula in 1976, declares that this story is too important for the audience to be distracted by dramatic clichés.

Box office: $54,641,191

The Weather Man (Gore Verbinsky, 2005, 102 minutes)

Nicolas Cage plays Chicago TV weatherman Dave Spritz as he passes through a mid-life crisis. Although on the verge of moving to a better-paid, higher-profile job in New York, he is separated from his wife and daughter and struggling to find himself. His media work is the backdrop to an emotional drama, and much less an element of the story than in Gus Van Sant's *To Die For*. Its key function is to enable a contrast to be drawn between Dave's humdrum work as the deliverer of weather news with the glamorous literary profile of his Pulitzer prize-winning father (Michael Caine). Throughout the film Dave is pelted with smoothies, cups of coffee and other soft objects by mocking audience members, as he struggles with the meaning of it all.

Box office: $19,039,770

Capote (Bennett Miller, 2005, 110 minutes)

This is the first of two films about Truman Capote and the writing of his book, *In Cold Blood*, which appeared in quick succession in 2005–6. Bennett Miller's *Capote*, co-executive produced by and starring Philip Seymour Hoffmann, who won an Oscar for his performance, follows the story from November 1959 when the news report of the Clutter family killings appeared in the *New York Times* to the execution in 1965 of killers Perry Smith and Dick Hickock – the event which permitted Capote to end the book and have it published. In the intervening time we see Capote – already a celebrated writer when the film opens, with acolytes hanging on his anecdotes and tales in New York literary salons – stumbling upon the Clutter story and gradually coming to sense the potential for what he characterises as 'a new kind of writing, the non-fiction novel'.

Capote and Nelle Harper Lee (Catherine Keener) travel to Holcombe, Kansas, and after some initial awkwardness work their way into the trust of the community, including the police. Capote's celebrity, and his tales of drinking with movie stars such as Humphrey Bogart, open doors and allow him to undertake research into how the Clutter crime has impacted on the community. Then, after the killers have been arrested and throughout their trial and appeal process, he interviews them with the aim, as he explains, of 'returning them to humanity'. He assists them in finding legal advice for their appeal, and provides them with reading material in jail. In short, he befriends his subjects.

Capote engages throughout with the nature of the writer's non-fiction writing – it is journalism, reportage, but also literature of the highest quality. We see the process of persuading sources to permit access, of interviewing and then writing up (Capote boasts that he has 94 per cent recall of conversations – 'I tested myself'). And then the film moves into the ethical dilemmas raised by the project. Capote sees one of the killers, Perry Smith, as a kind of alter ego, like him abandoned by parents, the victim of a troubled childhood, and he develops a genuine affection for him. But as the appeal process drags out, and the author is unable to complete his book, his frustration and personal conflict grow. By the end he is ignoring letters from Perry, and only at the last moment agrees to attend the execution. We also see him lying to Perry about the title of the book, and refusing to allow him to read drafts.

This is a subtle, understated account of a key moment in the history of twentieth-century journalism, boasting a script genuinely interested in the processes of research and writing, and the ethics of the kind of personalised reporting which would become routine later in the century. The clash of objectivity and subjectivity, the mix of factual reportage and authorial intervention and embellishment (if not fiction) which is now commonplace in journalism, did not begin in Holcombe, Kansas in 1959, but Capote is celebrated here as a pioneer of the style.

Box office: $49,233,161

Rag Tale (Mary McGuckian, 2005, 103 minutes)

If movies about journalism include what are widely regarded to be some of the greatest films ever made, they also include some of the worst, and *Rag Tale* has been judged by most critics to be among the latter. In his *Guardian* newspaper review Peter Bradshaw typified the critical response when he called it 'a boring mess', and 'intelligence-insulting nonsense'.[4] This is unfair. *Rag Tale* is neither boring nor insulting, though its frantic camera work could give some in the audience a headache. Described by director Mary McGuckian as 'a farcical depiction of life on a fictional newspaper', it has been under-rated in the sharpness and effectiveness with which it explores British tabloid news culture.

Released in 2005 and set on and around US presidential election day, 2004, the film tells the story of a few days in the life of a tabloid newspaper, *The Rag* (which could be any one of the UK red-top tabloids such as the *Sun*, the *Star* or the *Mirror*). As the film opens, the *Rag* editor, Eddy, is having a torrid affair with his deputy M. J. (Jennifer Jason Leigh), who also happens to be the wife of proprietor Richard Morton (Malcolm McDowell), the chairman of Global Media Incorporated. Mr Morton has discovered the affair, and warns Eddy to desist. There ensues a struggle over editorial control of the *Rag*, centred on whether the paper will pursue an anti- or pro-monarchy editorial line. The tone is black comic, and the film is accurately described on the DVD sleeve as 'darkly satirical'. The shooting style and *mise en scène* are influenced by the shaky camera angles of British sitcoms of the period such as *The Office*, and those of a nervous disposition are advised to watch with a supply of paracetamol at hand. Scenes shift constantly from colour to monochrome, and grainy video to saturated colour. The camera rarely rests in one place for more than a few seconds. Many of the film's negative reviews highlighted this feature of the production, although it can also be seen as an effective device for accentuating the confusing, paranoic atmosphere of the *Rag*'s newsroom, in which office intrigue and overheard conversations maintain the narrative tension throughout.

The camera work may not be to every viewer's taste, but this is a commendable film in many other respects. The cast is of exceptional quality, including Jennifer Jason Leigh in another of her many portrayals of female journalists, and, alongside McDowell, a host of great British actors such as Simon Callow, John Sessions, Bill Paterson, Rupert Graves, Ian Hart and David Hayman. Lucy Davis from *The Office* plays a scheming secretary, and Sara Stockbridge a ruthlessly believable celebrity and gossip news editor, apparently devoid of any hint of human decency. Mary McGuckian's script produces consistently good acting, and the reconstruction of a tabloid newsroom in early twenty-first century London is believable. *Rag Tale* is indeed one of the few films in recent times to capture the sterility and open-planned agrophobia of the modern newsroom.

The film is merciless in its portrayal of tabloid news values. We quickly learn that the US presidential election (Bush versus Kerry) is regarded by the editorial team as deadly boring. Stockbridge's ideas for stories based on celebrity and sport, and increasingly extreme suggestions for anti-royal stories (such as the headline, 'Bulldoze Buck Palace') are much more appealing to the editor, and mirror precisely the actual headlines regularly seen in the *Sun*, *Star* and elsewhere. In one scene we see how a 'serious' foreign story about the plight of Afghanistan is transformed into a campaign to find refugees a home in the UK, its political content stripped away until only human interest is left. Explaining this process, one editor points out that the *Rag*'s readers have difficulty telling the difference between Iraq and Afghanistan, and can relate to foreign stories only if they have an easily accessible angle.

The script also addresses the subject of class, snobbery and the taste demographics of newspaper readership. In one scene, Morton and a coked-up M. J. awkwardly entertain a group of advisors of the Prince of Wales. Morton aims to prepare the way for an honour, such as a peerage, but M. J. badly lets him down by flouting the elaborate protocol of such dinners, using four-letter words, smoking during the meal, and proclaiming loudly on matters such as European Monetary Union.

The film is also very good in depicting the thuggishness of the British tabloid news room. One might say 'macho' thuggishness, but several of the key villains of the piece are women, including Eddy's ex-wife (played by Kerry Fox), a rival editor who assists him in his illegal and immoral plot to frame Morton for incest.

Here and throughout, *Rag Tale* successfully, and quite chillingly, portrays a style of journalism from which all ethical and moral foundation has been removed, where objectivity and other normative concepts are entirely irrelevant and news-makers will do anything, including framing their proprietor on charges of drug abuse and incest, to get their story. This sub-plot, which occupies the final third of the film, descends into farce, and suspension of disbelief is required as we learn that Morton has married a woman who not only looks like a younger version of his first wife (not a problem, plot-wise, since trophy wives are well known to be one of the perks of power), but is in fact his daughter, leading to tragic (and deeply improbable) consequences all round. If viewed as a pastiche of Greek tragedy, this turn of events can, just, be borne, but it seems like an unnecessarily contrived and exaggerated solution to the plot problem of how to put the proprietor on the defensive.

Morton is not a convincing or credible global media baron, and the film's main flaw, from the perspective of its representation of this particular type of journalistic king-maker, is to under-state his proprietorial power. We are asked to believe that a figure of Murdoch-like proportions such as Richard Morton would permit an editor of one of his newspapers to ignore his commands, even after the latter has been caught sleeping with the boss's wife. Aside from this and its other flaws, however, *Rag Tale* did not deserve the critical disdain with which it was received, and stands up as a powerful satire about tabloid news culture – the most effective, indeed, to have been made in the period of this survey.

Box office: unavailable

2006

Infamous (Douglas McGrath, 2006, 113 minutes)

Based on the 1997 book by George Plimpton, *Infamous* was released one year after the Oscar-winning *Capote*, and addresses exactly the same episode in the writer's life – the writing of *In Cold Blood*. Starring Toby Jones as the author, *Infamous* is very different in tone to *Capote*. Where the latter is shot in autumnal shades appropriate to the Kansas winter in which the early parts of the story unfold, *Infamous* is more colourful, even gaudy. The clothes and personalities are bright and lurid, and the script plays Capote's personality for laughs. Toby Jones is generally agreed to look more like the real Capote than Philip Seymour Hoffmann in Bennett Miller's film, but his portrayal is more camp, comic, lispy and stereotyped to the point of distraction. In this version Capote invites mockery as much as critical admiration or emotional sympathy. As befits its title, *Infamous* is more melodramatic, with scenes of sexual violence, threatened rape, and even a passionate mouth-to-mouth kiss between Perry Smith (Daniel Craig) and the author. Here the Capote-Smith relationship is played like a Hollywood love story, right up to the execution scene with its flashbacks to happier times of Perry playing guitar. *Capote* also suggests a sexual attraction between Capote and Smith, but *Infamous* exaggerates and invents beyond what is credible. *Infamous* entertains, and tells the same story as *Capote*, if in a register which is less subtle and, for this viewer, less satisfying. Many critics prefer this version to Miller's, however, claiming it to be a more faithful representation of what Capote was actually like.

Like *Capote*, *Infamous* engages with the nature of the writer's project, if in a less satisfying manner. At one point Capote says, 'I'm trying to create a new kind of reportage' which incorporates the 'emotional and psychological detail' of the events being reported. Elsewhere, 'I want to bring fictional techniques to a non-fiction story'.

Box office: $2,613,717

Thank You for Smoking (Jason Reitman, 2006, 88 minutes)

This is a film about public relations, and the lobbying of Big Tobacco in particular. Aaron Eckhart plays Nick Naylor, ace lobbyist for the Academy of Tobacco Studies. Usefully compared to *The Insider*, it tells the (fictionalised) story of the people who were trying to smear Jeffrey Wigand and the evidence that nicotine is both harmful and addictive. In his attempts to 'spin the truth' for Big Tobacco Naylor makes the mistake of getting too close to *Washington Probe* reporter Heather Holloway, played by Katie Holmes. He is brought down by her exposé of his cynical methods, before a final act in which he redeems himself before his family, his friends and his own conscience.

The tone of the piece is satirical, and often effective, as in the scenes where three friends – Naylor, and the lobbyists for alcohol and firearms – compete as to which of their respective clients' products is the most dangerous. We see Naylor and a Hollywood agent discuss how to produce a movie in which cigarettes can be smoked by stars Brad Pitt and Catherine Zeta Jones, post-coitally, while circling the earth in a space station. More seriously, a case is made for the freedom of US citizens to choose whether they smoke or not, and some penetrating darts are fired against anti-smoking zealots. But the target is a straw man since, as we know when watching (and if we have seen *The Insider*, we will be even more convinced) that Big Tobacco has systematically lied for decades about the research evidence on smoking, and long ago conceded defeat on all the key arguments. Lobbying for tobacco is a lost cause, and Naylor's pleas for our sympathy are unconvincing, even to himself. In the end he abandons his employers, disgusted by their back stabbing.

The script is revealing on the techniques of spin and lobbying, though the ease with which the experienced and in-demand Naylor lets down his guard, sleeps with the reporter and divulges all she needs to know for her knocking copy lacks credibility. Her willingness to sleep with him to get her story likewise contradicts the notion that she is a principled journalist.

Thank You for Smoking is notable for its rare treatment of the subject of lobbying, rather than the depth of its engagement with the practice of investigative journalism. Like *The Insider*, this is the story of how the news media prise damaging information from a tobacco industry worker, and as a case study in the practice of lobbying in contemporary America it both educates and entertains. But it is a slight piece next to Mann's film.

Box office: $39,232,211

Scoop (Woody Allen, 2006, 93 minutes)

Scarlett Johanssen plays a journalism student on holiday on London, put on the trail of a potential serial killer by recently deceased investigative reporter Joe Strombel, who appears to her during a magic show by Sydney Waterman, the great Splendini (Woody Allen). Other than providing the vehicle for a comic thriller plot requiring its characters to indulge in investigation, the film says nothing about journalism. The 'scoop' comes to the central character by entirely supernatural means unlikely ever to be experienced by a real journalism student, and the ghost of Joe Strombel provides further assistance at key points as she goes along. Despite the involvement of a stellar cast, the film is a self-indulgent mess of badly improvised dialogue, poor editing and continuity, and ludicrous plot twists which insult the viewer's intelligence. The film is noteworthy only as an example of how bad Allen's films got before *Vicky Cristina Barcelona* rescued his reputation.

Box office: $39,215,642

The Good German (Steven Soderbergh, 2006, 107 minutes)

There are two kinds of film about foreign correspondents. One explores the nature of journalism in a war zone, and the role of the journalist in mediating conflict. *Welcome To Sarajevo* (Michael Winterbottom, 1997) exemplifies this type, with its account of journalistic confusion and frustration in the face of the siege of Sarajevo. The second type is that which employs the character of the journalist principally as a plot device, permitting the protagonist to be in exotic locations at exciting moments in world history. Steven Soderberg's *The Good German* falls into this latter category. It is not a film about foreign correspondence so much as a thriller in which the central character, a journalist working for the *New Republic* (George Clooney), arrives in 1945 Berlin to cover the Potsdam peace conference. There, he is embroiled in a mystery involving his driver Tully (Tobey Maguire), his ex-mistress Lena (Cate Blanchett) and her husband, a German rocket scientist wanted by all sides in the post-war frenzy to recruit talent for the emerging Cold War arms race. At no point in the script does Clooney's character discuss the nature of his work, nor do we as viewers gain any insight into the journalistic dilemmas such a figure may have faced in those days. Instead, he acts like a private eye, employing his investigative skills to the resolution of a whodunnit-and-why tale.

In this respect the film reminds us of Alfred Hitchcock's *Foreign Correspondent*, in which Joel McCrea plays a journalist in eve-of-war Europe, similarly drawn into intrigue. In both films the central character's journalistic status facilitates what are essentially spy thrillers, opening doors, permitting access. *The Good German* further encourages this comparison by being shot in monochrome, with many cinematographic references to 1940s film-making. The film is shot to look as if it belongs to another era, although the script is contemporary in tone and register (the 'f'-word crops up regularly). Clooney's character is regularly beaten to a pulp, and occasionally flees the scene of danger, in some contrast to the behaviour of 1940s celluloid heroes.

A work of homage by one group of film-makers to another, *The Good German* fails as a thriller, with a plot which is contrived and clumsy. As a film about journalism, it is of secondary interest only, and inferior to Clooney's other journalism-related projects in the decade covered by this appendix (*Good Night, and Good Luck*, and *Leatherheads*).

Box office: $5,914,908

The Devil Wears Prada (David Frankel, 2006, 106 minutes)

Towards the end of the 1997–2008 period a number of films appeared which took place in or around the world of style journalism. In this highly successful example Meryl Streep plays Miranda Priestley, reportedly inspired by Anna Wintour, the editor of *Vogue* in the United States. Priestley's magazine is called *Runway*, and shares *Vogue*'s (and Wintour's) seriousness about the culture and journalism of fashion. Anne Hathaway plays Andy Stark, a recent graduate and aspiring journalist who really wants to write what she regards as principled investigative pieces, but finds herself (and despite her obvious ignorance of the fashion industry) working as Priestley's assistant. Thus is set up the film's central tension, between the consensual view of worthy journalism as that which covers the injustices meted out to trade unions and workers, and Miranda Priestley's conviction that fashion is essential to life, and that standards of undisputed excellence must govern its coverage.

Andy has a boyfriend, and principled friends who, like her, scoff at her *Runway* job, confirming her view that it will do as a temporary bridge to better things. Then, as Andy gets sucked into the working rhythm and lifestyle of New York's fashion elite, they accuse her of betrayal and shallowness. Her colleague in the *Runway* office, Emily (Emily Blunt) has the film's funniest line, throwing out the accusation, 'You sold out when you tried on your first pair of Jimmy Choos'.

That the script takes fashion very seriously indeed, however, is demonstrated in a key scene where Andy, having scoffed at the care taken by Miranda and her advisors in choosing a belt for a designer dress they are going to photograph for the magazine, launches into a withering lecture on how this obscure accessory, and the detail of its colours and textures, perches at the top of a cultural pyramid from which all mainstream style and fashion flows. Andy learns her lesson and is soon to be seen ditching her 'grandmother's skirt' and wearing only the most exclusive of *haute couture*. Even if in the end Andy, having finally won the trust of Miranda, walks away from her glittering career to rediscover her boyfriend and take a job in a worthy left-of-centre newspaper, we are left in no doubt that style journalism is most certainly not frivolous or an easy option. On the contrary, at this level at least, its standards are almost impossibly high, the work hard enough to break up families.

One of the most moving scenes occurs when Miranda, having learnt of her husband's intention to divorce her, opens up to Andy about the difficulties of being a woman in her position – 'the dragon lady' who goes through husbands like outfits, and is always the subject of press gossip. 'Rupert Murdoch should write me a cheque', she says, 'for all the tabloid papers I've sold for him'.

This is a film which, though pitched as a comedy, engages with rare sophistication in the high-low culture debate, and the social role of style journalism in particular, as well as the status of women in a branch of journalism which has increased in economic power and cultural status with the rise of feminism.

Box office: $326,549,816.

Borat: cultural learnings of America for make benefit glorious nation of Kazakhstan (Larry Charles, 2006, 81 minutes)

The feature film of Sacha Baron Cohen's character created for TV in the UK and the US, Borat Sagdiyev, this mock-documentary takes the audience on a journey through America as seen through the eyes of a Kazakhstani TV journalist and his producer. What begins as a merciless assault on the sexual and identity politics of the central Asian country (so severe it provoked official protests from the Kazakh government) becomes an equally unsparing exposé of the worst of US racism, jingoism and class snobbery. Cohen's characters (Ali G, Borat, Bruno) typically operate by persuading their real-world interviewees first that they are real journalists, and then into revealing more about their social and political attitudes than is wise. Borat's encounters with a succession of individuals and groups, including 'veteran feminists' in New York, members of a fine dining club in Georgia, and an elderly gentleman at a rodeo in Virginia, serve to reveal a shocking level of racism displayed towards muslims, Arabs, and above all jews. As a jew himself, Cohen is licensed to entrap his subjects into breath-takingly anti-semitic remarks and gestures. In a gun shop, Borat asks what kind of weapon is best for 'shooting jews'. Astonishingly, he receives a polite and helpful answer.

Those who visited the further reaches of the old Soviet Union before its collapse will recognise the set of primitive ideas and attitudes towards mental disability, women's rights, homosexuality and other identity issues which Borat's character brings with him from Kazakhstan (albeit exaggerated for comic effect). The biggest target of Borat's fake journalism, however, is the United States itself, revealed to harbour more than its share of deeply reactionary attitudes. It was, nonetheless, very successful in that country, taking some \$130 million at the box office.

The film's style draws on the wave of first-person documentaries made both for TV and cinema from the 1990s on, utilising (or giving the appearance of using) cheap, portable cameras, minimal production values, and frequent video diary segments where Borat describes his feelings straight to camera.

Box office: \$261,572,717

Interview (Steve Buscemi, 2006, 75 minutes)

Based on an original work by the late Theo Van Gogh, *Interview* is a chamber piece of a movie, with the feel of a stage play and lasting only seventy-five minutes. Written, directed by and starring Steve Buscemi as a political correspondent in professional decline, it explores the culture of celebrity and the ethics of journalism, neither of which emerge particularly well. Sienna Miller plays Katya, a successful young TV and movie star, and Buscemi her reluctant interviewer. As Pierre Peder, he would rather be doing his proper job as political correspondent in Washington, following a breaking scandal within the president's administration. There is irony in this, since he makes it clear from the first frame that he is dismissive of celebrity journalism's triviality and shallowness, and sees this assignment as a punishment for his own professional sins. The world of political journalism, we might conclude from Pierre's fascination with political scandal, is hardly less salacious and sensational than the world of apolitical celebrity.

Katya is late for her interview in a chic restuarant, but Pierre has not bothered to prepare and is practically ignorant of his subject's back story and career profile. She rails at his unprofessionalism, which he does not even bother to deny, and abandons the interview, but when Pierre hurts his head in an accident, she takes pity and leads him back to her apartment, where the rest of the film unfolds.

In the course of the film Pierre reveals himself to be not only a lazy researcher when it comes to preparing for interviews, but a journalist prone to inventing facts. He admits to this, in explanation of why he is here, interviewing Katya, rather than in Washington where the big news is: 'My editor doesn't trust me anymore'. In an echo of the Stephen Glass story he admits to having invented sources in the course of his journalism, and we realise that he is in some kind of professional purgatory. To obtain material for his profile of Katya, he sneaks a look at what he believes to be her personal diary, and then prepares to reveal a secret she has shared with him in strictest confidence. Thus we see his untrust-worthiness in pursuit of a story, which is all the more damning because he has taken the moral high ground from the outset.

Katya's character is more sympathetic, and can be read as a riposte to those who place politics and the 'serious' issues of the public sphere (such as Pierre) above the fluff of celebrity. Katya is a serious, thoughtful actor, albeit blonde and physically attractive, with more integrity and honesty than Pierre, who routinely mixes fact and fiction in everything he does. She is proud of her B-movie roles, and her TV soap, where Pierre is full of self-loathing and cynicism. Their encounter ends with Katya's victory, in that Pierre's duplicity fails to get him the scoop he seeks (for all that he denies any interest in celebrity culture), and she retains the physical evidence of a damning secret which could destroy him.

The film is mainly shot within the confines of Katya's loft apartment in New York, and suffers from lazy editing (Pierre's whisky at one point changes magically into a glass of red wine). The script and acting are at times so histrionic as to challenge credibility. The film is notable, however, as a rare attempt to explore the taste distinctions so often applied to journalistic culture by lazy critics; distinctions which elevate the male worlds of politics, economics and the like to worthiness, while downgrading the feminised world of celebrity and entertainment. The two are not so far apart, says Buscemi. More than that, the trivial world of celebrity may be more honest and worthwhile than the one valued by Pierre.

Box office: $1,442,135

Superman Returns (Bryan Singer, 2006, 154 minutes)

The iconic Marvel superhero is re-invented to great effect for the twenty-first century. The most heroic of all journalistic heroes – a benign alien with super-human powers who uses his journalistic occupation as a means of masking his true identity – Superman and his adventures are deeply embedded in the news-room culture of the America in which they are set, and that of the *Daily Planet* in particular, where Clark Kent, Lois Lane and the other supporting cast spend their working time. From the first appearance of Superman in the 1930s he has been linked by scholars and critics to a view of journalism as a benevolent force (although, of course, it is not as journalist Clark Kent that Superman performs his most heroic deeds). More than any praise by association, however, the world of news journalism is a logical backdrop for a do-gooding super hero because it provides him with a convenient location for early warning of events requiring his attention. News is his vehicle for finding things out quickly. Moreover, this is a world in which the news is global, and events happening anywhere on the planet are instantly reported in the offices of the *Daily Planet*. Consequently, the twenty-first century Superman is globalised, able to be anywhere, anytime, just like the news from which he hears about this or that dastardly deed.

The film is alert to the changed cultural politics of its era, as compared with the late 1970s/early 1980s of the earlier *Superman* (Richard Donner, 1978). When at the start of the film Superman (Brandon Routh) appears back on earth after a five-year absence, the editor of the *Daily Planet* convenes an editorial meeting to demand coverage of his lifestyle, his tastes in clothes and food, his politics. In 2006 Superman is quickly incorporated into a popular news agenda dominated by human interest and celebrity. He becomes a celebrity, fielding news conferences and issuing sound bites wherever he goes. This is a superhero genre movie well aware of the nature of public relations and the dynamics of the celebrity media machine.

Also notable is Lois Lane's transformation from mere love interest in earlier versions of the tale to fully empowered equal of Superman. As the film opens, we learn that Lois (played by Kate Bosworth) is a single mother (she has a boyfriend, but does not wish to marry him), and that she has won a Pulitzer prize for an article entitled 'Why the World Doesn't Need Superman'. This choice of subject matter is because, on one level, she has been jilted five years before. But it allows for her character to be portrayed as an independent, more than averagely skilled professional – the *Daily Planet*'s star reporter, in fact. She is resourceful and fiercely protective of her young son. She is a better reporter than Clark Kent. More than that, it is she who saves Superman's life when evil Lex Luther has stabbed him with deadly Kryptonite. To the audience of post-feminist women who see the film, she is unambiguously the equal of Superman in courage and determination. She is, in fact, superwoman.

Box office: $391,081,192

Blood Diamond (Edward Zwick, 2006, 138 minutes)

Jennifer Connelly plays a foreign correspondent reporting the civil war in Sierra Leone, who becomes involved with a diamond smuggler (Leonardo Di Caprio). Her supporting role in the drama is to provide the liberal conscience to Di Caprio's mercenary mind set, gradually prevailing upon him to use the diamond he seeks to steal to help Sierra Leone and its people, rather than enrich himself. Journalist and smuggler help each other to gain access to information and logistical support respectively, and her insider knowledge allows the film to end with her journalistic exposé of the 'blood diamond' trade which continues to plague Africa. Connelly's character is that of the witness to appalling injustice and inhumanity, and thus heroic, although the script has little interest in the detail of her work.

Box office: $171,407,179

2007

Leatherheads (George Clooney, 2007, 105 minutes)

George Clooney's next film as actor-director after *Good Night, and Good Luck* is another period piece with journalism at its core. This time the tone is comic, in the tradition of classic screwball comedy, rather than the austere drama of the earlier film. A lovingly reconstructed 1920s setting stars Clooney as Dodge Connolly, a pro football team boss struggling to survive as the sport becomes more commercialised and rule-bound. The film is a mild attack on the celebrification of sport occurring in the 1920s, and also on the manufacture of celebrity. A central strand in the narrative is the 'war hero' status of star player Carter Rutherford, first created by journalists in the aftermath of World War One, but who now seek to bring him down with a damaging exposé. Reporter Lexie Lyttleton (Renee Zellwegger) is assigned the task of exposing Rutherford, but quickly realises that he is a nice guy and begins to feel the conflict of personal betrayal. 'You know, Harry', she says to her editor at one point, as he urges her to deliver the damaging story, 'sometimes this job stinks'.

The popular press are central to this story, implicated both as the manufacturers of myth such as 'war hero' Rutherford, and in the pressure they apply to undermine the integrity of authentic sporting culture with commercial sponsorship and celebrity. The film plays with journalistic stereotypes, in the form first of Lexie Lyttleton's girl reporter, who is aware of her status as a woman in a man's world and is determined to find professional success. To do so she must resist the urge to 'get out of this dull newspaper business' and get married to one or other of her suitors (Dodge and Carter both pursue her, in classic screwball manner). Feminist assumptions are embedded into the script. She is allowed to be much raunchier than, say, Rosalind Russell in *His Girl Friday*, and her character is never defeated. We also see, in Suds, the classic 'drunken journalist' type – a reporter who drinks more or less all the time, but is still lovable and friendly, as well as remarkably competent when it comes to delivering copy.

Combining Lexie's mission to bring down a war hero who is also a nice guy, and Suds' inebriation, we are presented with a film which presents a caustic, unflattering view of popular US journalism in the 1920s, already mired in commercial compromise and ethical inadequacy, already deserving of our contempt. In the end, Lexie and her editor are redeemed, but it is a hollow victory.

Leatherheads is shot, scripted and performed with skill, and works as an affectionate homage to the films of the period in which it is set (bar fights and extended fisticuffs in which no one is hurt, and so on). It suffers, however, from an unevenness of tone, slow pacing, and some confusing plot twists, and is inferior – as a film about journalism – to *Good Night, and Good Luck*. Part of its achievement is in demonstrating that contemporary concerns about the celebrification and commercialisation of sport, and the unholy alliance between journalism, business and sport, are far from new. Celebrity culture was alive and kicking in the 1920s, we see, as was the worst of sleaze journalism.

Box office: $41,299,492

Zodiac (David Fincher, 2007, 156 minutes)

A study of the real-life case of the Zodiac serial killer who preyed on the San Francisco Bay area in the late 1960s and early 1970s. From an early stage the killer used the media to communicate messages, and the film explores the respective frustrations and often conflicting agendas of journalists and police officers as they seek to decode the killers' ciphers and establish his identity (which remains unknown to this day). Like Stone's *Natural Born Killers*, the film is interested in the 'good business' which such a case provides for media and law enforcers alike, though this is a thriller rather than a satire, and much less critical of the press. Robert Downey Jr (Wayne Gale in Stone's film) plays the central journalistic character, Paul Avery, for whom the case proves to be a turning point in his descent into alcohol and drug addiction. He, like other characters, is brought to the edge of self-destruction by his obsession with the Zodiac.

The film's representation of editorial meetings and the early 1970s ambience of the *San Francisco Chronicle* news-room have been widely praised for their authenticity. The film is an effective thriller stepped in the print journalistic culture of the pre-digital, pre-mobile age where people still used public call boxes and not every office had a fax machine.

Box office: $84,785,914

A Mighty Heart (Michael Winterbottom, 2007, 103 minutes)

The prolific and stylistically versatile British director Michael Winterbottom returned to the subject of the foreign correspondent in this film about the post-9/11 'war on terror'. Based on the tragic, true story of *Wall Street Journal* correspondent Daniel Pearl (Dan Futterman), who was kidnapped and then executed by jihadi militants in Pakistan in 2002, the film is a moving tribute to the personal and professional courage of the correspondent in time of war, and a plea for the sanctity of the witness role to be upheld by all sides. The film is based on the book by Mariane Pearl (Angelina Jolie), who was with her husband in Karachi and was herself at the time a reporter for French public radio. The poignancy of the story is enhanced by the fact that she is heavily pregnant as the drama unfolds.

Daniel Pearl was the first western hostage of an islamic group, and the first journalist, to be a victim of the terror tactic of decapitation, carried out as if on an animal, filmed and then broadcast to the world. The nightmarish quality of the act made it far more horrific than the experiences of hostages such as Brian Keenan in 1980s Lebanon, and it became a much used tool of islamic groups in Iraq after the 2003 invasion.

Winterbottom's film begins by emphasising that Pearl and his wife are journalists who, in the immediate aftermath of 9/11 and the invasion of Afghanistan, genuinely want to know the jihadi side of the story, and to understand it. It is his desire to obtain one final interview, with an islamist leader known as Sheikh Gilani (who turns out to be unwitting bait placed in Pearl's way by a group led by UK-born islamist Omar Saaed Sheikh) which leads him to captivity and death. Pearl wants the interview because he wishes to report the islamist point of view. He is, in short, no propagandist, despite his status as a reporter for one of the United States' most politically conservative newspapers. This status is cited early on as a source of vulnerability. As Pakistani guests sit around Mariane Pearl's dinner table in Karachi, before she knows he has been kidnapped, one says, only half-joking, 'All American journalists are CIA agents'. When the kidnappers make contact, they accuse Pearl of being, first, a Mossad agent, then CIA. He is also jewish, which further exposes him as a target for the anti-semitic islamists. We are also informed, by way of explaining why this particular journalist was targeted, that the *Wall Street Journal* had provided the CIA with a computer containing information about jihadi suspects.

Pearl's professionalism as a journalist, his desire to report the conflict with a degree of objectivity, even at great risk to himself, are portrayed as quietly courageous. He and his wife are seekers after truth who, Winterbottom suggests, do not deserve this fate. Moreover, it is clear that they respect the culture they are working in. One of the film's most notable features, and one which sets it apart from many of the post-9/11 films which appeared around this time, is its sympathetic portrayal of the confusion, noise and chaos of Karachi. The police officers who investigate the kidnapping are shown torturing their suspects for information, but also as committed and competent. Although they are unable to save Pearl's life, they track down Omar Saaed and others involved. This is not a story of western knights coming to the rescue of Mariane's damsel in distress but of Pakistani police and security, notwithstanding their relaxed attitude to torture and other ethically dubious behaviour, doing their job with dedication and skill. The local US embassy staff are portrayed as helpless, and at times unsympathetic and intrusive.

As in his earlier *Welcome To Sarajevo* Winterbottom packages this tale of journalism in time of conflict within a very human drama. The earlier film spends most of its running time narrating the plight of the civilian victims of civil war. Here, the focus is on the suffering of Mariane Pearl, from her initial sense that something is wrong when her husband does not turn up for dinner as arranged, to the horror of being told that he has been beheaded. This strand of the story and the Pakistani police investigation take up by far the greatest proportion of the film's running time. Jolie's howls of anguish as her character digests this news makes for one of the most distressing scenes ever shot in a mainstream movie, and entirely redeems her earlier performance in the disposable rom com *Life or Something Like It*. In the end, in an interview given to an American news organisation, she reaches out to the Pakistani people with a declaration that they have suffered more from islamist kidnappings than foreigners. Then she states that terrorism feeds on poverty and injustice. She also attacks her interviewer for asking if she has watched the video of her husband being beheaded. 'Have you no decency?' she asks, in French, and then, in English. 'How can you ask me that?' Running through the film is a tone of disapproval at the way in which the western media treat the story and its victims.

The quiet courage of Daniel Pearl as depicted in this film and the dignity of his wife in dealing with such an appalling predicament make this one of the most heroic cinematic representations of journalism made in the 1997–2008 period, and in the context of the post-9/11 political environment, one of the most measured. The horror of the kidnappers' methods is not downplayed, but Winterbottom ensures that we are reminded of the link between this incident and the treatment of the Guantanamo detainees. Pearl is portrayed as a dedicated professional who gives his life in the pursuit of truth. Winterbottom's film is a plea for the combatants in such a conflict to respect that aspiration, if only for the selfish reason of having their views represented with some degree of objectivity.

Box office: $18,935,657

Dan in Real Life (Peter Hedges, 2007, 98 minutes)

In this romantic comedy Steve Carell plays Dan, a depressed advice columnist recovering from the death of his wife. He meets a woman – Juliette Binoche – who happens to be his brother's girlfriend. The humour extracted from the dilemma he thus faces – to pursue the woman he senses is the love of his life, but whom his brother is devoted to – is light rather than dark, and the film ends well, with Dan getting his girl and everyone living happily ever after.

Dan in Real Life is a minor representation of journalism, in so far as Dan's profession is never explored as an issue, or a practice. We never see him at work, and apart from a few words of wisdom extracted from his columns and delivered as voiceovers, we learn nothing about the journalism of lifestyle commentary. His journalistic status qualifies him as a writer, and there is irony in the fact that, as a lifestyle advice columnist, his own life is so chaotic, but is otherwise incidental. His lines are quoted here and there in the film, and he is cited as an inspirational figure by at least three other characters. His journalistic identity services the story by giving him depth and intellectual distinctiveness, in contrast to his brother, who eventually finds his true love in the arms of the local floozy.

Box office: $67,791,529

The Brave One (Neil Jordan, 2007, 117 minutes)

Jodie Foster stars as Erika Baine, a New York radio presenter who becomes a vigilante – the 'subway shooter' – following the murder of her fiancé. She sees herself as 'a different kind' of reporter, interested in capturing the sights and sounds of urban life, and moulding them into a broadcast show, *Street Walker*. After the attack which leaves her fiancé dead and her gravely wounded, the show becomes darker, her optimism and love for the city more guarded. She interviews the detective involved in the subway shootings case, and gradually he becomes suspicious of her.

Erika's status as a radio presenter functions in the script to provide a mechanism for her to articulate her rage at the impotence of the law in 'the safest big city in the world'. Her radio performances set out her motivation for the killings which, in the manner of Michael Winner's *Death Wish*, begin almost by accident but become more calculated as the vigilante gets sucked into the cycle of revenge and satisfaction. Being a journalist also gives Erika the opening to establish a relationship with Terrence Howard's detective, who shares her frustration with the slowness and inadequacy of the law and order process.

Although the film's ending is abrupt, and inconsistent with the tone of all that has gone before, Foster's is a convincing performance as the wounded journalist. Scenes of her at work are credible, and her radio scripts have the ring of authenticity. The film touches only rarely on the ethics of her very personal form of journalism, and there are some digs at the sensationalism of crime reporting in general. Neil Jordan's film says little that is new or profound about journalism, then, but effectively uses the ambience of the sound-deadened, darkened radio studio, and the access Erika's professional status allows the detective, to fashion a gripping thriller.

Box office: $69,787,663

Spider-Man 3 (Sam Raimi, 140 minutes)

The third in the franchise, and outdoing the first two in box-office receipts. Once again Peter Parker is engaged in a duel with J. Jonah Jameson and the *Daily Bugle*, which wants to expose Spider-Man as a criminal.

Box office: $890,871,626

Perfect Stranger (James Foley, 2007, 109 minutes)

Halle Berry plays Rowena, an investigative reporter for the *New York Courier*, specialising in exposés of the scandalous behaviour of powerful men such as the US senator she rudely 'outs' in the opening sequence. The film follows her as she investigates the role of advertising executive Harrison Hill (Bruce Willis) in the murder of her old childhood friend, Grace. With the help of her researcher Miles (Giovanni Ribisi), Rowena goes undercover as a temp at Hill's office. Assisted by Miles' skills in computer hacking, she embarks on an online chatroom relationship with her suspect, hacks into his personal email account, and eventually has him convicted of murder, before a final, unexpected twist.

Apart from a few references early in the film to journalism as 'the pursuit of truth' the script employs the world of investigative reportage primarily as the vehicle for a psychological thriller plot, since it allows Rowena and Miles to do things which no ordinary citizen could contemplate, such as impersonate people in chatrooms and steal private email. There is an exploration of the ethics of spying in pursuit of a story, and neither Rowena nor Miles emerge as particularly positive characters. Miles' computer skills come to be linked to sexual deviance, while Rowena's highly-sexed character invites disapproval.

The film misfires on many levels, satisfying neither as a thriller nor as an exploration of journalistic ethics. Bruce Willis is effective as the targeted executive, but disappears from the script after his (subsequently shown to be unjust) conviction for murder. Reviews were generally, and deservedly, negative.

Box office: $73,090,611

The Hunting Party (Richard Shepard, 2007, 101 minutes)

Loosely based on an *Esquire* feature article by TV news reporter Scott Anderson,[5] this is a fictionalised account of an expedition by a group of journalists into Serbia to find a fugitive war criminal, known as the Fox. Richard Gere plays Simon Hunt, a burnt-out TV news reporter whose pregnant lover has been killed by the forces of the fugitive in question (a character inspired by Radovan Karadzik), and who goes in search of him. Ostensibly, the aim is to gain an exclusive interview. In reality, he wishes to capture the fugitive. He brings along his old cameraman, Duck, who despite having become a successful network news staffer in the meantime, is persuaded to risk his life for what is clearly a wild goose chase, and a young, inexperienced son of a network vice-president just out of journalism school. The latter addition to the team allows for some easy jokes along 'journalism school won't teach you jackshit' lines. There are many other clichés – the too-smooth network anchorman who is by definition not a 'real' journalist; the evil Serb leader and his demonic associates; the several escapes from near-death which the journalists go through. In the end the film disappoints by being more boy's own adventure than a realistic account of a genuinely interesting episode in the murky and unprincipled aftermath of the wars in former Yugoslavia.

The original *Esquire* article dismisses conspiracy theories such as the allegation that Serbian war criminals were allowed to go free by the US and NATO forces at the end of the war, but this film takes them much more seriously. Hunt's contempt for what he sees as UN and US complicity in Serbian war crimes ends the film with a strong note of cynicism towards authority, and the final exchange between Hunt and his CIA rescuer bears little resemblance to the more measured account given in Anderson's article (Radovan Karadzik was finally taken into the custody of the Hague war crimes tribunal in 2008).

This is far from a 'true story', then, and suffers by comparison with the much more sombre and moving *A Mighty Heart*, released around the same time. The tone of the script veers uneasily from wacky comedy to scenes of torture and massacre, punctuated by the accentuated craziness of the central character, who in one scene risks death by shotgun for the sake of a stolen $20 bill. Hunt is a mixture of Hunter Thompson and Richard Boyle in Salvador, but without the magnetism or profundity of either. Although elements of the original source material are retained (and captions acknowledge that much of the story is invented), *The Hunting Party* has little to say about foreign and war correspondence, except that it is very dangerous and best undertaken by journalists who are practically insane to begin with.

Box office: $7,622,251

Control (Anton Corbijn, 2007, 113 minutes)

Telling the same story as Winterbottom's *Twenty Four Hour Party People* – the rise of Factory Records and Joy Division – Anton Corbijn's film is listed here for the same reason; one of its key characters, Tony Wilson, begins the film as a current affairs TV journalist. The script also has an important role for Ian Curtis' Belgian lover, Annik Honore, who first meets him in her capacity as a music journalist reviewing a Joy Division concert.

Global box office: $8,009,646

REC (Jaume Balaguero, Paco Plaza, 2007, 70 minutes)

A low-budget Spanish horror film in the tradition of *Blair Witch Project* and *Cloverfield*, premised on the expanded use of hand-held video technology by TV journalists. In this example of the sub-genre, a Barcelona-based documentary team working on the show *While You Sleep* – Pablo who holds the camera throughout and is never seen, and Angela, the increasingly distraught presenter – go out with a fire crew on a routine call to assist an elderly woman in an apartment block. Once inside the building, a policeman is bitten by the woman, and the firemen attempt to get medical help. The building has been sealed by the authorities, however, trapping firemen, journalists and residents inside. Eventually it is revealed that there is a contagious infection which causes those affected to become murderously violent. Angela and Pablo, having set out to make a routine fly-on-the-wall documentary, find themselves recording an escalating sequence of bloody attacks. With no route of escape from the building, they decide that their goal as journalists is to 'tape everything', to bear witness. This they do to the bitter end, and their own grisly demise.

The film uses the grainy, jerky quality of hand-held video to represent familiar genre movie scenes (people being chased, attacked, monsters being killed in appropriately bloody fashion) in a way which enhances their realism and heightens the horror for the YouTube generation. This is not a film about the ethics of such journalism, although it robustly defends the right of the journalist to report events which the authorities might prefer hidden. We see events through the journalists' eyes, as in *Blair Witch*, providing a degree of narrative distance which somehow intensifies the horror.

Box office: unavailable.

Lions for Lambs (Robert Redford, 2007, 98 minutes)

Robert Redford directs and stars in a critical study of US government policy in Iraq and Afghanistan, and the role of the US media in promoting the policy to the public. One of three narrative strands follows TV news reporter Janine Roth (Meryl Streep) as she interviews a pro-war senator about the opening of a new military offensive. The senator (Tom Cruise) wishes to enlist the support of Roth and her news organisation in order to 'change the subject' on the war on terror, and win back public support. He offers Roth an exclusive, if she will tell the story his way. She refuses, and is forced by her editor to choose between her own principles and her career. Streep's portrayal of the journalist is understated and sombre as she concedes that, despite her criticism of the senator's gung-ho approach, she and her organisation enthusiastically endorsed the 2003 invasion of Iraq. If the senator and his like are monsters, then she has contributed to their making.

The journalistic strand is engaging, but represents around one third of an overly didactic film which plays like a lecture on the political science taught by Redford's college professor, crammed with speeches and sermons designed to make the liberal, anti-war perspective on the war on terror seem self-evident. Made at a time when the unfinished Iraq war was the big story, and Afghanistan still a sideshow, the script has already been overtaken by events.

Box office: $63,215,872

The Bourne Ultimatum (Paul Greengrass, 2007, 110 minutes)

This action-hero film features features fictional investigative journalist Simon Ross (Paddy Considine), working for the real *Guardian*, in a supporting role alongside Matt Damon's Bourne. Ross gets on to Bourne's story, but is killed around twenty-five minutes in to the film.

Box office: $442,825,653

2008

Quarantine (John Erick Dowdle, 2008, 89 minutes)

A remake of *REC* (see above), relocated in Los Angeles and lacking the pace and scariness of the original. In this version we see the cameraman briefly (in *REC* he is never seen).

Box office: $39,769,976

Sex and the City (Michael Patrick King, 2008, 135 minutes)

Sex and the City was an era-defining success on American and global TV in the 1990s, signalling the rise of the young, professional woman with money to spend and sexual appetites to satisfy. Starring Sarah Jessica Parker, the series followed the lives and loves of four New York-based women, including Carrie Bradshaw, a successful sex and lifestyle columnist. The TV series was based on the *New York Observer* columns of Candace Bushnell.

This is not really a film about journalism, although its lead character is a journalist. Unlike *The Devil Wears Prada*, *Sex and the City* is about the life of a woman who happens to be a journalist, and whose journalism provides a narrative device for plot, as well as making credible her lifestyle of conspicuous consumerism and designer clothes.

The film's greater interest, for the purposes of this book, lies in its status as an index of the rise of the kind of 'new girl writing' which Carrie Bradshaw practises, and which is in turn one element of an expanding, post-feminist, post-Madonna culture of female consumption and sexual assertiveness. One can safely say that *Sex and the City*, and the kind of loose-living, free-thinking woman whom Carrie represents, would not have been possible without the previous thirty years of feminist activism. What she and her friends do with their economic power and social status, however, is far removed from what the pioneers of feminism thought they were fighting for, making this kind of 'post-feminism' a focus of intra-feminist debate in recent years.

Box office: $415,129,126

Definitely, Maybe (Adam Brook, 2008, 107 minutes)

A minor romantic comedy in which divorcee Will Hayes (Ryan Reynolds) attempts to explain the identity of her natural mother to his daughter. One candidate is journalist Summer Hart (Rachel Weisz) who features in the story as one of three women he may or may not have had a child with in the past. Summer's status as a journalist has significance to the film only in that, when they were pursuing their relationship, she had to write a critical story about the political candidate whom Will was working for as a paid party campaigner. Faced with the dilemma of writing the story and staying true to her journalistic principles, or suppressing it and saving the relationship, Summer opts for the former. Beyond this brief moment of ethical exploration, the resolution of which lacks credibility (would true lovers allow such an issue to separate them?) the film has nothing to say about journalism. The Rachel Weisz character is never seen engaged in her professional activity.

Box office: $55,447,968

How To Lose Friends and Alienate People (Robert B. Weide, 2008, 110 minutes)

This is the fifth in a series of big-budget Hollywood movies concerned with the world of style journalism released between 2002 and 2008. *How To Lose Friends and Alienate People* is based on the heavily fictionalised autobiography of British journalist and self-styled cultural guru Toby Young (renamed as Sydney Young in the film). Somewhat improbably, Sydney finds himself promoted from a dead-end editorship of the London-based *Postmodern Review* (the real-life Young edited a journal called *Modern Review*) to a much sought-after post at the high profile *Sparks* magazine (modelled on *Vanity Fair*). Although a complete newcomer, and bearing no obvious talent as a journalist, he has conveniently regular access to the editor, Claydon Carter (Jeff Bridges, based on *Vanity Fair*'s Graydon Carter), and gradually makes his way up the ladder of style magazine success, acquiring a journalistic girlfriend (Kirsten Dunst, as a copy editor) along the way.

The film is pitched near the style of British comedy Simon Pegg had success with in *Shaun of the Dead* and *Hot Fuzz*, but also has aspirations to satire at the expense of celebrity culture and the journalism which both fuels and is dependent on it. Sydney's self-appointed role at *Sparks* is to represent journalistic integrity in the face of a corrupt system of celebrity endorsement and PR puffery. He is, we are told, what Claydon Carter used to be – independent, critical, honest. The film takes us through a series of encounters with those who are the opposite, and thus traitors to the journalistic cause: Sydney's line manager, Laurence, the culture editor who sleeps with rising movie stars and promotes them shamelessly in the magazine; Gillian Anderson's publicist – 'I hate that word', she says, reminiscent of Tony Curtis' turn as Sydney Falco in *Sweet Smell of Success*; Sophie Maes (Megan Fox), the empty-headed starlet whose pet chihuahua Sydney inadvertently sends to meet its maker. The only characters, apart from Sydney, with whom we are allowed to sympathise are Kirsten Dunst's wannabe novelist, working on *Sparks* only to pay her bills until she finishes her novel, and *Sparks* editor Claydon himself – he may be jaded and cynical – but he is human enough to allow Sydney to make the kind of *faux pas* and professional balls-ups that would see him shown the door at any real-life magazine.

As light comedy, fusing British humour with *Sex and the City*/*Devil Wears Prada* locations, *How To Lose Friends* ... succeeds in providing two hours of pleasing entertainment. There are a few laugh-out-loud moments, and Simon Pegg is very likable as the initially unlikable protagonist. As satire, however, the jokes are obvious to anyone at all familiar with celebrity culture and its journalism. Its impact is undermined by the central character's fundamental lack of credibility – we never see any evidence of Sydney's talent, or what it is that allows him to cut such an iconoclastic swathe through *Sparks'* cosy inner world.

The film's broader significance is in its confirmation of the rise of style journalism as an important sub-sector within the media, linked of course to the rise of celebrity culture in the late twentieth century. Magazines such as *Vogue* and *Vanity Fair* were always glamorous, but rarely taken seriously as journalism, suffering from the low status attaching to women in the profession. In the post-feminist world, figures such as Carrie in *Sex and the City* or Miranda in *The Devil Wears Prada* can still be swooned over for their frocks, but have acquired a cultural weight in keeping with the size and affluence of their audience – young, professional women whose feminism is lived in work and at home, and who expect to be taken seriously by their entertainers. In this respect, too, *How To Lose Friends ...* fails. *The Devil Wears Prada* and *Sex and the City* feature strong women at their narrative core; *How To Lose Friends ...* is an old-fashioned film in which male characters dominate throughout. Kirsten Dunst's main function in the story is to be mistreated by the cad Laurence, then rescued, damsel-in-distress like, by Sydney. We are never in any doubt that this intelligent, ambitious woman, whose favourite film is the Fellini classic *La Dolce Vita*, needs a man much, much more than she needs a good job as a journalist.

Box office: $17,286,299

Gonzo: the life and work of Dr Hunter S. Thompson (Alex Gibney, 2008, 120 minutes)

This documentary (see *Control Room*, above) is one of two about journalism made for cinema in the 1997–2008 period. Alex Gibney had previously made *Enron: the smartest guys in the room*, and *Taxi to the Dark Side*, both part of the wave of big-screen documentaries which characterised global cinema from the late 1990s, and here turns his attention to one of the most iconic figures in the history of journalism. Hunter Thompson shot himself in 2005, in the spirit and in the manner of his hero, Ernest Hemingway. For forty years he produced a unique form of literary journalism, combining stylistic brilliance, iconoclastic satire and a perceptive eye for what was going in the world around him. His best years were over by 1975, as this film shows, but by then he had made 'gonzo' a byword for a new kind of reportorial style, appropriate to the postmodern sensibilities of the late twentieth century – difficult to define as either journalism or not-journalism, subjective or objective. Gonzo was aware of its capacity to change the world it was ostensibly observing, and put the interaction of the journalist and the real at the centre of its project. Wildly successful with *Hell's Angels*, *Fear and Loathing in Las Vegas* and *Fear and*

Loathing on the Campaign Trail, Thompson achieved the level of outlaw-ish celebrity hitherto reserved for rock stars, and became an inspiration to generations of would-be journalists who came after.

This account of his life and work provides admirers of Thompson's writing with rare access to home movie footage photographs, interviews with both of his wives (including the extraordinarily generous Sondi who, according to more than one biography suffered physical violence at Thompson's hands – here she remarks only that he could be 'difficult') – and with some of the key figures in supporting his career: Jann Wenner, the *Rolling Stone* editor who published *Fear and Loathing in Las Vegas*; Douglas Brinkley, his editor; Ralph Steadman, his illustrator on the key books. All of this is fascinating simply because we have not heard so much from them before, in this public context. There is little that a follower of Thompson's work would not already know, but it is engaging.

If the film has a flaw, it is that it spends rather too much time on the political journalism – the period after *Fear and Loathing in Las Vegas* up to the election of Jimmy Carter in 1976 – and not enough on the life behind the work. What fans of Thompson really want to know is: how did he do it? How did he produce such a volume of great writing when under the influence of so many drugs, and with such an apparently chaotic lifestyle? That he did so is self-evident, and the work will last forever. But for all that the director takes two hours to tell his story, the life remains elusive, touched on with nods and winks from the key players. We await the definitive account.

Box office: $1,491,958

Frost/Nixon (Ron Howard, 2008, 122 minutes)

The final film about journalism released during the period covered by this book was Ron Howard's adaptation of Peter Morgan's 2006 stage play. Its subject is the 1997 interviews of former president Richard Nixon undertaken by British journalist David Frost in California. The interviews are presented as a 'duel', with one of Nixon's minders conjuring up the image of a boxing match. The contest also has the feel of a chess match, or poker game, as the two opponents each seek to outsmart the other with smiles and wiles.

The central tension of the script lies in the contrast between Frost's allegedly light-touch style, his status as a comedian and satirist, and now an entertainer specialising in quirky, family-oriented programmes such as *Frost Over Australia*, and the demands of confronting one of the world's leading politicians (albeit a disgraced one). Can nice, smiling Frost get what he wants out of a Nixon still in denial – that is, a confession?

Ding, ding, seconds out for round one. Nixon dominates with banal anecdotes which last twenty-three minutes. Frost is unable to contain him, and the former president's handlers are ecstatic. Rounds two and three, more of the same. Nixon is in control, Frost unable to pin him down on issues such as his performance on the issue of Vietnam. As his researcher exclaims in exasperation, 'you're making him look good'. But then, in round four, as Frost faces financial ruin (as his own producer, he needs to sell the interviews, and will only succeed in doing so if they extract the confession), he comes across some key facts, and lands the killer blow. Nixon is forced on the defensive, and a kind of confession emerges. The suspicion that a 'talk show host' such as Frost could never succeed in pinning Nixon down is dispelled.

Writer Peter Morgan invented a key scene in which Nixon calls Frost late at night and reveals his motivation for doing the interviews, and there are other creatively imagined moments to propel the narrative. But this is a relatively faithful adaptation of a stage play, which effectively conveys the dynamic between a fallen emperor and the court jester who nailed him where so many others had failed.

Box office: $26,518,282

NOTES

1. Gilbey, Ryan, 'Open Mike', *Sight & Sound*, volume 14, number 10, October 2004.
2. Unless otherwise indicated, figures given are for global box office receipts on initial release, as supplied by the website Box Office Mojo.
3. Interview, *Vanity Fair*, March 2006.
4. *Guardian*, 7 October 2005.
5. Anderson, S., 'What I did on my summer holidays', *Esquire*, October 2001.

Bibliography

Allan, S. (2006), *Online News*, London: Sage.

Allan, S., Zelizer, B. (eds) (2002), *Journalism After September 11*, London: Routledge.

Allan, S., Zelizer, B. (eds) (2004), *Reporting War: journalism in wartime*, London: Routledge.

Arutunyan, A. (2009), *The Media in Russia*, Milton Keynes: Open University Press.

Bakewell, J., Garnham, N. (1970), *The New Priesthood: British television today*, London: Allen Lane.

Barris, A. (1976), *Stop the Presses! The Newspaperman in American Films*, New York: Barnes and Company.

Baudrillard, J. (1995), *The Gulf War Did Not Take Place*, Bloomington, Indiana University Press.

Bell, M. (1996), *In Harm's Way*, London: Penguin.

Blumler, J., Gurevitch, M. (1996), *The Crisis of Public Communication*, London: Routledge.

Bulman, David [1945] (2008): *Molders of Opinion*, Milwaukee: Bruce Publishing Company.

Brennen, B. (1998), 'Sweat and melodrama: reading the structure of feeling in *All the President's Men*', *Journalism*, vol. 4, no. 1, pp. 115–33.

Campbell, A. (2007), *The Blair Years*, London: Random House.

Capote, T. (1966), *In Cold Blood*, London: Penguin.

Carey, J. (1992), *The Intellectuals and the Masses*, London: Faber and Faber.

Chadwick, A., Howard, P. (eds) (2008), *Routledge Handbook of Internet Politics*, London: Routledge.

Chambers, D., Steiner, L., Fleming, C. (2004), *Women and Journalism*, London: Routledge.

Chomsky N. (1988), *Manufacturing Consent*, New York: Pantheon.

Chomsky, N., Herman, E. (1979), *The Political Economy of Human Rights*, vols 1 and 2, Boston: South End Press.

Conboy, M. (2004), *Journalism: a critical history*, London: Sage.

Davies, N. (2008), *Flat Earth News*, London: Chatto & Windus.

De Burgh, H. (ed.) (2005), *Making Journalists*, London: Routledge.

De Burgh, H. (ed.) (2008), *Investigative Journalism*, 2nd edn, London: Routledge.

Djerf-Pierre, M. (2007), 'The gender of journalism', *Nordicom Review*, vol. 28, pp. 81–104.

Ehrlich, M. (2004), *Journalism in the Movies*, Urbana and Chicago: University of Illinois Press.

Ehrlich, M. (2006), 'Facts, truth and bad journalists in the movies', *Journalism: theory, practice and criticism*, vol. 7, no. 4, pp. 501–19.

Eisenstein, E. (1983), *The Printing Revolution in Early Modern Europe*, Cambridge: Cambridge University Press.

Engel, M. (1996), *Tickle the Public*, London: Gollancz.

Fallows, J. (1996), *Breaking the News*, New York: Pantheon.

Frosh, Paul, Pinchevski, Amit (eds) (2008), *Media Witnessing: testimony in the age of mass communication*, London: Palgrave.

Fukuyama, F. (1992), *The End of History and the Last Man*, London: Hamish Hamilton.

Gabler, N. (1994), *Walter Winchell: gossip, power and the culture of celebrity*, London: Picador.

Ghiglione, L. (1990a), 'The American Journalist: paradox of the press', Washington, DC: Library of Congress.

Ghiglione, L. (1990b), 'The American journalist: fiction versus fact', unpublished paper (ijpc.org/ghiglione.htm).

Glasgow University Media Group (1976), *Bad News*, London: Routledge & Kegan Paul.

Glasgow University Media Group (1978), *More Bad News*, London: Routledge & Kegan Paul.

Glover, S. (ed.) (1999), *Secrets of the Press: journalists on journalism*, London: Penguin Press.

Good, H. (1989), *Outcasts: the image of journalists in contemporary film*, Lanham, MD: Scarecrow.

Good, H. (1998), *Girl Reporter: gender, journalism and movies*, Lanham, MD: Scarecrow.

Good, H. (2000), *The Drunken Journalist: biography of a film stereotype*, Lanham, MD: Scarecrow.

Good, H., Dillon, M. J. (2002), *Media Ethics Goes to the Movies*, New York: Praeger.

Greer, G. (1981), *The Obstacle Race*, London: Picador.

Hartley, J. (1996), *Understanding Popular Culture*, London: Arnold.

Hammill, F. (2004), 'Round the World Without a Man: feminism and decadence in Sara Jeannette Duncan's *A Social Departure*, *The Yearbook of English Studies*, vol. 34, pp. 112–36.

Hammill, F. (2007), *Women, Celebrity and Literary Culture Between the Wars*, Austin: University of Texas Press.

Hayward, A. (2008), *Breaking the Silence: the television reporting of John Pilger*, London: Network.

Hersh, S. (1997), *The Dark Side of Camelot*, New York: Little Brown.

Higgins, M. (2008), *Media and Their Publics*, Milton Keynes: Open University Press.

Hill, A. (2005), *Reality TV: audiences and popular factual television*, London: Routledge.

Hill, A. (2007), *Restyling Factual TV: the reception of news, documentary and reality genres*, London: Routledge.

Joad, R. (1996), *The Invention of the Newspaper*, Oxford: Clarendon Press.

Keeble, R., Wheeler, S. (eds) (2008), *The Journalistic Imagination: literary journalists from Defoe to Capote and Carter*, London: Routledge.

Keen, A. (2008): *The Cult of the Amateur: how blogs, Myspace, YouTube, and the rest of today's user-generated media are destroying our economy, our culture, and our values*, New York: Doubleday.

Lichtenberg, J. (1991), 'In defence of objectivity', in Curran, J., Gurevitch, M. (eds), *Mass Media and Society*, London: Edward Arnold.

Lippmann, W. [1922] (1954), *Public Opinion*, New York: Macmillan.

Lloyd, J. (2004), *What the Media Are Doing To Our Politics*, London: Constable.

Luhmann, N. (2000), *The Reality of the Mass Media*, Cambridge: Polity Press.

Lule, J. (2001), *Daily News, Eternal Stories: the mythological role of journalism*, New York: Guilford.

Lumby, C. (1999), *Gotcha: life in a tabloid world*, Sydney: Allen & Unwin.

McKeen, W. (2008), *Outlaw Journalist: the life and times of Hunter S. Thompson*, London: Aurum Press.

McLaughlin, G. (2002), *The War Correspondent*, London: Pluto.

McNair, B. (1991), *Glasnost, Perestroika and the Soviet Media*, London: Routledge.

McNair, B. (2000), *Journalism and Democracy: a qualitative evaluation of the political public sphere*, London: Routledge.

McNair, B. (2001), 'Public relations and broadcast news: an evolutionary approach', in Bromley, M. (ed.), *No News Is Bad News*, Harlow: Longman, pp. 175–90.

McNair, B. (2002), *Striptease Culture: sex, media and the democratisation of desire*, London: Routledge.

McNair, B. (2005), 'What is journalism?', in De Burgh, H. (ed.), *Making Journalists*, London: Routledge, pp. 11–27.

McNair, B. (2006), *Cultural Chaos: journalism, news and power in a globalised world*, London: Routledge.

McNair, B. (2007), *An Introduction to Political Communication*, 4th edn, London: Routledge.

McNair, B. (2009) *News & Journalism in the UK*, 5th edn, London: Routledge.

Maltby, S., Keeble, R. (eds) (2007), *Communicating War: memory, media and military*, London: Arima.

Marx, K. (2007), *Dispatches for the New York Tribune: selected journalism of Karl Marx*, London: Penguin Classics.

Miller, D., Dinan, W. (2007), *Thinker, Faker, Spinner, Spy*, London: Pluto Press.

Moeller, S. D. (1999), *Compassion Fatigue: how the media sell disease, famine, war and death*, London: Routledge.

Morris, T., Goldsworthy, S. (2008), *PR: a persuasive industry?*, Houndmills: Palgrave Macmillan.

Mulvey, L. (1994), *Citizen Kane*, London: British Film Institute.

Mulvey, L. (1996), *Fetishism and Curiosity*, London: British Film Institute.

Ness, R. M. (1997), *From Headline Hunter to Superman: a journalism filmography*, Lanham, MD: Scarecrow.

Oates, S. (2008), *Introduction To Media and Politics*, London: Sage.

O'Brien, J. C. (2008), 'Lapsed liberal', in Bulman, D. (ed.), *Molders of Opinion*, Milwaukee: Bruce Publishing Companu, pp. 36–47.

Raymond, J. (1996), *The Invention of the Newspaper*, Oxford: Clarendon Press.

Reed, J. (2007), *Ten Days That Shook the World*, London: Penguin.

Sanders, K. (2008), *Communicating Politics in the Twenty-First Century*, London: Palgrave Macmillan.

Schiller, D. (1981), *Objectivity and the News*, Philadelphia: University of Pennsylvania Press.

Schudson, M. (1978), *The Discovery of News*, New York: Basic Books.

Schudson, M. (1992), *Watergate in American Memory*, New York: Basic Books.

Schudson, M. (1995), *The Power of News*, Cambridge, MA: Harvard University Press.

Seib, P. (2004), *Beyond the Front Lines: how the news media cover a world shaped by war*, New York: Palgrave Macmillan.

Shirky, C. (2008), *Here Comes Everybody*, New York: Penguin.

Starr, P. (2004), *The Creation of the Media*, New York: Basic Books.

Steadman, R. (2007), *The Joke's Over*, London: Heinemann.

Thompson, H. S. (1979), *The Great Shark Hunt*, London: Picador.

Thompson, H. S. (1997), *The Proud Highway*, New York: Villard.

Thompson, H. S. (2001), *Fear and Loathing in America*, New York: Villard.

Tiffen, R. (1989), *News and Power*, Sydney: Allen & Unwin.

Tuchmann, G. (1972), 'Objectivity as strategic ritual: an examination of newsmen's notions of objectivity', *Amerian Journal of Sociology*, vol. 77, no. 4, pp. 660–70.

Tulloch, J. (2007), 'Charles Dickens and the voices of journalism', in Keeble and Wheeler (eds), *The Journalistic Imagination*, London: Routledge, pp. 58–73.

Varty, A. (ed.) (2004), *Eve's Century*, London: Routledge.

Wahl-Jorgensen, K., Hanitzsch, T. (2008), *The Handbook of Journalism Studies*, London, Routledge.

Weber, R. (1974), *The Reporter As Artist: a look at the New Journalism controversy*, New York: Hastings House.

Wenner, J., Seymour, C. (eds) (2007), *Gonzo: the life of Hunter S. Thompson*, London, Sphere.

Wilson, T. (2002), *24 Hour Party People*, London: Channel 4 Books.

Wolfe, T., Johnson, E. W. (eds) (1975), *The New Journalism*, London: Picador.

Wolfe, T. (2000), *Hooking Up*, London: Picador.

Wolff, M. (2008), *The Man Who Owns the News*, London: Bodley Head.

Zynda, T. (1979), 'The Holywood Version: movie portrayals of the press', *Journalism History*, vol. 6, no. 2, pp. 16–25.

Index